International Pra

Susanna Haink - South Author - Illustrator - wrc read [Accountability]. It has made quite an impact on me. Your style, vocabulary, sentence structure, the whole nuance of similarities and metaphors - all a delight to read."

"The misrepresentation of judicial power is mind-boggling. That the authorities did not take into account the individual case, is a crime in itself," exclaimed Melanie Schmitz - Malaysian - Psychologist.

"Normally, I'm in bed with a book by ten and I usually read two or three lines before my eyes start to close," said Nicola Ferger-Andrews - British - PYP Early Years Coordinator, "but I was up into the wee hours reading this story - I had to find out what happens!"

"At first, like Aurora, I couldn't relate to the violence that prevails in our society. But the suggestions in the program about communicating with your partner, resonated deeply with me. I think that anyone in a relationship, not necessarily a hostile one, can benefit greatly from the lessons and guidelines laid out in the program," said Lydia Rickard - Australian - Librarian.

Carolin Heider - German - German Translation Proof Reader/Editor - read the book in English and said, "Ich bin so begeistert! Es ist echt ein tolles Erlebnis. I can't wait for the book to come out in German so I can give it to my mother and sister!"

Sabine Rohr - German - Learning Assistant - said about the author, "You really opened yourself up. I guess the whole process made you grow a lot."

Accountability

"I juggled my laptop on the train ride to work because I couldn't put the book down," said Liz Sanchez - German - Cuban/American - Early Years Teacher.

Kathy Kukura - American - EAL Coordinator - is quoted saying, "You've got a way with writing that kept me engaged throughout the whole (!) book. I connected to what happened. It impacted you; no matter how you tried to see it from the outside."

Louise Hart - British - Elementary Education Assistant - wasn't shocked at the story. "It reminds me of 'Orange Is The New Black'," she said with a nodding smile. "It may have been a terrible ordeal, but I was sure it would turn out well; knowing how her story ends!"

"It's a winner!" proclaimed Margi Desmond - American Author - Editor - when she read the first draft.

Accountability
Facing the truth to discover self-empowerment

By

Laura Strobel

Accountability

Copyright © Accountability 2020 Laura Strobel

All rights reserved. The author has used creative license in this nonfiction narrative. The events and people in the story are real, so names have been changed to protect their privacy. No part of this publication may be reproduced, distributed, or transmitted in any form or by any means, including photocopying, or other electronic or mechanical methods, without the prior written permission of the author, except in the case of brief quotations embodied in critical reviews and certain other noncommercial uses permitted by copyright law.

ISBN: 9798519007276 (Paperback)

Book cover integrity and design by Farrukh_Bala.

Printed independently in the United States of America.

Available on audio and eBook.

Coming soon in German and Spanish translation.

For further information go to www.laurastrobelauthor.com

Laura Strobel

For my mom, my sister, and every woman who's been there.

Foreword

I wrote the first draft of this book in 2000.

In a fury, I jotted down all the facts for an outline. I was feverish to expel the story; to throw it all up and get the poison out of me so I would feel better. Then I got on with my life and the manuscript lay dormant for almost ten years.

In 2009, I answered the beckoning call to take the project further. I worked hard to give voice to the story. When the last chapter was completed, I felt confident that I was ready for the next step.

The perky youngish woman at the library was eager to assist me in finding a reference book on literary agents. She and I got to talking and she ended up offering to edit my text.

When the copy came back with scribbles and sentences circled with a bold yellow highlighter, I read through it, and cried. I became incensed to see that on nearly every page of my precious body of work this stranger had written, 'Show me - don't tell me'.

I was outraged as I ranted and raved, "Even if she is a professional, who does she think she is, criticizing my work when she doesn't even know me?"

Then I reread her notes. And it became obvious. The long narratives were flat. And boring. I realized that this practical criticism had done me a great service. The simple instruction, to *show* the reader what you want them to *see*, enabled a more focused writer in me to immerge. With much appreciation I thank her for that valuable advice, because it transformed my whole writing technique.

I dabbled at the text over the next decade, but it didn't become a priority until 2019.

When my family became more self-sufficient, I set to work diligently, and finally refined and finished the job.

Now at this point, the author would write about what a visionary their agent was, how invaluable their editor proved to be, and how privileged they feel to have been offered the deal to publish their book.

But that space for me, is empty.

Oh, I drafted the infamous query; that enticement; that bait to hook an agent, rewording my pitch many times. I sent it out and some of the agents responded with a quick, professional refusal. Others sent a kinder, more personal sounding refusal.

It didn't take me long to find out that gaining passage into the elite world of traditional publishing, is like winning the lottery. I actually play the lottery sometimes, but I rarely, if ever, look to see if I've won.

I decided that it was vital to find out whether my story had an appeal; if it held enough merit in pursuing publication, so I shyly sought some of my close colleagues and asked them to read it. It's important to clarify that I work amongst very bright, educated individuals. I am merely a wannabe. Asking them for help felt awkward and embarrassing.

Acclamation is a delicious, intoxicating tonic. Validation and accreditation combined are a sugarcoated confection that an undernourished writer can gobble up. I got fat on the positive feedback that came from each person who kindly took on the task of reading my work.

It had only been intended that my associates read it, but many went further and surprised me with edited, notated copies. Susanna Haink, God bless her spirit, read, and proofed the text half a dozen times for grammar and punctuation. She's been my steadfast champion and mentor in production as well.

With genuine cheer, these goodhearted people laughed at me when I got teary-eyed about being so blessed, and they hugged me when I wept with gratitude and couldn't stop hiccupping.

Accountability

I want to thank you all most kindly; Susanna Haink, Nicola Ferger-Andrews, Liz Sanchez, Mel Schmitz, Louise Hart, Lydia Rickard, Carolin Heider, Sam Rodd, Kathy Kukura and a special thanks to Sabine Rohr for her x-ray-vision in seeing many hidden errors.

Without such mindful analysis, criticism, and encouragement, I would have remained stagnant and uncertain.

I feel as fortunate as winning the lottery,
finding myself so rich in friends as these.

Laura Strobel

Accountability
Facing the truth to discover self-empowerment

Table of Contents

Part One: Shock 1

Chapter One: The Call 3
Chapter Two: The Police 14
Chapter Three: Jail 38
Chapter Four: An Angel? 49
Chapter Five: Processing 68
Chapter Six: The Cell 73
Chapter Seven: Diana 77
Chapter Eight: Inmates 86
Chapter Nine: A day in the Life 99
Chapter Ten: Court 108
Chapter Eleven: Release 121
The Wallet Photos 132

Part Two: Denial 133

Chapter Twelve: Home 135
Chapter Thirteen: Real Court 144
Chapter Fourteen: Rules and Regulations 157
Chapter Fifteen: Spring Assessment 169
Chapter Sixteen: Diversion Class 101 182
Chapter Seventeen: Power and Control 194
Chapter Eighteen: The Cycle 210
The Adventuress 229
Chapter Nineteen: Mathematics of Battering 230
Chapter Twenty: Criticism and Manipulation 238
Chapter Twenty-One: Open Negotiation 258

Part Three: Acceptance 265

Chapter Twenty-two: Accountability 267
Chapter Twenty-Three: Control Log 281
Chapter Twenty-Four: Self-Talk 289
Chapter Twenty-Five: Me, Myself, and I 301
Chapter Twenty-Six: Faith 315

Postscript..320

Group Discussion Questions.......................................325

SELF-TALK...327

PERSONAL BILL OF RIGHTS 329

Accountability

Laura Strobel

Introduction

Domestic violence is prevalent in every society. Indiscriminate of economic levels, age, race, or religious preference. It occurs behind closed doors or blatantly broadcasted in the public eye, ever the struggle and fight from opposing forces for power and control.

The Domestic Violence Prevention Program, which is widely available, gives a truly eye-opening view of the cause and effect of domestic disharmony. It offers insightful guidelines to a positive approach at another way of going forward from an oppressive environment.

This is a true account.
People's names have been changed to assure their anonymity.

Accountability

Part One: Shock

Laura Strobel

Chapter One: The Call

"How much longer, Aurora?"

The urgency in his voice is unmistakable. It's more of a command than a question.

Aurora hesitates, alert. Suddenly dizzy, the tiny cabin-like space slopes. A rumble under her feet, the cracking of linoleum tiles breaking and the feeling of tumbling into a dark abyss, is very real. With the back of her forearm she swipes the sweat dripping from her upper lip, straightens her gritty yellow apron and tries to steady herself.

I can't -

Aurora silently appeals to the imaginary judge who's glowering at her. She can almost see his arms crossed in stoic contempt for her failure to persevere. She can't quell the escalating panic clambering in her head. The patterns on the kitchen wallpaper are wiggling and flashing too blindingly loud.

***

Gripping the edge of the stove, she bows her head toward the pot of boiling water and the steam fogs her glasses. Within the brief escape from behind the mist, she can see clearly that her well-ordered plan is starting to break down, becoming gray and murky like the juices and the meat congealing on the counter.

Aurora takes stock of her plight and decides that she'd better get a move on and finish the job as quickly as possible. Spaghetti gets thrown into the pot, her lenses clear, and she notes that the faded green curtains adorning the side window could use a good washing. She shakes her head frowning at the dirty little dust bunnies huddling in the corners and marvels with distaste at the grimy baubles sitting on the counter, serving no purpose in a kitchen.

Aurora fights an urge to tidy up, but then she'd have to give the whole place a swift going over, and that wasn't part of the deal.

She picks up her pace and swiftly slices the plump chicken breasts cooling on a board. Eyeing the pans hanging above her, the rack's rickety-looking hinges invite morbid images. She can almost hear the creaky squeaks of the bolts turning and see the equipment sliding off; clang, clang, clang, toppling down on her head. *The timing would be perfect* - she thinks stepping out of the way sneering, as if she's daring the inanimate objects to move.

William's heavy tread is palpable. Aurora can feel a vibrating tremor as his demanding steps trample over the books, games and apparel that are strewn across the narrow living room of his parent's house. He's grunting with displeasure trying to find a spot amongst the chaos to plunk himself down. She pictures her husband as an uppity bull gnashing his teeth, banging his bulky shoulders against the walls, in an attempt to escape the domestic mayhem.

"Just a little longer and we'll be out of here," she murmurs uneasily, quickening her step.

A sports commentator's voice enthusiastically broadcasts the evening's highlights, and Aurora senses that the din is unnerving William's mother who has come to talk to him.

"Turn that racket down, so that I can speak to you," she says with a sharp snip in her voice. The sound hovers at a high level until the news is over and then the volume lessens.

Aurora closes her eyes and listens because she knows.

Her husband is drawn to all sports with the same craving

as a serious addict and even without sound he will continue to watch. She's sure that his eyes have been glued to the screen as she hears him say, "That's not necessary Mom, we're fine. Aurora's almost done. We'll be going soon. Do you need any help with Dad?"

Aurora's father-in-law is laid up in bed from quintuple bypass surgery. He's aggravated by the painfully throbbing scar running down his torso from being filleted like a side of beef. His voice rattles as he calls, "Nancy - I'm thirsty - where *are* you? Are you coming?"

"Yes, yes, Barry - I'm coming - *coming*!"

Aurora's mother-in-law is not used to being 'On Call' and looks visibly haggard. Nancy's mascara is smudged giving her complexion the ghoulish look of a zombie.

Her purple velour jumpsuit jiggles as her hand flaps with forced enthusiasm at her grandchildren before hurrying down the hall in fuzzy pink slippers. On leave from her insurance job to assist her husband's recovery, Nancy is overwhelmed by the daily tasks that William's father has always been home to do. Barry is the domestic in their household, Nancy the breadwinner.

When the hospital nutritionist implored the family to establish a healthier food regime for Barry, Aurora was the obvious choice to do it. As a personal chef, she knows that preparing numerous meals can take a lot of time, often running longer than expected. Aurora's harried now trying to get the job done as fast as she can because William and the children have been sitting around for hours anxiously waiting for her. And everyone is tired and getting agitated.

"Almost done honey, it won't be long now," she calls out in a strained attempt to be civil, suppressing the urge to scream, *Keep it together for God's sake - I'm going as fast as I can!*

She takes a breath and stirs the caramelizing onions. They smell tantalizing, but she resists slowing to taste them; hustling to finish the dish. "Almost done," she moans faintly, putting a lid on the pan.

Aurora seals more Tupperware containers and labels them with heating instructions. Peering over the breakfast bar, she watches her husband stretch his arms out wide and sigh audibly. William is restless. He sits, gets back up, and paces. His long fingers comb through the salt and pepper hair fallen on his high forehead. Aurora retrieves the runaway wisps that have escaped her bandana, tidies herself up, and continues to assemble a few more meals. She gets it that William would much rather be at home on this Sunday evening, lounging in front of his widescreen TV with his multi-continental sports channels. If the children were tucked neatly in their beds, the obligation to mind them would not be his burden. Her annoyance is mounting because William seems so 'put out' even though he'd made all the arrangements. Aurora wishes that he would just suck it up and deal with it - like she's doing.

Preoccupied amid her task she observes with detached curiosity, William striding over to the children. The boys have been building a Lego wall for over an hour, but a tinkling, a jangle, and one of the large green foundation pieces whizzing past her work area signals to Aurora that peace time may very soon be over and the threat of war forthcoming. Just as an image of diminutive soldiers with swords in hand sporting fierce expressions crosses her mind, her pint-sized Titans clash and a ruckus ensues.

"That's *mine* - let go!"

The television blares with raucous cheers and Aurora can picture the fans going crazy. Whatever the success is, be it a goal or touchdown or home run, the bravado's crescendo helps to drown out the children's whining and ever-growing cache of accusations and charges.

At first Aurora is unmoved; shrieks and bouts of hysteria are often the background melody between the feisty siblings. Still, she works faster. The two weeks of meals for her father-in-law are nearly completed.

"Simmer down boys, I'm almost done. Start cleaning up now," she calls out to them.

"You let go - it's *mine*!"

"No - it is *mine*. Give it back! You've had it long enough!"

Aurora's six-and-a-half-year-old, born with a benevolent disposition, rules over the one minion in his little realm generously, to a point, but now he wants his treasure back while his three-year-old rival jealously covets the prize he's conquered, and will not give it up. They tussle and tug, and the smaller one strikes and punches with itty bitty white-knuckle fists.

"Hey, enough already! Now *Stop*!"

William's imposing voice booms and Aurora is incited to look up right as her husband leans down to slap her toddler. A shrilling scream pierces Aurora's ears and she winces as she sees William swatting the boy on his backside, tossing him like a flimsy rag doll. As the child springs forward, an electric jolt and gush of heat like fireworks of red explode in Aurora's head, blinding her. She loses her equilibrium and sways like a drunkard toward the counter.

"Jesus - what - in the name of God - are you *doing*?" Aurora's cry is a high-pitched outburst; she's trembling, still holding tightly to the knife.

Looking over at his mother, the astonished little boy is white- faced with shock at the newness of never having been physically disciplined before. Enticed to react by Aurora's exclamation, he lets out an agonizing squeal, "Papa *hit* me!"

And both boys start to howl.

The pot of boiling pasta is foaming. The pan of onions is steaming. Aurora quickly turns the heat off both burners and dashes from the kitchen in determined pursuit of her husband.

Heads simultaneously turn, and miniature bowtie mouths silently open wide in wonder, as the children's eyes trail the blurry yellow streak of their mother's unrelenting form racing toward their father.

Aurora is in a flurry of such fury, as they have never seen before.

"Ooh, come on," says the older boy gravely. Taking his charge's hand, the little brothers scamper down the hall to their grandparent's bedroom. Aurora sees her son squaring his shoulders as he reaches to knock on the door. "Grandma, Mama and Papa are *arguing*," he announces at the opening, his small chest puffed up, chin raised, sounding authoritative.

After a few seconds Aurora hears her mother-in-law's voice, "Come in boys and sit on the bed with grandpa. We'll find something for you on the television."

Aurora has a mental picture of her boys being sucked into a void, their slender bodies shrinking to fit through the keyhole as the door closes with a thud.

Shaky and apprehensive, Aurora rushes up to William. Wary of advancing any closer, she stands about a foot away and yells at him. "You - you - what was *that* all about? And why did you have to *hit* him?"

In a fit of haste, as if her hand is moving without her command, Aurora strikes at William with fierce viciousness. It's a stretch, but as fast as a snake bite she connects with his lower lip and her fingernail slashes a tiny bit of flesh.

Instantly blood oozes from William's pursed lip. Blackish droplets plop onto the beige carpet making dark little stains. The surging flow is mesmerizing.

Aurora stares at William's face, then at the floor; both scared and fascinated.

William seems stunned as well. His look visibly changes like captions in a sequence of still photos from surprise to disbelief to annoyance. He wipes his mouth and examines the blood on his fingers. He slowly grabs a towel from the counter to dab at the cut, never taking his suspicious, scowling eyes off his wife. "For Christ's sake Aurora, what was *that* for?"

Puzzled and awkward, Aurora inadvertently lowers her head and draws a hand up toward her brow.

In reflexive defense William's hands shoot out and clamp down on Aurora's wrists, immobilizing her. "What-the-*fuck* - you wanna hit me again? Man - what's up with you?"

"Hey - I wasn't going to - I just - let go of me!"

Aurora's fingers whiten and go numb as William applies pressure. She grunts and moans trying to push against him as he effortlessly forces her down onto the floor between the living room and the kitchen walkway. Painful electric sparks shoot up her arm when her elbow hits the hard surface. Fiery brown eyes squint furiously at her husband. "Oww - you're hurting me - you - you, *animal* - get your hands off me - if you don't let go right this minute I swear - I'll - I'll call 911 - or something - I mean it - let *go* -"

"Whoa - stop it - all right? Come on Aurora - I just reacted -"

Aurora recoils as William's spittle sprays her face. She tries to shoulder him away, but he bears down on her and presses his knee against her thigh.

"Hey - calm down -" he says hoarsely, trying to keep her down.

"Calm down?" she yells at him. "You're telling *me* to calm down? *You* calm down and - let - go - of - me -"

Aurora wriggles out of William's stronghold and staggers to her feet. Seeing the cordless phone on the counter, she scrambles to get it. Wild eyes flit from her husband to the phone. With a sudden impulse, she hits the numbers 911 - but in that same instant she steps back, aghast.

Aurora freezes.

She stares at the device in her hand thinking, *What am I doing? This is crazy!*

Paralyzed and dumbfounded with fright, she lets go of the phone and it slips from her hand, dropping with a thumping sound onto the carpet.

William's face is flushed as he sidesteps Aurora and bends down to pick up the phone. "Oh, right - is that it? You think there's a threat here? That I'm a *threat* to all of you? Well then baby, maybe you should call!"

He taunts Aurora by waving the phone above her head.

"Nooo -" she wails. Aurora claws at William's arm frantically trying to retrieve the remote, but he whirls away.

He hits the off button cancelling the connection, and throws the beeping handset onto the countertop where it bounces a few times toppling jars and figurines, sending them flying.

"Good God woman, what's gotten into you? It was a smack on the popo. Do you seriously think I'd *harm* my son?" He stares at Aurora; the blood continuing to drip from his lip.

Aurora's legs turn to jelly. "No," she whispers, dropping with despair into a nearby chair.

"NO is right, Aurora. It's ridiculous." William returns the phone to its cradle and crouches down. "Are you okay? You must know that I would never hurt any of you - don't you?"

Aurora can't look at her husband because she can hear the torment in his voice. If he *ever* - he could do much damage with one blow. And she knows he would never harm any of them. She wants to say that, but she can't speak. She wants to explain her actions, but she doesn't know why she reacted like that. All she can do is lower her head and nod in acquiescence.

William tentatively brushes a lock of hair from Aurora's down-turned face and tenderly tucks it behind her ear. Laying a hand on her shoulder and squeezing gently he says, "Listen baby, it's been a long day - we need to get home. You finish up, I'll get the boys, and then we'll get out of here - okay?"

Sitting listlessly twisting the hem of her apron, Aurora's tightened knuckles begin to burn, and she faintly hears the worn fabric start to tear.

She cannot move, cannot think.

"Come on Aurora - no more of this - it's over."

William puts his arm protectively around her bent body, quickly kisses her cheek, and rises.

Aurora measures the back of his frame as William treads heavily down the hallway to gather up the children. She closes her eyes and can taste a sourness of bile in her throat.

Gulping for air, she looks around disoriented.

Everything is blurry.

Accountability

The collection of family portraits hanging in the living room look like they're tilting. The faces of her husband's relatives are leering at her. Knick-knacks scattered on the bookshelves seem to be jiggling. She pulls the elastic band at the nape of her neck, and the thick mass of golden hair escapes the tension from the bun. She drops her head into her hands and covers her ears hoping that the rumbling thunder pounding in her head, will stop. Behind her closed eyelids the dramatic scene, clip by clip reenacts in her mind: *His form looming over the child - His arm raised - That awful scream -*

Aurora knows she's overprotective of her children, but she shudders realizing what she could be capable of doing if anyone ever posed a real threat to her precious family.

***

In a daze, the rest of the meals are completed, assembled, and everything is put away. William grips Aurora's arm helping her down the path. She leans heavily on him, grateful that he's holding her tight; she's weak and unsteady going down the bumpy stone walkway.

His father is consigned to his bed, but William's mother comes out with them. Laying a coat over her shoulders she seeks and commandeers her youngest grandson, taking his hand. "It's late - you must be very tired - when you get home, go straight to bed."

The little rascal nods obediently, smiles sweetly, swiftly breaks loose and runs to his brother. They dash gaily down the sloping yard.

At the car, Nancy's staid expression and evading eye contact speak to Aurora, but William seems unaffected by his mother's silent reproach.

Nancy helps to buckle the kids into their seats, and fussily nuzzles an ivory powdered cheek against each of their faces. The boys respond in kind by lightly patting her face and giggling. Without comment, she hands her son a tissue for his unremitting bloody lip.

Aurora is embarrassed and thinks she should make an attempt to explain, but the opportunity is lost when Nancy loops around William, embraces her and says, "Thanks for cooking all those meals, Aurora. I know it wasn't ideal to do it here; we do appreciate it. Now it's late, you'd better get on your way."

***

William and Aurora watch, arms entwined, as Nancy climbs the short hill to her house. Halfway up the lawn she turns and waves them on, indicating they needn't dally any longer.

Aurora can't help but wonder how much her in-laws could have heard.

She thinks, *Okay, the door was closed, but the noise would have been hard to ignore.*

She exhales, and tries to put it out of her mind.

William plays with the buttons on the side of his leather seat and fiddles with his shoulder strap.

Aurora turns around to check on her sons before swiveling to clip her own belt in. "Settle down now boys, we'll be home soon," she says in a soothing voice.

William waves to his mother who is waiting on the paved terrace in front of her entrance.

"Drive safely - no more arguing -" Nancy calls out from her landing, waving back at them.

"Oh yeah, she heard it all. Loud and clear," Aurora says softly, but William doesn't hear.

"Don't worry, Mom, we're fine." William closes the window, winks at his wife, and turns smiling to his sons. "Okay space cowboys, we're ready for takeoff. Time to go home."

He leans over and lays a protective hand on his wife's leg.

Their eyes lock and they sigh at the same time.

William adjusts his rearview mirror, motioning for Aurora to look back at the boys.

Their flopping little heads are nestled against the padded car seats; their eyes are closed; they're steadily drifting off into dreamland.

Aurora wiggles in the cushioned seat, tucking her legs up, getting comfy. With a long, ample yawn she relaxes into the chair.

"Finally, this day is done. I can't wait to get home," she says, exhaling slowly.

Their car starts to back down the drive, but William has to brake for an oncoming vehicle.

The flash of car lights arouses Aurora. She leans forward, straining in her seat to see out of the driver's side window, and catches a glimpse of lettering on the side-door of the oncoming car. Her breath catches and she sits up straighter.

William puts the car into park, turns off the engine and focuses on the road as well.

In sudden recognition, Aurora's hands shoot to her mouth and she whispers, "Oh, my -" as a black and white police car slowly advances toward them.

Chapter Two: The Police

Ground lights strategically dispersed amongst hedges and flowerbeds on the neighboring lawns illuminate the dark road, sending shadows with spidery tentacles across their yards. The palm fronds dance and sway to a perky breeze; glowing in luminous greens and yellows under the stage setting. It's a starry night, the sky sparkling silver, the energy almost visible.

Aurora's heart starts to race. She wraps her arms around herself and shivers. They sit strapped in their seats as the police car pulls up and onto the driveway blocking their way.

William tweaks his outer mirror and says, "I can see the cop's face; he's scouting house numbers." He shuts off the car lights, and takes Aurora's hand in his. With their backs to the road, they wait. The children are snoozing. One boy has a raspy chest rattle; the onset of a cold.

Aurora hears a car door slam. Then another. She quickly turns to see two officers approaching their vehicle. William and Aurora exchange a silent, probing inquiry. *This can't be about us,* she thinks, *the call didn't go through - but maybe one of the neighbors heard and called- no that couldn't be - it was over too fast -* She fidgets uncomfortably.

Nothing happens for a moment, and Aurora thinks maybe they have the wrong house, the wrong street. Maybe they'll get back in their car and drive down another block, looking for another address.

Her older son stirs, and his hopes rise, as a blur of a blue uniform passes his window. He swivels, straining to see where the intriguing figure is headed. "Look Mama - a poleeceman!" he says excitedly.

"Ooh - I want to see -"Aurora's whining toddler demands. He's awake as well and squirms in his secured seat, trying to undo the harness buckle.

Aurora knows that her boys would love to witness some action, and they'd be thrilled if the sirens started blaring.

Dear God, help me - she prays. "Hush now boys," she says trying to maintain order. "There's nothing to see. Sit still and don't try to wiggle out of your seats - I mean it - you hear me? We're going home."

The disappointment in her son's eyes is so pure, so honest, she covers a guilty smile.

At the beckoning rap on the rear side of the car, William begins to roll down his window. He motions for Aurora to lean over and look.

In the rear-view mirror is an elderly officer; he's hunched over, slowly inching hand over hand up the car's frame. It looks as if he's travailing a perilous path.

They both sit back as the exhausted-looking man, huffing and puffing, peers into the car.

"Evening folks. I'm Sergeant Rafferty and my partner there, is Officer Manning. We need to verify an address."

The Sergeant, breathing heavy, rubs hard at his glistening stubble as if his beard itches badly and then unclips a black flashlight from his hip holster and waves the long-stemmed metal club inside the Tahoe.

"Ooooh -" the boys squeal as the blinding light passes over the family's squinting faces.

William shadows his eyes with the back of his hand.

"Yes officer, you are at that address."

William is seemingly respectful, but to Aurora his voice is cutting.

She reaches over and lays her hand over his hoping to allay the incessant drumming of his fingers on his thigh.

"Would you both step out of the vehicle please," Sergeant Rafferty says taking off his cap, poking a balding head in through the window, crowding William for a closer peek at Aurora. Carefully replacing his hat and refastening his flashlight to his belt, the cop tugs on the door handle and stands aside to allow William room to emerge.

William hoists his left leg up by the knee and pivots in his seat to release the lengthy appendage from its confinement, thus freeing the rest of his body mass as well.

"Oh," Sergeant Rafferty says tilting his head back as he follows William's gaining height. The officer coughs, clears his throat, reaches into his coat pocket, pulls out a shiny blue metallic tinted confection, examines it, unwraps it, and pops the ball into his gaping mouth. He chomps loudly as his gaze examines William intently.

Officer Manning springs to Aurora's side, pulls on the door handle, and glides into the open passage. Inquisitive eyes run up and down and over Aurora before reaching for her elbow. "Can I help you out Ma'am?" asks the officer, grinning in a helpful tone.

Aurora notices that the cop's bulging athletic physique seems to be in bondage within his tightly fitting attire; the first three buttons on his shirt may simultaneously split wide open.

Smiling warily at the robust young man, she takes the extended hand that he's offering her, and she steps down from the high running platform. Coming into his closer proximity, Aurora is instantly assaulted by a blast of conflicting odors. Hair gel and aftershave make her gasp for air; her eyes well up, and she succumbs to a huffing horn blowing sneeze.

The perfumed cop starts to say, "Bless y-" but Aurora turns track before he finishes saying, "Hold on."

She hops back up on the running board and leans in between the two front seats to address her wide-eyed children. "Don't worry boys," she says reassuringly, "Papa and I are right here. Stay put, we won't be long."

Aurora's worried thinking, *I hope this won't take long - I can't leave them sitting there in the car* - She sighs in relief as her mother-in-law comes rushing down from her house. Nancy dashes past the policemen, acknowledges Aurora, and scrambles into the car with the children.

***

Assembled in a rough semicircle a few feet apart, William stands tall on the high side of the hill like a centurion, towering over everyone. An awkward silence hangs over them.

"Sir, could you move over here?" asks Sergeant Rafferty, stepping forward looking up at William through thick bifocals. "Yes, here. A bit further away from your wife if you will."

The officers seem uneasy as William moves down the hill.

Stepping with purpose up the hill to meet William's eye level, Officer Manning only makes it to his chin. "Thank you, sir," he says, looking away.

Aurora watches both officials size her husband up. Then they take in her measure as well.

"Well now. We need to see some identification folks. Your driver's license or something with a picture will do." The policemen remain immobile, but the veins in both of their necks are visibly pulsing.

Aurora can see that they are anxious. While their probing eyes scan the surrounding area, scoping the neighborhood, Aurora decides to run quickly to the car so she can talk to her children. She sprints, calling over her shoulder, "I'm getting my wallet officers - I'll be right back."

As she hops onto the seat and retrieves her bag, Aurora shrugs and shakes her head at Nancy's silent inquiry. They both turn and smile at the boys, pretending that everything is fine. Aurora squeezes Nancy's hand and says, "I'm sure this is just some misunderstanding."

Still, she's uneasy.

"Grandma says the cops are real," her six-year-old reports like she's a true authority.

"I want to touch one," Aurora's toddler insists, his jaw set with fervent conviction.

Aurora reaches out and pats the chubby little fingers thumping restlessly on the quilted bolster of their car seats and says, "Nothing's happening here guys, we're just talking. Sit tight, we'll be going soon."

She pivots quickly, slides off the high cushioned seat, and drops down to the ground. She turns back and leans into the cab, low enough that the boys can't see her face, and whispers, "Thanks for being here Nancy. I don't know how long this will take."

***

"Mr. Sabel is it?" The senior officer asks William. He scans their licenses, flipping them in his hand. "The address on your driver's license differs from here. Whose place is this?"

"It's my folk's house, sir. We've been visiting. Now we're headed home." William retrieves his license, slips it into his wallet and returns the billfold to his back pocket. He starts to walk down the little hill and stops where he is closer aligned to his wife. He readdresses Sergeant Rafferty saying, "Anything else, sir? If not, we'd like to be on our way."

The leading officer pulls out a starched white linen handkerchief and Aurora sees elegantly embroidered monogram letters in bright blue: E on the left, large R center, F on the right.

She vaguely wonders what his first and middle name could be. Edward? Frances?

Sergeant Rafferty studies the finely-crafted piece of linen before honking loudly into it. He takes his time folding the used swatch of fabric into a neat little square before sighing noticeably and returning it to his trousers.

"First things first," he says, frowning a bit sternly.

Accountability

A shiny black Pontiac convertible cruises slowly down the road, evidently on the prowl. The young driver's elbow casually rests on the ledge of the open window. His lengthy staring, and lack of attention to the road in front of him, almost causes a run-in with a parked car.

"Nothing's happening here buddy. Move along," Officer Manning shouts, waving the curious kid on.

The jumpy junior cop rubs his palms down the legs of his tight navy pants and leans toward Aurora. The glint in his eyes betrays his eagerness. "So Ma'am, was there a disturbance here?" Officer Manning asks.

Aurora's radar switches on. She detects a wolf-like hunger in his demeanor as he licks his lips. He looks at her with a longing, a need for something. She gawks at him, tongue-tied.

"Actually officers, there was a slight problem earlier," William replies, as he steps adroitly around the policemen and puts an arm around his wife. "But as you can see everything is okay now. Our boys are in the car, it's been a long day, and we need to get them home."

"Just a moment folks."

The officers step aside and put their heads together talking in whispers.

Aurora and William exchange a furtive look. The damp perspiration under her arms gives her a chill.

The rookie cop advances to Aurora and gently steers her away from William. He lowers his volume, but his voice squeaks with anticipation. "Ma'am did your husband hit you?"

Aurora interprets his tone as malicious, intended to incriminate, making her defensive.

"Of course not!" she says indignantly, openly miffed that he has the gall to ask her such a thing.

Officer Manning stoops to study Aurora.

Her brows crease and eyes narrow challenging him.

"Uh - Okay. Let's just step over here," he says in a quiet, suggestive tone.

As his hand secures her by the elbow and he guides her, Aurora feels like a helpless animal tangled in a hunter's snare.

"Yes. Here's good. Thank you," he says good-naturedly.

Officer Manning seems puzzled. His eyebrows arch as his eyes trail over to William and then back to Aurora. He inhales, exhales, and sighs. In a smooth coaxing voice he asks, "All right Ma'am, then how about you tell me. Why was 911 called?"

Now at this point, if things had gone differently, there wouldn't be a story to tell.

***

William can't stand still.

He takes a step, stops, and turns around, waiting for further instructions from Sergeant Rafferty.

"Let's go inside Mr. Sabel and find out what all this is about."

He strides briskly ahead to place himself first. Waving a liver-spotted hand, he motions for William to follow him up the lawn.

Aurora sees William turn at the doorway, shrouding the porch light, darkening the landing.

She hears him ask, "Sir, if you please, can I tell my mother to bring our boys inside?"

"Yes, yes of course," Sergeant Rafferty replies; he seems anxious to get through the door.

"Let's go in as well Ma'am," the subordinate official tells Aurora, pulling on her arm.

"Officer, please, okay yes, 911 was *dialed*," Aurora appeals to Officer Manning as they start up the path, her hands clenched as if in prayer, "but you have to believe me, it was an unfortunate mistake. I really didn't need to do it. I hung up before I talked to anyone."

Officer Manning caresses the top of his bristly crew cut, but doesn't respond to Aurora.

"I'm sorry that you had to come out here on a false tip," Aurora continues, her beaded sandals planted firmly in the walkway, "but as my husband said, we're on our way home." She thinks bitterly, *Home - If we'd left five minutes earlier, we would've missed these guys completely.*

Officer Manning sets his shoulders, standing his ground. "I'm sorry too Mrs. Sabel, but you have to understand that when 911 is called, we have to follow through. *Every* time." He saunters up the pathway then turns on his heel, bows slightly, and extends a hand in an exaggerated princely offer for Aurora to follow. "Let me assist you inside Ma'am," he says with a smirking grin, "and you can take your time and tell me what happened here tonight."

***

As she walks on tiptoe past the officer, ignoring his proffered hand, Aurora is now quite worried thinking, *How do I explain all this to them without making William look like a child beater?*

***

Secure in the grip of their grandmother's hands, the children's heads crane for a final glimpse at the men in uniform before being conducted down the hall.

Aurora waves to them, blowing air kisses. "Be good now you two, this won't take long and then we'll be on our way home." She wants to cry seeing them mimic her by pressing their little hands to their mouths and slobbering on themselves before throwing kisses her way. She sighs watching them romp out of the room.

Sergeant Rafferty sits gingerly at the dining room table across from William. He adjusts the lopsided tablecloth, smoothing the maroon colored damask before setting his pile of papers down. "We'll sit here, if that's all right, and start with the standard report sheet."

Although the couch in the adjacent living room is quite long, Officer Manning chooses to sit chummy next to Aurora. She can smell his spicy cologne as he leans unnecessarily over her lap to place some papers on the coffee table. Should she offer him a band-aid for the huge pimple she can see festering on his neck right at his blue-collar line? It looks ripe and ready to burst. No, she decides, she'll let him deal with that on his own. She quietly tucks into the soft cushions of the couch and places a pillow barrier between them. The cop is too busy lining up his papers to notice. Officer Manning is undoubtedly finicky about the order of things.

"Sooo?" his voice coaxes, dragging out the single vowel to urge Aurora to commence. His attention is intensely fixed on her face. His eyes run the length of her frigid body as if he's measuring how long it will take to gobble her up. Is it possible that he's unaware of his leg sliding along Aurora's thigh as he edges nearer?

Hairs prickle the back of Aurora's neck and she thinks, *Hey, that's a little too close for my comfort.* She scoots further away and snatches a scratchy wool shawl laying on the sofa's edge. Draping her shoulders she covers herself, but it doesn't relieve the feeling of nakedness; the overwhelming awkwardness of being on display.

How do I begin? she wonders. She's panicked by the blatant expectation for a juicy, sordid story to unfold. She has never been this close to a cop before, let alone this kind of interrogation. She fidgets with the pillows lined up along the couch cushions, rearranging them again and again.

Officer Manning has the guise of a dogged predator. Baring his teeth, he nods encouragingly while patting Aurora's leg. "Go ahead, I won't bite," he says, smiling wryly.

Wrapping the long-haired coverlet tighter about her body, Aurora sighs.

"Today has been a rather busy day, officer," she says picking up a pillow, laying it down and picking it up again.

Squirming, she tries to inch her way down the length of the couch, but the officer, like in a game of cat and mouse, nimbly advances as she clumsily retreats. His heavy cologne permeates the air making her nose tickle again. Aurora turns her head and inhales deeply through her mouth. Letting the air out slowly, she sighs and positions herself facing the man. At this angle, their knees are almost touching.

"So as not to bore you with all the details Officer, I'll just say that we've been out all day. We left our home in Lakeland early to go to Tarpon Springs where we spent the whole day at my father's house. It was his birthday you see. Then we drove here to Brandon this evening on our return to help my in-laws. My father-in-law just had open-heart surgery. Now it's very late and we just want to get home to put our children to bed."

Aurora holds her breath saying to herself, *That's enough - now don't say another word.*

"*And* ?" the cop urges with his eyebrows raised in what looks like impatience for a juicy finale.

"*And* - And nothing. Well, actually, I mean, so, I had to do all this cooking - here - and my family has been waiting for hours for me to finish and -" Aurora inhales and the words hover as she looks to see how the officer is faring so far.

"Please understand, officer, it's been a long day and my boys are worn out. We're all worn out. My husband is a tolerant man, but the boys got cranky and when he hit our son, solely in a disciplinary manner mind you, I rushed in to intervene and, uh, I slapped him because, well, because I wasn't keen on his action toward our boy."

She waits, inhaling deeply, looking at the cop timidly.

He stares at Aurora with an expression of sudden clarity.

Okay, that didn't sound too bad - she thinks, exhaling slowly, with an imperceptible whimper.

Then he frowns.

And sighs.

The Officer's penetrating dark eyes scrutinize Aurora as he massages a hairless chin and shakes his head a bit.

Seeing that her explanation isn't up to par with what the policeman has been waiting for, Aurora tries to expound. "I was disturbed -" her tongue seizes; she instantly regrets the insinuation of that word. "I mean I was upset - by - by my husband's uncharacteristic behavior."

Man-o-man, I'm making a mess of this! She berates herself internally clenching her jaw, grinding her teeth to shut her mouth and not say another word.

Officer Manning's focus is resolved as Aurora watches him study her like she's a rare new species. She can almost see tiny, oiled wheels spinning in his head. "Ah," the young official says finally, his voice sounding unconvinced.

Aurora is sure that "Ah" means that he doesn't believe a word of what she's said. She tries to control herself, to hold back on his tacit baiting, but she can't. "It was a rash impulse and I lost control," she blurts out. "But my husband didn't hurt our son - he was just disciplining -"

Geez, stop babbling - it's pointless - she says to herself biting her lip hard.

"Uh hum," mumbles the policeman as he picks up the report, and scans the sheet.

Aurora watches expectantly, letting the officer systematically digest her statement. She waits, refolding her hands in her lap.

He seems remote now, intensely interested in his papers.

Taking a new tack, Officer Manning becomes all business, initiating a series of questions that could have come from an old detective movie. Clearing his throat while scanning his sheet he asks, "During this time, Mrs. Sabel, was anyone under the influence of alcohol?"

Aurora's eyes widen. She shakes her head slowly, cautious as to this new objective.

"Drugs?" Officer Manning's eyebrows are raised in what appears to be unsuppressed hope.

Aurora's body stiffens.

She isn't sure why the cross-examination is headed in this direction, but it irritates her terribly.

"Now you listen here," she barks, quite perturbed, "we haven't had any alcohol, that's absurd; I've been *cooking*. I'm a personal chef and I made some meals for my father-in-law who is recovering from open-heart surgery. My husband and our children had to wait for me. A long time. It got to be a strain. The boys fought and then my husband and I argued. There's nothing more to it than that. The call was a fluke. I don't know what got into me, but I assure you it wasn't necessary. And for the record, we don't do drugs."

Aurora is huffing angrily.

Officer Manning seems quite startled. He eyes her, nodding slowly. Evidently placated enough by her statement he says, "Okay Mrs. Sabel, enough of that for now. Let's move on." Shifting his weight on the sofa, the officer repositions himself in an offensive position. "It's pretty clear how this evening went down Ma'am, but I still have a few more questions and you need to clarify a few things." He studies the sheet in his hand. "So, during the alleged incident between you and your husband were any weapons involved?" He looks up and sits back abruptly.

Aurora can see he's bracing himself; he looks anxious. She explodes, "Incident! Weapons!"

The officer stares at her with wide eyes.

She starts to shriek, "What kind of *incident* do you think we had here? And *weapons*? Good heavens, what would we be doing with *weapons*?" She pulls the blanket up, her body's shaking. She's shocked at how vivid menacing weapons come to mind at the suggestion. "Please officer, nothing happened here - we just want to go home."

She trembles with growing anxiety thinking, *What else can I say? He's not hearing me.*

Officer Manning shakes his head and looks away, presumably deep in thought. Straightening his collar, he pulls at his shirt sleeves and runs his hands down the length of his torso smoothing invisible wrinkles, avoiding eye contact.

Aurora lowers her eyes and waits.

Sergeant Rafferty, seated at the dining room table with William, stirs in his chair. The rotund man shifts from hip to hip with great effort to find a comfortable position. He pushes the chair back aggressively, extends his legs, and rests his arms over his protruding belly. "Okay, let's get started," he says slowly expelling the air in his lungs, waving an impatient hand. "So, Mr. Sabel, how tall are you?"

"A tad under six foot four, Sergeant."

"And how much do you weigh?"

"Two forty, or maybe closer to two hundred forty-five pounds, sir."

Aurora looks up when she hears her husband's answer.

Simultaneously the men from across the room turn their attention upon her.

She smiles calmly at them.

They nod at her.

Unaware of this interaction, Officer Manning, looking at his file sheet and then at Aurora, begins on the same line of inquiry. "Okay then, let's leave the other questions for later and get on with these preliminaries. Alright then - so - Ma'am - how tall are you?"

"Uh - I'm five-three - almost five-four," Aurora says shyly, feeling William's eyes on her.

"And how much do you weigh?"

"Oh - well, I - I weigh something like one hundred forty pounds, officer," she says quietly jutting her chin, gazing purposely away from her husband's glinting eyes.

Nodding, she discreetly shakes her head knowing William is watching her. She hopes he's in accord with her view that the variable between a few pounds, plus or minus, means nothing in lieu of the situation. She returns her attention to her interrogator.

He hasn't noticed a thing.

Both parties finish filling out the paperwork. Only one thing remains. Her husband's red swollen lip must be photographed. He keeps dabbing at the dribbling mess with a tissue. It won't stop bleeding.

Geez, it's only a scrape - Aurora complains to herself.

William steals a glance at Aurora and shrugs; powerless to do anything.

He's about to say something when Sergeant Rafferty huffs and growls, "Hey, concentrate. It's late. Let's get this done."

A few Polaroids of William's formidable lip are taken from an ancient camera; the negatives pulled out and set on the dining room table to develop within a few minutes.

At rising, the lackluster-looking policeman runs both hands over his balding freckled head kneading his scalp as he walks into the living room area motioning for William to follow.

Aurora's eyes are fixated on the long wiry bristles of hair sprouting from Officer Rafferty's knuckles as he takes off his glasses and drops them carelessly onto the low coffee table; they collide with Officer Manning's papers, ruining their order.

With his hands on his hips the Sergeant arches his back and stretches opening his mouth so wide that Aurora can count many nuggets of old silver fillings.

He yawns noisily.

He motions for William to sit on the couch, but when William moves to sit next to his wife, the officer barks, "No! That - will - not - do," and makes him get up and move to a chair across from her.

The disagreeable Sergeant appears to be contemplative as he yanks at the bunched-up material at the crotch of his navy-blue pants.

"Listen up folks, we have a serious situation here," he says tugging on his pant leg. "There are new rules in the state of Florida now. Abiding statutes concerning domestic violence."

"What do you mean, *domestic violence*?" Aurora exclaims jumping up from her seat.

"Mrs. Sabel, please, sit down," Sergeant Rafferty orders promptly, "and listen."

The senior Officer turns his full attention upon Aurora.

"As I was trying to explain, this new law in the state of Florida concerning domestic disputes is called, Zero Tolerance. Now, if 911 is called, or merely dialed," he nods at Aurora, "and if any family member has been struck," keeping his eyes fixed on her, "and or injured, the assaulting person and sometimes both parties will be judiciously taken into custody."

"Sir," Aurora says sitting back on the sofa, "you're mistaken. We didn't do anything -"

Officer Manning turns to William and Aurora, and tries to mediate with pertinent statistics.

"You see folks, since the national attention of the O.J Simpson trial, Florida and other states are cracking down on domestic violence. It protects everyone involved in scenarios like this."

"*Scenarios* like *this*?" Aurora cries, her beseeching eyes darting from William to the cop.

William raises a hand motioning for her to stop talking. Her hands clamp over her mouth.

Aurora and William wait for the policemen to continue talking, but Officer Manning simply rises and both policemen retreat into their own thoughts. They gather up their papers without another word.

William waves at Aurora to stay seated. He stands up and waits to talk to them.

"I'm sorry about this Mrs. Sabel," says Officer Manning, lowering his head toward her.

She can see he's embarrassed as he steps around the coffee table. "I wish we didn't have to do this - but - well - could you please get your things together? We have to leave now."

What? Aurora stares at him. She doesn't understand.

William starts to object, but Sergeant Rafferty holds up his hand. "Mr. Sabel, it's the law."

With huge, questioning eyes, Aurora whispers, "What do you mean? You mean *me* - go with *you*? For how long? What about my children? We have to take them home!"

Accountability

She's pleading now, grabbing onto Manning's arm. Her body is twitching, her voice rising to a hysterical pitch. "Holy Mother of God - you can't be serious - you're taking me to go to jail because I *slapped* my husband? For God's sake - you've got to be kidding - look at him!"

The novice turns to the veteran and says in earnest, "Sir, this doesn't seem right, these people are not a threat to each other in any way. Why do we have to do this?"

Sergeant Rafferty takes off his glasses again and shakes his head closing bloodshot eyes. "Kid, this is the way it goes now. These are the new rules, and we have to enforce them."

Officer Manning drops his shoulders in defeat because he won't challenge his superior.

William tries to approach his wife, but his path is obstructed. His hostility is clear as he stands tall; his countenance fierce as a sentry trying to defend his wife's honor. "How can you do this?" He complains loudly. "You've heard our story. This is wrong. You know it's wrong. Don't take my wife. Take me instead!"

The law enforcers, hunched together rigid as a wall, wave him off with the strength of their authoritative influence. "Be warned Mr. Sabel, if you do not calm down, we will take *you* in as well," says Sergeant Rafferty with the stern voice of undisputable power.

William moves, but he won't back down. "Why are you doing this?" he asks again. "We've told you what happened here. Why can't you let it go? Why can't you just let us go home?"

Sergeant Rafferty displays all the empathy a well-seasoned officer should bestow upon unfortunate victims or ignorant wrongdoers.

"Mr. Sabel, let me explain it to you and your wife in clearer terms. Your behavior toward your child as a disciplinarian is not in question here. The altercation between you and your wife though, is. Unfortunately, this became a domestic violence dispute when your wife attacked you, unprovoked."

"But -" Aurora clutches her throat as her heart quickens.

The facts stated the way Sergeant Rafferty proclaims are irrefutable, but she can't understand his objective in building a case. She tries to stand but her legs won't support her.

Dropping back down onto the couch she begs, "Please sir, *please*."

Questions with the heat of a brush fire rush through Aurora's brain but she cannot seem to articulate any of them.

Her voice is dry and hoarse. "Sir, this is not what you think - I did not *attack* my husband."

She forces herself to stand face to face with the officer.
"I was - I - Sir, haven't you ever been in a state - or agitated enough to -" Aurora stops herself thinking, *Oh no - putting your foot in it again -*
"Sir, please - you can't take me - take me to *jail* - my gosh - you can see for yourself that my husband is unharmed -"

***

Aurora sits down hard.

The unexpected turn of events makes her whole body shudder. *This can't be possible - It just can't be -* she cries inside.

Suddenly she blushes thinking, *Oh, no! I need to change!* She's only wearing the t-shirt and sweatpants that Nancy lent her when she started cooking. Her undergarments and party outfit are in the boy's travel bag. "Oh, thank Goodness," she mumbles seeing the bag leaning against the wall at the front door.

***

Officer Manning is baffled by the unusual request.

"I don't get it Ma'am, you look fine to me," he says with a crooked peek, looking uncomfortable for the first time all evening. "You were already in your car ready to go home, Mrs. Sabel, why do you need to do this now?"

"Because if I have to go to - go with you - it will be in my own clothes," Aurora says jutting her chin out, mustering her last bit of self-righteousness to make her point.

Officer Manning shakes his head with an obstinate air. "No. No, it's impossible. It's against procedure. You have to remain in my sight at all times. What you're wearing is -"

"Please, you don't understand," she interrupts, "I can't go to that place half-naked -"

"Mrs. Sabel, you will have to change into the county uniform once you get there anyway."

His voice is cutting, but Aurora doesn't care; she stares at him, silently pleading.

"Oh, all right - just make it fast - wait -"

He stops Aurora as she's about to dash down the hallway and reaches for her bag.

"First I have to check your bag and secure the room. Are there are any firearms in the house?"

"*Firearms*? What kind of people do you think we *are*?" she reprimands, jerking it away.

"Ma'am, it's policy. I have to check." He looks inside quickly and gives the bag back. "Okay, see, all done. Now, please Mrs. Sabel, go change so we can get out of here."

***

William is trying to bargain with the Sergeant, but they're merely talking at each other; the decision is final.

Aurora walks back into the room in her party outfit and the men turn at once.

Sergeant Rafferty appraises Aurora, but he can't quite register the change.

Officer Manning raises an eyebrow, smiles, and imperceptibly nods at her.

William leaves the Sergeant mid-sentence and crosses the room. He gathers Aurora in his arms before anyone can stop him. He tightens his grip, brushes his bristly cheek against hers, and runs his lips down her neck.

"I'm so sorry Love, I can't change his mind. Please try not to worry, I'll get you out of there as soon as I can."

Aurora leans into his body and buries her face in his chest. She whispers, "Oh my God - please, William - don't let them take me -"

Sergeant Rafferty reels toward them visibly displeased. "Alright now, enough of that. Get your things Ma'am, we need to leave. Pronto." He tries to pass by William who's planted firmly in the middle of the room. "Excuse me Mr. Sabel, but you must let us through."

William reluctantly steps aside.

Sergeant Rafferty reaches for Aurora's elbow, but she spins away from him and grabs Officer Manning's arm.

The Sergeant huffs.

Officer Manning, noticeably uneasy, casually tucks Aurora's elbow securely into his hold. "Okay, well then," he utters as they advance toward the door.

Outside on the landing, Aurora turns and calls out, "William!" in a moaning wail of agony. She needs to see her husband's face, but the portly Sergeant is standing unyielding in the doorway.

With his hands on his hips, he's an imposing figure of resolve. "Let's go -" he says starting briskly down the path.

Grabbing Aurora by the arm and taking her from the junior cop like he's cutting in at a dance, he drags her further on in a powerful course.

As she trots unsteadily beside him she thinks, *The boys -* Aurora panics. And stumbles. She twists her body and calls over her shoulder as Sergeant Rafferty pulls her on, "William! What about the boys? Don't tell them anything - just tell them I love them - tell them I - tell them -"

"That's enough Mrs. Sabel," the Sergeant snaps. "Stop all this drama - it's not like you're going to the *moon*."

Aurora's heart is thumping, her fear is building, and a rush of lightheadedness makes her knees give way and she slips to the ground. She can't stop thinking of her children. Without her.

Accountability

With a firm grip and a jerk up, Rafferty pulls Aurora to her feet. In an uncharacteristically kind gesture, he leans down to brush some gravel off her shins.

Aurora swats his hand away and wrenches the elbow he's still gripping. Resentment turns to burning anger.

"Do you have children Sergeant?" she asks spitting the words at him. "Well mine are still babies - *babies*! They won't understand any of this. They'll ask, 'Where's Mama?' They won't know where I've gone, and they'll be inconsolable thinking I left them."

Sergeant Rafferty looks overthrown by surprise. He has no response.

Aurora glares at him, squares her shoulders, and walks away from the policeman with his mouth hanging open.

From the doorway William waves calling to Aurora. "Don't worry Love, the boys will be alright. When we're home, I'll call the station to find out how to get you out of there."

Aurora tries to wave back, but her arms feel like lead. "Yes - okay - but - oh -"

***

Aurora starts to cry when the handcuffs come out.

Officer Manning tries to fasten the cold metal braces loosely, but they clamp down tight and cut into her wrists right away.

William cautiously tries to make his way toward them, but Sergeant Rafferty holds his hand up to warn him away.

Aurora feels faint. She sways and bumps against the side of the car.

Officer Manning grabs her by the elbow, opens the door, and settles her into the seat. "Sir, can't you see this is -" he calls over the open doorframe. "Come on - do we have to do this?" Officer Manning's hands are on the roof of the car.

Aurora stares at his belt buckle and hopes that Rafferty will relent.

The Sergeant will not budge.

"Let's not do this kid, okay? It's the rules of the game now."

Aurora looks up to see the veins in his neck throbbing and she knows that Officer Manning is annoyed by Sergeant Rafferty's mind-set.

"I'm really sorry about this," he says, scooping up a bit of her skirt and laying it on her lap before closing the door.

***

Aurora is encased in the heavy vinyl seat. It sticks to her bare thighs when she tries to move.

The engine starts with a roar and they launch slowly down the road.

Aurora strains to see over the high back seat and keep William in her sights until the car must turn. He's at the apex of the lawn, shaking his head. The glow of the streetlamp lengthens his frame to a substantial shadow.

As they start to round the corner a ray of light flashes from the opening door.

Aurora has a fleeting glimpse of her little boys coming out of the house. She sees them stop and stare at the police car, as they wrap their arms about their father's legs.

***

The police car reeks of vomit.

Aurora's mouth is salivating and she's praying not to throw up.

Sergeant Rafferty swings his left arm over the low front seat and becomes talkative.

"Yeah," he says, as if he's continuing an ongoing conversation. "We had a guy in here a few hours ago. He beat his family up bad. He was so drunk that after he beat up his wife and kids, he even hit the dog. He got sick in here. We tried to clean it up, but it still stinks."

Accountability

Sergeant Rafferty tugs on the collar of his starched white shirt. He looks relatively satisfied with himself; apparently with his concerted effort at being civil.

"Why aren't you listening to me?" Aurora says, not loud enough for them to hear over the din of traffic. "We've *never, ever* hit each other -" She tries to get closer to the door handle, to reach the knob to turn the crank and get some fresh air, but it's impossible to do shackled. "Can't you take these off? They hurt," she whines rubbing her wrists. She drops back into the seat, frustrated at her inability to do such a simple task.

Aurora sees Officer Manning in the mirror deliberating over her request. He looks over at his partner calmly dozing. The consigned swishing of his head reveals his decision even before he speaks. "Sorry Ma'am, I can't do that, but I can stop and roll down the window, if you'd like."

"It doesn't matter," Aurora says exhaling. She turns her head away and looks out at the passing cars. She's exhausted.

Officer Manning adjusts his mirror repeatedly and Aurora catches his eyes darting from the road back to her. "I gotta tell you Mrs. Sabel, we've had some pretty bad cases. It's crazy how unpredictable people are - it starts out with an argument and then we'll get a call because someone's dead."

Startled, Aurora maintains an anxious fix on his face in the little mirror. *Dead? Geez, that's extreme,* she thinks. She's too tired and shocked at his words to ask any questions, but her look is enquiring.

As if he's read her mind he says, "You know, some scenarios hit a dangerous level, but this new law saves lives. The Zero Tolerance Act protects people. It works, I've seen it."

Aurora shifts in her seat. The vinyl clings to her skin like a greedy lover. "You have to believe that, I'll bet, to sleep at night. But in this case, you're way off the mark," she says with disgust.

The cop and Aurora's eyes lock for a moment and he solemnly nods at her.

"I can't believe that you've ignored everything we've been telling you," she continues becoming more agitated. "We aren't at all like the people or situations you're describing."

Officer Manning swivels to face Aurora at a red light. "You know Mrs. Sabel, in most cases the volatile factors are alcohol, drugs or people off balance in some way. But sometimes the impulsive nature of hostility in individuals is enough cause for deflective action. Now, if 911 is called, the authorities are obligated to go and investigate and separate the parties involved."

The light changes and he continues to talk; his eyes on the road and on her. "And you know what? Even if they've been removed from the scene, people are often compelled to return and because they go back to pursue the issue, someone, more often than not, ends up dead."

Aurora starts to cry saying to herself, *God, how awful.*

"I get what you're saying," she says sniveling. "A lot of bad things can happen between two heated individuals, but this isn't - we aren't - this was not that way. I can see that you know that. So how can you do this, knowing it's a farce? Even if your boss has the authority, why can't you say something when we get to the - get to the - jail?"

Raising her bound wrists to use a bare forearm to wipe away tears and snot running down her cheeks, Aurora sulks back into the seat, depleted of energy to plead her case any further.

Officer Manning looks again at his snoozing partner and readjusts his mirror.

Aurora notes that he has disengaged as well.

She sighs heavily.

She's worn out.

They travel the rest of the way in silence.

***

With silent tears Aurora plummets into a deep despair.

Accountability

She feels the shame of being considered a criminal.

She moans silently - *Assaulting my husband, unprovoked* - It's impossible for her to fathom.

Aurora can't stop hiccupping.

She needs air.

She tries to breathe slower.

She's afraid of what's coming - where she's going - what might happen to her in *there*.

She closes her eyes, puts her hands together, and prays:

Oh my God, I am heartily sorry for having offended Thee,
And I detest all my sins because of Thy just punishments,
but most of all because they offend you, my God,
Who art all-good and deserving of all my love.
I firmly resolve, with the help of Thy grace, to confess my
sins, to do penance and to amend my life. Amen.

Aurora can still recall the Act of Contrition from her childhood bible classes at St. A's.

The nuns had the catechism students recite the prayer over and over again.

Aurora dutifully memorized all the words, but she's never given the prayers much credence.

Until now.

Now she can feel the weight of it in keeping her Faith as shelter from a storm.

Chapter Three: Jail

Wheels crunch on the gravel at the county jail and shoot up under Aurora's seat. The parking lot is busy, full of transportation vehicles. Aurora stares grimly as handcuffed men and women are being escorted by uniformed guards toward the entrance of the facility. Colossal spotlights shine down on the grounds outlining the perimeters. Barbed wires coil along the high cement walls.

This is a mistake - It can't be happening - she whines to herself.

Officer Manning opens the door to retrieve Aurora. He takes a cuffed hand and tries to help her out of the car, but she won't budge. Like a thief holding her hostage, the seat won't release her. The strong officer pulls with more force, and with a slow farting sound, she's out.

Now Aurora is standing in the last place on earth that she ever expected to be.

***

Sergeant Rafferty is sitting in the front seat with his door hanging open, yawning. He scratches his head and picks his nose and flicks the muck into the jail yard. He says to no one in particular, "What a night, I'm beat. Thank God I have tomorrow off."

He stands and looks contemplatively over at Aurora.

"You better take care, little lady; it can get pretty rough in there."

Straightening his tie and adjusting his glasses, Sergeant Rafferty makes the mockery of a salute to Aurora and says to Officer Manning, "Get her processed. I'm headed home."

***

When they reach the reception counter, Officer Manning takes a clipboard off the wall and signs Aurora in. He says to the guard on duty, "Evenin' Joe, busy night, right; I see them coming in by the boatload. Hey, take it easy on this one here okay; she's nice and really scared."

Aurora lowers her head self-consciously. *Yes, I am nice - and yes, I am really scared* - she says, not loud enough for anyone to hear.

The cop's frown looks like a permanent fixture on his face as he peers down at Aurora.

"Yeah, sure, they're all nice until they kill someone," he grumbles with unconcealed disdain.

Aurora is shaking and can only scream inside, *Oh God, help me, I'm standing at the gates of hell !*

Officer Manning sneers at his coworker, but the cop named Joe, just shrugs.

Aurora is thankful that he spoke on her behalf and tells him so.

Inhaling slowly, he hesitates; it seems like he has something vital to impart.

Aurora stares at the man that only an hour ago flirted with her outrageously. *He doesn't seem so pompous here* - she thinks.

Officer Manning takes Aurora's wrists and carefully removes the hand cuffs. He thoughtfully massages the red scuffed skin.

"I really am sorry about all this Mrs. Sabel. If it were only up to me - be careful and look after yourself," he says softly, dropping his hold on her. "You're tougher than you think."

Officer Manning shrugs his shoulders and turns away, disappearing into the bustling mainstream of traffic.

The man at the front desk leaves his post, grabs his black cap from a rack on the wall, and advances toward Aurora. At first he appears to have a dense shadow of beard, but a closer look reveals deep purple craters littered across his face.

Aurora cannot hide her surprise and steps back.

His eyes narrow as he sees her reaction; the revulsion on Aurora's face is obvious. "What's the matter poppet? Haven't you ever seen a real blue beard before?"

Aurora's *'Oh - My - Gosh'* expression speaks for itself. She does think that he looks a little like one of Jack Sparrow's shipmates though. Even his demeanor seems blasphemous.

"How long will I be here?" she blurts out hoping that he doesn't hear the quiver in her shaky voice.

The pirate-cop named Joe grins crookedly flashing a bit of gold, and winks. He says with a snide grin, "Wouldn't you like to know," before motioning for Aurora to follow him.

They come to a huge room the size of a gymnasium.

He points with a flourish at the cavernous space. "Take a seat little miss and for your own safety, make yourself scarce. The amount of trouble you get into is up to you. An officer will call out names for processing in due time."

"Righty-oh," she murmurs, shrugging her shoulders.

Cocking his head to the side he sniggers, turns on his heel, and leaves Aurora to fend for herself.

The room is noisy.

People are congregating socially.

The place is buzzing with activity.

Groups are forming; chairs and a table are being added to accommodate a large party.

Guards carrying long serious-looking clubs are patrolling the area.

Aurora lingers in the doorway; she can't bring herself to step into the vast and uncharted territory of this strange new world.

Sometime later, the rangy figure of a man saunters into the room straight toward Aurora. He's wearing a standard uniform, but it isn't cut the same as his fellow officers. The jacket has been tapered; it's been altered to the style of a morning coat. The collar on his white shirt is stiff and winged and instead of a tie there seems to be an ascot cravat tied at his neck.

With grace and good diction he beckons, "Good evening young woman, might you be Mrs. Sabel?"

Stepping out of the corner from which she has been hiding, Aurora nods, "Yes, I am."

She has an urge to say, "Yes, it is I," but she doesn't think he'd catch the vernacular.

"Then let us commence," he says, clicking his heels and taking her up by the elbow. They begin to sashay - Aurora awkwardly stumbling alongside him - as he brings her to another station in an outer vestibule.

She wants to ask him who he is - where he's from - if he's ever read Jane Austen - but there's no time; they're moving too fast to make conversation.

They arrive at the designated area.

With a half turn and a pirouette he releases her and bows. "A fine evening to you Ma'am."

He adjusts his collar, turns on his heel and waltzes away.

Aurora watches marveling at his manner as he saunters around the corner. *Oh my word,* she says to herself.

***

Behind the desk at the Items Station stands a prominent looking man. His beefy hands are extended on the counter, his thick torso bent at the hips as he leans out to watch and observe. An intake of air fills his lungs, and his upper body puffs up showing the muscle definition of a man who works out regularly. His chest is broad and commanding. Like a great armor-plated gladiator, he looks big, powerful.

Until Aurora walks up to the desk. And sees the platform.

Gosh, that's strange, she thinks trying to be discreet, comparing his size against the height of the counter. *Ah, he's on some kind of elevation device,* she realizes.

The policeman has his hands on his hips glaring critically at Aurora, as if he's challenging her silent query.

Aurora, ashamed, turns away.

"Tisk, tisk," he admonishes shaking his head.

Aurora can see he is rebuking her; she feels like a spy who's been caught stumbling upon a national secret.

As she starts to say, "I'm sorry, I -" the clerk interrupts Aurora, brushing a lion's mane of bouncy curls away from his face. "Please hand over your purse and jewelry," he says with the hearty voice of a larger man. He looks like a Greek god and has the presence of a staunch leader.

Aurora begins to dismantle her life.

She takes off her wedding ring, looks at it, and sighs. She sets it down on the counter along with her earrings, necklace, and watch. She takes the contents out of her purse. A small bag of makeup, a comb, some hard candy, and her wallet. She starts to babble. "These things are - they're not valuable - but - well, they're quite valuable to *me* - where are you going to put them? Will they be safe? Could anyone come in and take them? When will I get them back? Can't I just keep the pictures in my wallet? I'm just so - so terribly - so nervous - sorry," she stammers breathlessly.

Arresting green eyes settle upon Aurora. He waves nonchalantly with benevolent charm. "Your treasures will be safe Ma'am. I am here to guard them, but everything must go in the bag. Everything."

The rich baritone of his voice seems incongruous to his body, but it works; Aurora is instantly more at ease as he hands her the claim papers and a big brown paper bag.

"Oh. Well. Yes. Okay. Thank you," she whispers feeling a little less insubstantial.

Before putting her wallet into the bag, she pulls out the two photos that she always carries with her.

She loves this one of her little guys at the beach.

Accountability

They're making a drip castle. She'd asked them to give her their best smiles. Her older boy is looking straight into the camera with a warm indulging radiance. Her little fireball, with his tongue sticking out in a dimpled grin, defiant and mischievous as always, has a sparkle in his eye. *Typical* - she thinks, smiling. Aurora slowly lets out a weary sigh, longing for them.

The picture of William is comical as well. He's standing turned away from the camera having dropped his shorts to show the tan line between his broad tanned back and his white backside. He's such a showoff. Each photo is priceless.

Aurora puts a hand to her mouth to stifle the voice that wants to scream, *This just can't be - dear God - please - get me out of here !*

***

After gathering up the bag and Aurora's claim forms, the officer punches a few numbers into his intercom and calls the next station. Nodding at Aurora, he says authoritatively, "We're done here Ma'am. After printing you'll be issued facility clothing. All of your belongings will be put into a bin for safekeeping until you're released."

He steps down from the platform and walks into the storage room with her things.

Suddenly, the room looks a lot bigger.

***

Right then a female guard comes into the room.

"You Mrs. Sabel? I'm to take you to the holding area Ma'am. We're running late, so let's get a move on."

She has a disagreeable scowl and sucks her lips as if she's eaten sour lemons.

Aurora is already so tired she barely registers the command. "Yes, alright," she says and follows the woman to an adjoining room.

The dour policewoman is about to abandon Aurora, but then she remembers her duty and before she retreats says, "Find a seat. It may be a while. Then we'll get you processed."

***

Shallow partitions divide the space into orange and blue sections. Drug Intervention and Alcohol Prevention posters are mounted in steel frames on the grey walls around the room.

Aurora spots an empty corner and takes a seat.

Televisions are bolted to the floor in each area. Every screen shows Richard Dreyfus soaked in jungle khakis balancing on a pile of rock off the coast of Ecuador. The documentary is running without audio, only a bold yellow band of subtitles.

The actor seems exhilarated. He speaks to the camera as Aurora reads that he's searching for the Galapagos lizards.

She tries to comprehend what she'll do while she waits. Watch Richard Dreyfus? Forceful waves are thrashing up on the glistening black volcanic jetty set against a cloudless azure sky. Even with sound she'd have no interest.

She plays with the knobs to change the channel, but the buttons don't respond. She looks around for something to read, but there's only twelve-step AA and NA pamphlets.

Dejected, Aurora clasps her hands together, lowers her head, closes her eyes, and prays:

Dear Lord, if You just get me out of this place, I promise to be better. I'll be more agreeable - less impulsive -

The list of reformations is long, her sincerity genuine.

Ah, the vows we make in desperation, begging to be saved.

***

Time passes.

Accountability

Aurora looks up and scans the ever-active room. Displaced men and women are floating around the facility. A few are paired up, two by two, walking the perimeter; panting like caged animals. Others with less anxiety are lying in a fetal position on the carpeted floor, sleeping. An obese woman has collapsed across a walkway. Her enormous multi-colored dress is spread out like a blanket at a picnic, obstructing public passage. People are mumbling obscenities; they're not pleased to dodge around her to get to the corridor. The woman is oblivious to their catcalls; Aurora can see that her eyes are glassy black pools.

Many of those milling about seem to be familiar with each other; they're even cordial.

Aurora hears, "Hey, man, no shit, you here again? How's it going? Seen Harry lately?"

She knows how horrified she'd be if she heard someone call out, "Hey Aurora, what are you doing here?"

***

For a while there's only white noise.

She closes her eyes and rubs her temples.

A shuffling sound makes Aurora look up right as a man in torn jeans and a dirty shirt is crossing the room; he's headed straight at her. He's unsteady on his feet, like walking on a tightrope. He teeters and totters and tumbles onto the seat next to her. He tries to right himself, unsuccessfully. Slicking back his long stringy hair, he looks her over slowly. "Yo baybee, how you doin?" With the back of his hand he wipes drool from his bushy mustache and smears it on his pants. Gawking at Aurora he winks with hopeful anticipation. "What's say we go somewherz and -"

Good God, what's this now? she wonders, as Aurora sits back in her seat with the force of being pushed. "Please. Go away-" she murmurs in a low voice, arching her body away from the man.

She's penned in.

He's tilting into her.

His intrusion startles her, gluing her to the seat. *What kind of derelict is this?* she asks herself.

Until now the people Aurora has encountered have been relatively kind and harmless, but this guy seems sinister in an, 'I could take you right here', kind of way, and Aurora can't help but be afraid that he may try to grab her.

The man reeks of alcohol.

His breath is rancid.

He's snorting air like a pig, huffing deeply, and puffing it out in a strained effort.

Aurora crosses her arms over her chest. She remembers drunken guys like this one when she bartended years ago in a rowdy country-western bar. She knows what to do. She leans in a little toward the man and bellows, "Listen buster - listen! You better move - move it! Or I'll call a - a bouncer -" She grips the chair rail pulling back, bracing herself for his response.

Back in those bar days, it was all she needed to say, but sizeable bouncers were watching over the young female bartenders, just waiting for a signal to bully the rough guys out.

Who's going to save me now ? she wonders crossing her arms, hugging herself tightly, sitting upright in the seat.

The dazed man clears his throat loudly, his bloodshot eyes wandering haphazardly around the room.

The scene has aroused the attention of a few curious people. They stop what they're doing briefly to look over at Aurora, but no one says a word, and no one makes a move to help her.

The drunkard's reaction is a blank-eyed vacant shrug; all the pomp has gone out of him. He glances in the vicinity of Aurora, but his watery eyes move sluggishly past her. It looks like he's trying to figure out where he is, as if he's just arrived in a foreign land and can't read the signs. She can see the dulled mechanisms in his brain toiling, but nothing registers.

"Wow man, like, yeah, okay," he mumbles in a delayed reaction rubbing his forehead. He scratches the stubble on his shadowy chin, and he hoists himself up. He weaves in a zig-zag toward the nearest bench and drops down, almost missing the mark, onto a vacant seat.

Aurora sits up a little straighter trying to regain her composure; hoping to quiet her thumping heart.

After a long wait, a female officer with bright eyes, a full head of cornrows, and a heavy Jamaican accent, greets Aurora in a welcoming way. "Hey ah, Aurora Sabel? I'm offissa Golden. How ah ya girl? Yous ta come wit me ova heeya an' we'll juss take cara some tings." Her tone is like Caribbean music. The scent of roses emanating from her, is heavenly.

Aurora inhales and sighs and takes the extended hand of the friendly woman. They move together like dance partners across the room. Aurora feels like her feet aren't touching the ground. She wishes they could stroll right out the door.

Officer Golden holds Aurora at arm's length and gives her a thorough looking over. "So, baby, hows doin'? You doin' awl raht?"

In a shrill voice Aurora's cries, "Oh sure - I'm great - I -" and pitches over, about to fall.

"Whoa -" says the policewoman catching Aurora by the waist, steadying her upright.

"Actually -" Aurora says as bile shoots up her throat, "I think - I'm going to be sick -"

Without hesitation the police lady turns Aurora around and envelops her in an embrace. She holds her tight and rocks Aurora gently in her arms. "Come on now, you'll be okay baby. We juss need to get a handle on tings and then we'll git you all sorted out."

The kind official gives Aurora a squeeze and gently helps her to be seated. Aurora silently complies.

Officer Golden is pleasant and encouraging. "How 'bout you step ova heeya. Take your shoes off my deeya, then we'll measha ya -" she says in a singsong, melodic voice.

Aurora wants to oblige the nice policewoman, to do everything she asks, but the thought of her bare feet on the dirty linoleum tiles - she just can't do.

"Oh, please Ma'am," she pleads, pulling her pink sandals under her chair, "Don't make me take them off - look at this floor -"

The policewoman studies the floor, gazes at her ward and beams. "Ah, yeahya - I see what cha mean girl, no problem; go ahead an' keep yur pretty shoes on, it won't kill nobody."

Aurora's height, with the heels, is about one and a half inches taller on the report.

After concluding their business, officer Golden leads Aurora down a hallway to an area where more people are gathered.

It's freezing in the building; to shake off the chill, Aurora walks faster to stay close to the female official because she seems to emit her own heat.

When they're standing in the doorway Aurora asks, "What should I do - where do I go?"

Officer Golden reaches for Aurora's hand. She squeezes it and in a gentle command says, "Go find a quiet spot and wait there. Noone'll botha ya - I've gotta an eye on ya."

Aurora feels like she's being hypnotized.

The officer's soft, tranquilizing voice and those kind, penetrating eyes looking right into her soul, seem to insist that there's no need to worry. "Don't fret now baby; no-ting bad will happen to ya." She embraces Aurora with thorough reassurance. "Trust me. I know what I'm talkin' about."

Aurora walks over to a vacant corner of the room and stands there. She watches the charismatic woman's arms raise slightly as she turns gracefully, and glides down the hall.

Soon she's out of sight.

Aurora hugs herself and wonders.

The distinctive, blessedly sweet smell of roses, lingers.

Chapter Four: An Angel?

A wastepaper basket smolders in the corner of the room. Little flashes of fire lick at the rim.

Two officers rush to put it out.

"Bill, find the asshole who did this," says one man to the other guy.

An adolescent starts to move with hunched shoulders, out of the room.

Oh, he's just a kid - she thinks. No, Aurora sees that he's not a kid; he's short and slender, but middle-aged; his temples grey.

His eyes dart suspiciously with guilt written on his face.

The larger of the two guards spots him slithering away and shouts, "Hey-boy-oh-Mr.- stop right there! Don't even try to leave."

The man stops in his tracks. He raises his hands, open palms up. "What? I didn't do nothin' -"

"Just stay where you are Mister."

The smaller officer pats down the guys pants and sure enough he has a pack of matches in his pocket.

"What the hell do you think you're doing setting fire to a garbage bin?"

The guard waits, but the man says nothing; he silently shakes his head and shrugs.

As the boy-man is ushered out, Aurora looks around the room.

A group of women are seated at a big table. They're chatting amiably as if they meet there often. Leaning against a wall, a bunch of men are apparently enjoying a rather lewd joke. The snorts of laughter turn into such a howling that it causes one of the guys to choke violently on his own saliva.

Aurora's exhausted; she's been waiting for hours. She wants to go home. *When is this processing over?* she wonders. She stands to stretch her legs; they're stiff from being sedentary. Questions bounce in Aurora's head: *Will they take my statement and then let me go? How will William know where to find me?* Her mind wanders and her eyes fix upon the biggest, blackest man she's ever seen. *Wow - that's a big guy,* she thinks. *I'll bet he could lift a Volkswagen. He'd be my first choice for a body guard.* She angles herself at a covert viewpoint, curious to compare his size to the others.

The massive man is sitting at a large round table at the far end of the room. He outweighs the motley crew around him by a hundred pounds. At least. They plainly see him as King Pin, hanging on his every move. Something funny makes them all laugh. The big man joins in laughing heartily and pounds a fist that sounds like a clap of thunder, sending plastic cups flying off the table. He becomes serious, pensive, no longer amused. The festive mood is immediately stilled.

Aurora wonders why he's there. Her imagination runs wild at the possibilities. *Don't think about that,* she says to herself. *Who cares about him; I just want to get out of here.*

She turns from the hustle and bustle of activity and shuffles back to her corner to brood.

***

Much later, a very tall guard covered in tawny freckles strides into the area. Her gait bends inward; the knees of a giraffe. She brushes ringlets the color of carrots off her face as thick eyelashes blink slowly. She plants her legs in an inverted V and calls out, "Sabel - Aurora Sabel here?"

Aurora sits up at attention when she hears her name called. "I'm here -" she answers in a whisper because her throat is so dry.

The guard doesn't hear her and starts to walk back toward the other end of the room.

"That's me - I'm - here - please -" Aurora shouts quite a bit louder, waving to the officer.

Some heads turn to see what sounds like a cry for help, but it doesn't hold their attention.

The policewoman signals to Aurora and struts toward her. "Ah, good. Okay. Mrs. Sabel, you need to go over there and sit down." She points to an area blocked off by blue partitions. "Relax, it won't be long now; soon you'll get your tags and then we'll get you printed."

The long-legged officer strides out of the room.

Tags? Printed? she wonders.

Aurora has much to learn.

***

Aurora is surprised to see the man who she was spying on, seated where she has been sent.

His considerable frame dwarfs the bench under him. He lounges, legs like felled tree trunks extended and arms crossed over an abdomen that's straining the t-shirt he's wearing. His eyes are closed, his breathing sedate; he's napping.

Aurora retreats, not wanting to alert him of her presence and thinks, *Now what do I do? There's no other vacant seats?*

Noiselessly she walks around the bench and stands at the only empty seat; right under him. She watches him breath: in and out - in and out. When he stirs and reaches up to scratch an itch; rubbing his scalp and his fuzzy gray halo, Aurora slips quickly into the spot.

He drops his arm, changes position slightly, and now she's stuck. Pinned under him.

"Uh - excuse me - sir - can I - could you - sorry – there's nowhere else to sit -" she says quietly, more than a little afraid of waking the sleeping giant.

The man seems unimpressed noticing Aurora. He lifts an elbow and gazes under his armpit, then rubs his nubby beard and yawns. As he tries to turn, the seat underneath him moans as if in pain. The task evidently enervates him; he yawns again and then closes his eyes dismissing the whole matter.

Aurora doesn't want to move.

Ever.

She secretly measures their arms and thinks, *Geez, he's even bigger than William.* She exhales deeply and relaxes into the tight little seat. *You can't beat this kind of security,* she thinks.

For a long time, they remain that way.

***

In an instant the room is alive with noise.

And action.

Two male guards are bringing in a rather disheveled man dressed in women's clothes.

His dress, belt and blouse are caked with mud, his fishnet stockings torn to shreds. A blonde wig hangs jauntily askew, revealing a shadow of dark stubble underneath.

Lips smeared red, eyes coaled with black liner, and a deep cut on his cheek pronounce the man's pathetic appearance.

He looks lost, no clue where he is.

His legs are elastic. One of the heels on his Patten leather boots has broken off. He hobbles unevenly making it difficult for the guards to keep a hold on him. He seems slippery because they keep dropping him as his arms flap from side to side.

The large man next to Aurora awakens at the commotion. Finding the scene humorous, he chuckles, rocking back and forth.

The bench creaks jostling Aurora as if she were riding in a bumper car. She grabs the rail, anticipating falling off, but his sheer mass holds her in place.

"That's terrible," she says hesitantly to the man who's restraining her. "Terrible for all of them."

The man peers down at Aurora.

She smiles meekly.

He nods soberly, without comment.

When they question the rubbery man, all that comes out is gibberish.

"Man, let's process this wacko fast and throw him into Detox," says one frustrated-looking cop to his harried-looking partner.

Gumby is so inebriated his body won't stay upright.

Like a vaudeville act, one cop tries to hold the boneless body, while the other cop grips the lifeless hand trying to work his fingers. The ink pad slips off the desk and papers scatter to the floor.

Gumby almost goes down too.

"Yo - Ma'am - buddy - hey - help us out here -" says the annoyed guard.

Gumby doesn't hear him.

"*Hey* - why does *he* get to go ahead of *us* -" asks a pinched faced woman whose been waiting to be processed. "I've been here much longer than that dope." She taps her foot on the floor, the cadence conveying her impatience.

The officers are too busy to respond to her.

The tap-tap-tap continues but there's no reply. "Figures," she says in a huff turning on her heel.

"I saw 'em bring that guy in earlier - he's wearin' high heels - the queer - whatever he got - he deserves -" says a scrawny-looking young man wandering into the area to no one in particular. An unpleasant stench seems to surround him; the odor so overwhelming that it looks like he has a kind of greenish glow.

Aurora discreetly covers her nostrils and breaths from her mouth.

He sees her, and with a taunting glare, he pulls on the snaps of his sleeveless plaid shirt, opening it. He flaps the sides as if to air himself out.

Aurora turns away, but not before she notices the skull and bones tattooed on his skinny arm.

The word 'Freedom' is etched into his bicep as well; the ragged lettering probably self-inscribed with his own knife. The rough teen's Doc Martins are unlaced, the strings snapping under his feet as he treads toward the partition's ledge to rest an elbow. He strokes a shaved head without remark. After hacking loudly, he shuffles onward with a mouth full of snot in search of a place to spit. Aurora sees him hurl his mucus but miss the bin by inches, the muck landing on the carpet. Wiping the slobber off his face, he looks around, laughs, and stomps away.

Disgusting. What a punk, Aurora thinks, turning her head, looking away.

"I heard they found him in an alley around Ybor City. Gay area," says a leathery faced man, walking to where the arrogant youth was moments before.

He licks both index fingertips and flattens down the gray wisps of electrically charged hair spiked on his head.

"What a revolting way to live," he says lazily taking in the scene.

He coughs open-mouthed and walks away.

Aurora feels the bench give a little squeal as the big man squirms in the cramped space. The weight of his hard muscle traps her as he reaches across her chest for the chair rail to pull himself up. Aurora can smell the familiar brand of William's cologne as the man's body presses close to hers.

"Fuckin' cheap city can't even build decent size benches." He adjusts his t-shirt and wedges himself back into the inadequate space. Tight jeans outline a toned thigh muscle when he stretches his legs out.

Aurora can see that he's huge, but he isn't fat. He's rock solid. Her sandals next to his gigantic black on black Converse high-tops are half the size.

Accountability

He flexes feet that look like paddles in big wobbly movements; back and forth, back, and forth. He seems to be contemplating.

Aurora wants to get away from the whole situation, but she's too afraid to move. She tells herself to stay put even though her backside is numb with pins and needles and her neck is aching. Aurora's thinking, *It's a circus in here; a bunch of oddballs roaming around* - and sighs loudly trying to shift her position.

The man tilts his head and looks curiously at Aurora.

She mutters to herself, *I didn't say that out loud, did I?*

They make eye contact.

He nods.

She nods and smiles shyly.

Her face flushes as he smiles benignly back at her. "So, what's someone like you doing here?" His voice is deep, rich, unambiguous.

Instantly Aurora has an image of the man in an elegant tuxedo, puffing on a fat Cuban cigar, leaning on a baby grand piano in a classy jazz bar saying, "So, doll, what's a girl like you doing in a place like this?"

It makes her light-headed.

He watches her carefully and waits.

Aurora starts to speak, "Well, it's a long story, I'm not sure you want to hear it all -"

At the same time, an orderly in baggy white overalls pushes a cart into the waiting area. Heads turn as the man with the food sets up his station, surely preparing for an onslaught.

"Saved by the bell," Aurora says to the man next to her trying to be funny, but he's no longer listening.

The triple-decker cart with the logo 'Food Wise' in bright green letters has stacks of thick white Texas toast and bologna sandwiches piled high.

The name Frank is embroidered in blue script on the man's shirt pocket. Frank has an air of pride adjusting the hygienic netting over his hair.

"Sandwiches, sandwiches here," he calls out like a vendor at a ball game. "But only *one* -" Frank cautions the crowd coming toward him, pointing a finger at the throng of people tromping in a rumble to the cart.

Aurora's stomach is churning, beginning to ache. She covers her mouth thinking, *Oh no, if I smell food now, I know I'll be sick* - "Uh - would you like my sandwich?" Aurora asks the man next to her; she can see by his size that he must have quite an appetite.

He smiles and nods encouragingly.

Aurora goes over to where Frank is handing out the goods, points toward the big man and explains her plan to him. He nods and quickly hands her two blocks of bread.

Giving over their sandwiches she says, "Geez, I've heard tell that prison food is atrocious, but this - gosh - this won't even make a dent, will it big guy?"

The man pauses mid-bite. His eyes narrow, his face puckers like has a bad taste in his mouth. He lays the sandwich down on his thigh and leans toward Aurora with a knitted brow.

The hairs on her neck stand up as she thinks, *Oh no - he thinks I'm insulting him.*

With palms up, Aurora shrugs her shoulders in an attempt to be funny and smiles broadly.

His expression and demeanor gradually soften. He chuckles. Between recommenced chewing he asks, "Okay, so tell me. What are you doing in here?"

Aurora doesn't know how to start. She thinks, *How do I tell this stranger anything? I don't even know his name.* "Well, gee, first - I'm Aurora," she says, thrusting her hand at him. "Aurora Sabel."

"Kenny Bensen," he says, settling her hand in his.

They sit there.

And time stands still.

***

Accountability

Aurora closes her eyes.

She can't believe that twenty-four hours ago she was home in bed.

In a flash she sees the start of the day, very early that morning when the house was quiet.

While William was sleeping, she'd lain in bed appreciating God's handy work at the stripes of sunshine filtering through the blinds. She recalls it being so blissfully tranquil that she'd wished she could cancel the day's obligations and stay home.

She remembers hearing the padding of little feet and the sweet melody of voices from down the hall. She'd nudged William. "Do you hear them? No, don't move - pretend you're asleep so they can jump you. Honey roll over, so they don't hit you in the - oh, here they are!" She can see the boys pouncing on their father.

"Gotcha, Papa!" they'd cried with pure joy.

"Oh yeah," William had moaned, shielding his privates, "you got me alright."

The heady feeling Aurora gets is heavenly; her heart pounds when she revels in the miracle of that unconditional love. *This is my home, this is my family,* she recalls saying to herself.

She remembers William gazing at the three of them with a satisfied look on his face.

"Look at these two - what more is there?" He'd rolled back to make more room and the boys nestled between them. "I keep telling you Aurora, this is all that's important. Let the other stuff go."

She'd smelled the cocoa butter he'd rubbed on their skin after their bath the night before; William would squeeze their hands and toes with cream and make them hoot with delight and beg for more.

Smiling, she'd whispered, "You're right. No, I know. You're *right*. I just hope no one blows up today -"

"Let your father enjoy your children. That's all you have to do," William had said grabbing the boys, tickling them.

Leaving that haven had been tough, but they'd had to go to the party.

Aurora remembers being frantic watching William slowly sip his coffee.

She'd paced the room testily, "Come *on* already!"

She'd been in a panic to get there on time knowing full well that her father's displeasure could, with a disdainful nod and well-known frown, reduce her to self-loathing.

William had tried to placate her. "Baby, relax, will you? It'll all work out. Stop stressing."

Aurora thinks of the quarrels they've had; sometimes explosive, most times with quick resolution.

She smiles recalling the catch-me-if-you-can game they play often.

"Why are you taking so long - you know what going to my father's house does to me -" she remembers saying. "You're doing this on purpose to make me crazy - let's get going - *What*? You're smiling - why are you smiling?"

She'd had her hands on her hips.

He'd been scanning her body with a lustful appraisal.

"Okay, sure - yeah - let's get going -" she recalls William saying with a gleam in his eyes moving toward her.

"Ohhh - nooo - there's no time for *that* -" Aurora had said giggling, backing away.

"Sure, there's time," he'd said grinning, scooping her up by the waist. "We'll *make* time."

She can feel her face heat up.

He'd been very persuasive, and they'd made time.

***

Now she sees her father's face when he opened the door, pointing at his watch. She knew that the humorous gesture masked his disapproval. He'd ushered them in and teased his grandchildren. "Look at you handsome guys, you're lookin' more like your ole grandpa every day."

He'd leaned down and pinched their cheeks.

The boys had wiggled and giggled.

"Give your grandpa a kiss," she'd said pushing them forward. She'd given her father a peck on the cheek and said, "Happy birthday Daddy," before hurrying off to put the food she'd brought to an outside table.

William must have told him a funny story, because Aurora remembers hearing her father's laughter as they'd gone outside to join the party.

The day had passed pleasantly, and she'd been relieved.

Anxiety had reared its ugly head that morning, taunting her like a bully, trying to dishearten her hopes for restored kinship with her estranged family.

It had been a terrible divorce; the shattering of lives so devastating that even decades later unresolved issues would resurface. Sadly, she wonders but can't remember if her parents ever touched each other. Remarried to nice people, the new spouses are a good fit, but ancient history comes out of hiding like a mean, vindictive monster, gnashing at old wounds to remind them that there once was another alliance. The past is painful and new family affairs often begin with the hope and promise of a first date only to end in bitter disillusionment.

***

Aurora remembers how much she wanted to go straight home after the party.

Returning by way of his parent's house though, had made it viable for Aurora to help William's father. She'd created the menu and William's mother had shopped. Everything was set. All Aurora had to do was cook for a few hours and make two weeks' worth of meals.

"Geez, I wish we hadn't set this up," Aurora recalls saying to William that afternoon. "I really want to help your dad, it's just so late and we've been out all day. The boys are pooped." She'd hoped he'd consider cancelling, but she knew that the commitment had been made.

"I'll take care of the boys Aurora. You just do your thing," William had said. "My Dad needs our help, Love. He can't change bad habits without our support. What you're going to do for him is really important. It will definitely put him on the right track."

She knew then that she couldn't let any of them down.

William's parents, being married for thirty-seven years, and his whole family being close, is a blessing to Aurora. Sure, they quarrel, but they *talk*, and *get over it*. Their commitment to each other is what she envies.

Aurora doesn't trust herself opening this Pandora's box; to expose all the complicated intricacies of the day's events to the man sitting next to her. She's finally calmed down and wants to remain that way. But the warmth emitted from Kenny's hand, and the intent look in his eyes are like a beaconing; a gentle luring, lighting the way. The words spill out in a flourish and she tells him everything. A waterfall of tears stream down her cheeks.

He releases his grip on her so she can wipe her eyes with the back of her hand. When it appears that she's done, Kenny gets up. "Hang on a minute," he says.

Aurora watches his wide shoulders sway in rhythm with his relatively slender hips as he gracefully maneuvers through the maze of intermittent groups splattered in his path.

He disappears into what must be the men's room and returns with a wad of toilet paper.

"Here, take this, you're blubbering all over everything."

"Gosh, that's nice of you," Aurora says. She honks loudly into the tissue, then hiccups.

Her face is red and puffy.

Her eyes burn from fatigue.

She wants to lay down and let it all go.

"It's fucked up, you know, your shit playin' out like that," Kenny says, standing over Aurora. "The cops're all corrupt. They're just fillin' a monthly quota. Legally they can't do what they did to you. You should call your old man and get him to call a bail bondsman to spring you outta this place."

Accountability

Kenny scratches his head and looks about the surrounding area.

"A bail- geez, I haven't a clue what that is," Aurora says, seeing only the shadow cast upon Kenny's face from the harsh ceiling lights.

"Okay," she says. "I'll call my husband. He'll know what to do. Thanks Kenny, you've been very kind."

Kenny shakes his head agreeably and finagles his way back into the little seat. He crosses his legs, adjusts his weight to get sufficiently comfortable, rests his arms over his broad chest, and closes his eyes.

Aurora gets up and heads toward the phones.

Kenny bolts upright and cups his hands over his mouth like a loudspeaker, beckoning her before she's out of earshot. "Hey - Aurora! It's called a bail bondsman - remember that name."

***

The sign above the four telephones mounted along a padded wall reads in black letters: COLLECT CALLS ONLY.

Aurora wipes the telephone's mouthpiece with the edge of her dress, dials zero, and talks to the operator.

She hears her husband accepting the call.

"Aurora, baby, are you there? Where did they take you? Are you alright?"

Aurora's breath catches at the sound of William's voice. She starts to cry; she can't stop.

"Oh Love, don't cry. I'm so sorry. I can't believe they took you in after we explained everything to them," William says. "I even tried calling the local precinct, but they said they couldn't help me."

"I can't believe the 911 call went through," Aurora sniffles. "What a mess I've made."

For a moment they seem to have been disconnected.

"Baby, are you there?" William asks.

Aurora hesitates.

"How're the boys? Have they asked about me? Are they upset I'm not home? You didn't tell them the police took me, did you? I'll *kill* you if you did -"

She looks around the room to see if anyone is within earshot and thinks, *God, I hope no one heard that.*

"No, of course not Aurora. I put them right to bed when we got home. They're fast asleep now. I told them you went shopping -"

"*Shopping*? At eleven o'clock at night?"

"I didn't know what else to say - I said they'd see you in the morning, but now I have to make something else up when they wake up." Aurora can hear that William's tired as he sighs. "Anyway," he says, "a public defender called already; he's been assigned to your case. He relayed a few preliminary things that we'll need to do when you get home." William sounds exhausted, no longer positive and reassuring.

Aurora's nerves are frayed. She's exhausted too, but she still has to relay the information that Kenny has given her.

"William, honey, I met a man in here - he's nice - we've been talking - I told him everything - do you know what a bail bondsman is?"

"Aurora - wait - what? You met a man? There in the jail?" William's octave rises; he seems as agitated as a jealous lover. "Did he - are you - I mean, you're okay - aren't you?"

"William, sweetheart, I'm fine. Just terribly tired. The man's name is Kenny Benson. I told him the whole story and he said that we need this bondsman. Do you know what that is?"

"Uh, yes, I know what a bail bondsman is Aurora, but it won't do us any good."

Through a lengthy discourse, William explains why.

The facts deject both their spirits.

William is silent.

Aurora stews.

"Well, if I'm to be stuck in here, at least I know now that I can take care of myself," she finally says looking out into the room.

"What do you mean Aurora? Did something happen?"

"Oh, I just had a little run-in with a drunken idiot," she says. "He was bothersome for a short time, but I got rid of him."

"Wait - *What*? What happened? A guy in there - a man *attacked* you? Did he hurt you?"

Aurora can't help feeling empowered by her husband's shock and worry.

"No, no. It was nothing like that. Don't worry Lovey, I'm okay, really."

As they talk further, William conveys what the attorney told him about her case.

Aurora sighs.

"Well, my status as a felon isn't as devastating as it would be if you were branded for life."

Her voice cracks at the realization, *Geez, and I've never even had a parking ticket.*

***

The operator comes on the line to tell them their ten minutes are almost up.

"William, please forgive me. I'm so sorry that I slapped you," she says sincerely.

"You know Love, I didn't think you could reach that high," he says trying to be funny.

"Oh, I hate you," she says.

"But I love *you*," he tells her.

Aurora hangs up the phone with a little more information on the legalities concerning the state of her affairs, and a lot more faith that no matter what, they'll face it together.

***

Kenny seems oblivious to his surroundings, staring into space with a serious look on his face as Aurora squeezes in next to him.

He acknowledges her presence by shifting his weight and swaying, making the bench tip, to give her a bit more room.

She's settled in like a mouse in a hole, and doesn't mind it at all.

A few minutes pass in a treading-water like state, but she can't contain herself any longer.

Tapping his shoulder, she hopes he'll look down at her, but he doesn't respond. She uses a more aggressive tact to get his attention by jabbing him in the side with her elbow.

At first he seems aggravated, but his face softens when he sees her bursting to deliver the information she's acquired.

"What's got you all worked up?" he says yawning.

She's so relieved he's asked her, that she grabs his arm, and squeezes the iron-hard muscle.

"Okay, I found out a whole lot of things. First of all, I can't get a bail bondsman like you said because it's a domestic violence case. The law states that in these situations the arrested person must remain incarcerated for a minimum of twenty-four hours."

Kenny appraises Aurora with a banal expression.

He mouths the words, "I know that."

She waves an impatient hand at him.

"This guy, the state-appointed attorney that called William, my husband," Aurora says becoming agitated, "said that nothing can be done to facilitate my release until Tuesday because Monday is a holiday. Everyone incarcerated will have to lay over the two days. Two days! No one's getting out."

"I know that too," he says smugly rubbing his beard, pulling on the hairs under his chin.

"But I can't stay here - I'll go berserk if I have to stay cooped up in here -" Aurora shouts.

A few cops look up from their stations to see where the commotion is coming from. Seeing the outburst is insignificant, their attention wanes, and they go back to their own business.

Kenny though, looks visibly affected by her rising temper.

He shifts away from her, a frown of concern and unease making deep creases on his forehead. He tells Aurora to calm down.

"Calm down - *calm down*?" Aurora yells, "that's what my husband kept saying!"

Kenny stares at her wordlessly, then scrambles to hoist his body out of the seat.

Aurora feels a whoosh of warm air as he steps away. She watches him move away; her mouth open in bewilderment. In long strides he stomps all the way to the end of the room.

She sees, as he heads back to her, that his expression continually changes.

He's talking to himself.

He can't fix this - he has his own problems - Aurora thinks. She grabs her head and squeezes her temples. *Oh God, I'm losing it!* she moans silently.

Kenny walks back and sits beside Aurora. He gently lays a hand on her back. His body heat gives off a rich musky scent, but the warmth of the contact doesn't soothe her, it makes her anxious. "Listen," he says patting her lightly, then removing his hand, "it's going to be okay. You're gonna be all right. In the end, you'll go home."

Aurora explores his face. He's smiling and nodding with an expression of assurance. She can't understand why he looks so pleased with himself; it aggravates her. "What do you mean I'm going home?" she says irritably. "Of course I'm going home. We're all going home - eventually."

"Yeah, well," he says leaning back in the cramped seat, wiping some sweat off his brow and smearing it on his jeans, refraining from saying anything more.

Aurora stands, crosses her arms on her chest, and faces the big man. Now she has to know. "Okay big guy, I know you're not my fairy godmother, so what are you doing here?"

"Good sense of humor Aurora," he laughs, "but you wouldn't believe it, if I told you."

"Oh, come on, tell me, it can't be that bad," Aurora asks hoping it won't be really terrible.

He sighs, and acquiesces.

"The whole thing is bullshit. My wife and I were moving. We rented a truck, had to move fast to get it back on time. We've got a lot of junk I coulda done without, but my wife has these ducks that're important to her."

He rubs the finger where his wedding ring would be.

Aurora is at his side, waiting for him to continue, but he doesn't. "She has what?" she asks, squeezing into the seat next to Kenny.

He smiles at her.

"Ducks. *Ducks*. She has this crazy collection of ducks. It fills a fucking bookshelf. Full. She's been lugging the shit around since she was a kid."

He scratches his head, and sighs.

"Go on," Aurora says wondering how an assortment of ducks could land a man in jail.

"Fucking furniture started the whole thing," Kenny says rubbing his bristly beard. "She wanted a chair near the door; I wanted it next to the television. I accidentally hit a picture my wife had hung on the wall while I was backing out the door. Glass went everywhere. My wife went wacko. She started screaming at me. I was tired man, so tired. I tried to calm her. I said I was sorry. Told her I loved her. She said how could I love her if I didn't respect her things? I said I did love her, but then I - I said I hated those fucking ducks." He frowns and looks away.

Putting a hand to her mouth, Aurora is desperate to suppress the urge to find humor in his unfortunate tale, looking away too.

"When my wife started slapping me, I grabbed her wrists. That's when it got real bad." Kenny leans back on the seat. It creaks under his weight. He takes a long drag on the air. "It was like de ja vu, man, ya know. We had a fight last year and she told the cops I hit her. I was shit outta luck then and totally fucked today." He shakes his head. His gray puff of hair shimmers under the ceiling lights. "Eh, it's not so bad, I was ready for a rest anyway."

Just as Aurora is about to say how sorry she is for Kenny, and the injustice of it all, a small dark-skinned man ambles into the area, pulling on the excess material under his feet.

"Are you Sabel?" he asks as he slips and slides to a halt.

Turning their attention to the man's failing attempt to pull his feet out from under his baggy trousers, suspends their conversation.

"Yes, I'm Aurora Sabel," Aurora answers.

"Okay then, come with me," he says waddling rapidly past her, his legs tipping from side to side as if he's straddling a horse.

Aurora shoots a questioning look at Kenny.

He dips his head and shrugs with a quirky smile.

"Go on now, this guy doesn't look like he can wait." He looks up and says, "Just remember what I said Aurora - you'll be okay. You're going home."

The guard is waving for her to join him, so Aurora gets up. She pauses, standing next to Kenny. She looks over at him; his back is hunched, his elbows resting on his knees; they're at the same level. Aurora wants to say something, but words escape her. She starts to reach out and touch his shoulder, but the gesture seems too intimate.

The fidgeting man is waiting in the doorway.

All Aurora has to do is take one step away from Kenny and she'll be on her way. She takes off, but has an immediate impulse to turn back; to see Kenny's face one more time, but she decides that it's not necessary. His image will stay with her, it's that vivid.

Aurora remembers a prayer she used to recite as a child:

Angel of God, my guardian dear, to whom His love entrusts me here. Ever this day be at my side, to light and guard, to rule and guide. Amen.

She says the prayer three times thinking, *I want to believe.* But she still has to get through the next couple of days.

Chapter Five: Processing

Being finger-printed is a relatively quick procedure.

A young fresh-faced boy-man officer in a crisp new uniform has the telltale signs of his job: blackened fingertips and ink splotches speckled on his shirt. He stands proudly behind a counter with an assortment of printing utensils and stacks of paper. "This way Ma'am," he calls out to Aurora in good cheer. He extends his hand, but seeing Aurora hesitate at the sight of his stained fingers, he nods, smiles, and withdraws the gesture. "I'm officer Goodman, Ma'am, I'll be doing your processing."

Picky about where he wants Aurora to stand, he orders her back and forth until she's right where he wants her to be, and then he asks to inspect her hands. "Nice, clean hands you got here Ma'am. No need to wash 'em first," he says smiling with approval. Pressing Aurora's fingers onto a small black pad he sets each of the wet digits onto the report sheet, working methodically at his task. Absorbed in the precision of correct print placement, he is unaware of the smudge on his forehead from wiping a wisp of blond hair out of his eyes.

Aurora stifles a smile as an image of the young man wearing a black visor and shirt clips, working in an ancient newspaper room, on an old-fashioned printer comes to mind.

"You can wash your hands at that small sink on the wall over there by the drinking fountain," he says, dipping his fingers into a jar of cleaning cream when they've finished.

Accountability

Aurora scrubs the remaining dye in the crevices around her nails and thinks, *Now I'm a registered felon. I have a record. My reputation is tarnished forever - so what the hell -* She waits until the man's back is turned, scoots to the water fountain before he can say otherwise, and glugs, slurping; the water dripping down her chin. She hasn't had a thing to eat or drink for hours.

***

Towering next to a row of seats is a gigantic stainless-steel computerized photo shop.

"This is a do-it-yourself job Ma'am," says officer Goodman beaming as he brings Aurora around the corner to the photo station. "We're pretty proud of this baby; it saves us a lot of time." He takes Aurora's elbow, positions her in front of the unit, and presses a button. Waiting for the red light in the center of the box to turn green, he nods encouragingly at Aurora.

For a second Aurora wants to see what she looks like and tidy up a bit, but the sink with a mirror is around the corner and she's afraid the machine is on a timer.

"Stand up straight and look directly into the lenses," a voice like the robot in 'Lost in Space' directs.

Aurora follows the order and adjusts her stance. The machine peeps. *Oh, it's radar,* she thinks to herself. At first Aurora hopes that her photo comes out well. Then she huffs and says to herself, *Who cares? I know I've looked better, and I'm sure the police have seen worse.*

Keeping still to focus on the spot, she's sure that when the burst of a flash goes off her startled expression will leave an impression similar to that of a deer-caught-in-headlights.

***

The female dressing room is active; one big, open space where everyone is hurrying to change clothes.

Aurora heads to the end of a long line of women who are still in street clothes waiting to get the county-ordered regulation duds.

The hunch-backed, gray-haired woman perched behind a screened cage is thrusting stacks of folded parcels and growling, "I can figur yur meashaments by juss one look. So no squabblin' 'bout whats I gives ya, it ain't gonna do no good. Juss take what comes and move along."

A tall skinny woman nudges the others waiting in line and works her way to the window. She handles the garments as if they are dirty, thrusting the bundle of clothes into the opening.

"Ma'am, I can't wear these, the shirt's too big and the pants're too short," she complains.

"You listen heeyah," says the police lady with a deep southern drawl, "stop yur fussin', this ain't no beauty contest. Juss give me the paynts and ah'll bring youah nothah payah."

A few women in line start to laugh.

"Quiet!" shouts the aged official, "there's nothin' funny 'bout this."

Aurora is giddy hearing the woman's twang. She doesn't speak when she reaches the cage; she just nods at the grumpy woman with a polite smile and waits. The officer rapidly sizes Aurora up and issues her a stack of clothes.

Aurora heads back to the changing room and promptly swaps all of her clothing because she was told that every item must be switched out. *Geez*, she thinks, *after all the fuss I made about getting back into my own clothes.*

***

Aurora neatly folds her things and puts them into the brown paper sack she was given. With a fat, black marker she writes her name on the outside of the bag.

Adjusting the new ensemble, she tightens the straps of her new crisscross cotton bra and pulls up the wide elastic band on the waist-high cotton underwear.

Accountability

The drawstring on the orange pants is tangled; it takes a good tug to get it to work. A button on the orange top is cracked in half; the one right at that crucial spot where it secures the middle of the shirt. Aurora buttons the collar hoping it will fix the problem. If she doesn't move too fast, it won't open. *It'll have to do*, she thinks, because she has no intention of asking the grouchy woman for another shirt. She'd have a hard time shuffling back there anyway, seeing as the white plastic shower shoes are too loose on her bare feet, and she wasn't issued socks.

Gosh, she wonders, *How long has the uniform been orange? I thought it was always black and white stripes - Man, I need to lie down. I hope the next place they take me to, is a bed.*

***

"Those who've finished changing must leave promptly and wait in the hall to be taken back," calls out a self-superior faced guard leaning against the doorframe.

Her trim blue uniform hugs her powerful-looking body. She crosses one leg over the other: a suave gesture. The female cop has a lustful air about her; a sexual energy that the other women seem to notice because they turn their backs on her as they disrobe. She runs her palms down the front of her trousers almost obscenely, and licks at her lips, smiling as if she's anticipating the taste of something sweet. When a woman tries to exit, the officer makes it difficult to pass through the doorway by swaying close to the individual, almost touching her.

Aurora watches the scene, standing in the vestibule against the cold hard wall. Taking a roundabout route through another corridor, she bypasses the perverted guard.

Aurora re-enters the waiting room, stands at the perimeter and searches for Kenny.

Her heart jumps spotting him seated at a corner table with other men; he's dressed in orange as well.

She restrains from flapping her arms and calling to him seeing that he's enthralled in his current conversation; bent down to the waist, he's focusing on the man talking.

She slumps to an unoccupied bench, sits and stares hard at Kenny, willing him to notice her.

But he doesn't.

A short time later the 'Food Wise' man comes back. With the same enthusiasm Frank offers up the identical snack and Aurora takes her share with the intention of giving it to Kenny. Just as she decides to be bold and go to his table, the loudspeaker shouts his name. Aurora watches as he slowly rises from his seat. She raises a hand and waves until he notices. Kenny heads her way in a slow easy-going strut.

Aurora pops up and dashes to the big man, excited to talk to him again.

"You hear that? I gotta go, they're singin' my song," he says, eyes twinkling at Aurora.

Wordlessly she hands him the sandwich.

"That was nice of you," he says. He takes a bite and more than half of it disappears. "That color looks good on you," he says with a bobbing nod.

He smiles and moves to go but Aurora clutches his free arm, trying but unable to grab the whole mass. "Wait - what happens now? Will I see you again? And me - what about me?"

"Don't worry - I told you. It's all gonna work out. Okay?"

Kenny lays his hand on her hand.

Aurora wants to let go of his arm and free him, but her fingers won't relinquish him. She's embarrassed by her behavior but can't help herself. "Okay," she whispers, reluctantly releasing her grip.

With dramatic flair, Kenny lifts a stiff hand to his brow and salutes Aurora before turning to cross the room. He heads over to a pensively poised guard at the doorway.

The policeman is drumming a pen on a clip board, the tempo undoubtedly to the tune of his impatience.

Chapter Six: The Cell

At five-thirty the next morning, a floor buffer starts to whirr. The black furry brushes under the device rotate inward like it's masticating. An elderly attendant in grey overalls, donning padded headphones, pushes the vibrating gadget along the corridor polishing the scuffed linoleum.

My gosh, the workday starts early here, she thinks yawning.

The sound of the motorized cleaner is boisterous, rousing several individuals who are camped out on the benches dozing, to stir.

Aurora watches the public servant grooving along, his hips gyrating to the music playing in his head. He guides the dancing machine down the hall and around the corner.

The echo of annoying humming disappears, and in the restored quiet, the county jail facility awakens.

Aurora stands, throws her arms out, and arches her back. She stretches from side to side, and then bends down to touch her toes. She remains in this rag-doll pose until she hears her back crack, then she returns to an upright position.

Aurora is stiff and her body aches from loitering on the hard bench. For hours she's been drifting in and out of a meditative state; not asleep, yet not able to stay alert and awake.

She sees through heavy eyelids, the activity in the room; the vista is a haze. Shadowy bodies shift like spirits in a mist.

Aurora counts scores of vacant expressions and thinks, *They all look like the walking dead.*

"Sabel!"

"Here -" Aurora says, loudly so this official doesn't miss her; she won't be left behind.

The officer nods as she treads nimbly in the direction of her ward. Watching the perky policewoman, it's obvious that she's an athlete. She glides with the grace of a long-distance runner; her arms swinging to keep pace. "Morning. Mrs. Sabel, right? Ready? Let's go then." The guard bounces on her heels, checking her watch. "We should make good time getting to the pod where you'll be put into a cell." The young police lady bobs her head with a hopeful grin and puts a check mark on the manila folder she's carrying.

"The - *pod?*" asks Aurora incredulously. "What in the world is, 'the pod'?"

"It's a term for the whole section of the female holding facility," says the cop with bright, intelligent-looking eyes. "We need to hurry now, to get you there before the first bell."

Aurora moves quickly trying to keep up with the energy infused policewoman. They trail through passageways to what Aurora privately dubs her 'awaiting confinement'.

Panting at times, the officer jogs in place waiting for Aurora to catch up; she's the embodiment of verve.

***

Opening into the room is a split-level structure with a long balcony gated by steel rails. The top level is dark, with doors battened down. The ground floor has a glassed-in cement court with a basketball hoop; the net's tattered strings are dangling limply. It faces a lounging site with two metal framed couches and a coffee table: vacant at this hour of the day. Staircases are positioned at either end of the huge space. In the middle of the compound are tables and chairs. On the corner wall of the community area is a sign stating 'Showers' with a big black arrow.

"Your cell is on this level," says the cop. "But first we need to pick up something."

Aurora follows the policewoman to a door that reads 'Utility Room' in dark red letters.

The official takes a set of keys out of her front pocket and unlocks the metal entry. "I may need some assistance Ma'am; this one often sticks." she says to Aurora while pulling on the handle. "Yup, it's quite stiff. It needs some WD40," says the officer.

Aurora and the policewoman pull on the door and it slowly opens with a hair-raising grating sound like nails scraping a blackboard. "I have to remember to get this thing oiled," says the officer huffing.

She walks into the utility closet and for a moment Aurora is standing alone thinking, *Holy, Moley, I'm in a Pod going to a Cell.*

The officer comes out tugging an inflated rubber mattress.

"Can I - get a hand - here please?" she asks, panting.

At the sight of the air pad, Aurora gasps open-mouthed at the officer; her expression wordlessly saying, *What? I'm not going to have a bed?*

The guard nods in a sympathetic way as if she's heard Aurora's disgruntled plea. "Let's move this into place and settle you in, eh?" she says in a quiet voice.

Together they drag the heavy canvas like a dead body over to an already open doorway. They bump heads while peeking into the cell at the same time. As they drop the mattress and simultaneously put hands to their heads the room comes into focus.

"Ow - sorry," says the guard begrudgingly.

"Geez, I'm sorry too," Aurora replies, patting the exact spot she hit earlier in the police car.

They have to tug hard on the mattress. It's difficult to push it through the doorway. The rubber makes a smooching, kissing sound when Aurora and the guard finally shove it in. Aurora watches as the officer runs a hand up the wall of the inner doorframe, apparently searching for the light switch.

"There's bedding somewhere in here," she says.

Aurora notices that the only bed is occupied.

"Ma'am, please don't turn the light on - there's someone in that bed sleeping - can't we do all of this without disturbing her?" she whispers. Aurora is baffled as to why, but bestowing this small act of kindness suddenly seems to be quite important to her.

The officer's eyes soften. "Hey, sure, why not. You'll all be getting up in an hour anyway."

With a sudden whirl she turns and trots away, leaving Aurora to make her own way in the dark.

Chapter Seven: Diana

She's never felt so sedate and weightless; her body seems powerless to move. The current is calm on this sea in the middle of nowhere. Aurora sways, comfortably drifting. A cool breeze sweeps across her face as a sail is being hoisted - or is that a sheet being shaken out and laid back down? She faintly remembers the long walk to get here and there's something about her not going home for a while, but at this moment she's simply grateful to just float. She wants to dip her fingertips in the water and drag lazy circles, making little whirlpools off the side of the raft, but what she touches feels like sand - or is that gritty dirt? The sun feels bright, she can see multi colors swirling on her closed eyelids and almost smell the salty air. It's so refreshing Aurora rolls over to let her body slip into the water. She immediately slips off the rubber bed hitting the floor. She's blinded by a blaze of fluorescent ceiling lights.

***

Oh shit, she moans silently.
Gong: a bell sounds.
Click: the cell door slides open automatically.
Aurora moves back onto the air bed, pulls the wool blanket that smells of mildew over her head, and tries to recall what she did to deserve this.

She hears a cacophony of unrest in the outer area; the buzz like an assault of bees vibrating in her ears.

Anxiety like a villain, seizes her throat.

She hops up quickly and tries to close the door, but the hinge is frozen in place. She tugs and tugs. *Oh God, please help me! I have to close - this - door - keep out - whatever's out there -* she cries to herself.

Exhausted from the failed attempt, Aurora jumps back under the covers hoping that no one will notice the lump under the blanket on the rubber mattress in the middle of the tiny room.

Stifled underneath the dense protective cover, she begins to wheeze. Gasping for fresh air, she throws over the cover, and scans the room. There isn't much in the little space. Only the single bed, a metal chair, and a desk with a pad of lined paper. Aurora wonders absently, why paper would be issued without writing tools, and the flashing image of a morose scene plays in Aurora's mind: the metal chair has been kicked to the floor, a limp body hangs from the light-fixture, and a suicide note sits on the desk, (but how did the note get written?) and Aurora's head starts to throb.

***

A six by eight-inch porcelain sink, is mounted crookedly on the wall. A little wire mesh basket holds a tiny white toothbrush sealed in plastic, a tiny tube of toothpaste and shampoo, a mini comb, and a matchbox bar of soap. A dingy scrap of a washcloth sits precariously on the edge of the sink. A mirror the size of a five by seven-inch picture frame is above the sink. The bed is made up, the blanket pulled tight in military style-bounce-the-quarter compliance.

The woman who was sleeping there, is gone.

Aurora wonders distractedly, how her missing roommate got out of a room, that was locked from the outside.

***

Accountability

A moment later the smell of laundry starch tickles Aurora's nose and she notices a pert young official poking her head into the doorway. Her crisp white shirt is open at the neck, the collar flipped up preppy style, a little hat with a shiny black brim sits rakishly on her head. "Hey - You - Breakfast - Now -" she commands, pointing a bright red fingernail at Aurora. 'Security Guard' is stitched in the same color on the sleeve of her dark grey uniform. The trim-looking guard scans the room, her eyes unblinking.

Aurora suspects she's taking a head count. The guard doesn't ask about the previous occupant, so it appears that the authorities must be aware of the missing person's whereabouts.

Aurora wiggles to sit up on the rubber bed to make a polite inquiry. "Excuse me miss - uh - ma'am, I was hoping that I didn't have to attend the breakfast assembly - I'm not at all hungry. Would it be all right if I remain here?" Feeling her heart pumping; the thump, thump, thump palpitating under her shirt, Aurora stares at the guard, her eyes pleading as she prays on the steward's sympathy for an automatic dismissal.

The young woman looks at Aurora sharply. Her nostrils flare, her cheeks flush, but then she smiles. A slight twinkle sparks in her eyes, but a frown quickly replaces the impish grin. "Ah, well, why not princess; you don't have to get out of bed at all, there's room service all day in this hotel," she snaps. She adjusts her hat, swivels curtly, and marches out the door.

***

Aurora stays in the cell all morning; the escape afforded her is intoxicating. She dozes off. Eventually she has to use the lavatory and ventures out into the communal area.

There's a bustle of motion; flashes of orange everywhere. No one gives Aurora a second glance as she finds her way to the combination toilet and shower room.

The mushroom smell of mildew is overpowering. Dim lighting casts shadows on the cracked tiled walls; the plastic shower curtains dripping with black slime seem to squirm as if a demon could reach out and grab her. Aurora shudders at the image of a gateway to hell.

Her plastic slip-ons squelch as she swishes along the sticky floor. The toilet stall smells like sewage; the toilet bowl is stained black and she thinks, *This is disgusting - and in a government building.* Rolling up her pant legs as if she's going to tread through a swamp, Aurora balances on tippy-toes hoping that she doesn't slip and flop on the seat.

***

Back at her cell Aurora comes upon a young gal stretched out on the rubber mattress.

The leggy girl wobbles like a young colt to a standing position. Unsteady at first, she sways and totters and lunges at Aurora with an extended hand. "Hi - Diana - birthday yesterday - nineteen - your new roomie -" says the gangly teenager, pausing, mouth open, like she has more to say.

"I'm Aurora and I feel ancient," she says looking into Diana's clear blue eyes sighing.

Side-stepping the rubber air-pad on the floor, Aurora kicks off her slippers and drops heavily onto the bed. Scooting further onto the mattress she puts her back against the wall.

Diana, mimicking Aurora, plops onto the bed and leans back against the wall as well. She stretches out her long slender legs, crosses her ankles and tucks her arms behind her head. "I've been in jail for eighteen months now," she says with a seemingly smug grin. She pauses, giving Aurora a sideways glance. "I'm waiting to transfer to a larger facility. I've been on the upper level, but they moved me today to put two pregnant women together. It's okay, I like change." Diana smiles at Aurora; her eyes jutting around the room while twirling her ash-blonde ringlets.

Accountability

"So, what about you? What are you in for? How long have you been here? When will you be released?" she asks Aurora, clearly not really interested in a response. "So, you probably want to know what's what around here, hum?" She smiles brightly. "Well I can teach you a thing or two. I know just about everything that goes on in here."

Diana is glowing with good health; she's rosy-cheeked with an affable energy. "First there's the proper procedure of making a bed. Who made this bed? It's perfect," she says with authoritative approval.

Aurora has the questioning look of a lost lamb.

"Okay, let me make this easier for you. There'll be an inspection twice a day. If you rest on your bed, it doesn't have to be made, but the room must be maintained all day long. If you leave your room, it has to be in order. Everyone belongs to a section and each section is judged daily. At the end of the week the winners get pizza for dinner instead of the usual cafeteria meal - get it? Am I talking too fast for you?"

She sighs seeing that Aurora's confused expression has not changed.

"Don't worry, I'll be here for you, every step of the way."

Diana fiddles with the bra under her shirt, pulls it out through the sleeve, wings it onto the air mattress and smiles innocently at Aurora. "Ah, that's better," she says. It appears that she may say more, but she just grins at Aurora.

Feeling she should interact in some way, Aurora says, "Ah, well, I'm sure that information is important to anyone staying on, but I won't be here that long. I'm only here because of a terrible fluke, so none of that really concerns me."

Aurora doesn't want to be unfriendly, but she truly can't fathom doing a Pizza Night with the other inmates.

Diana looks at Aurora with curiosity mixed with what undoubtedly looks like pity.

Aurora can see by her lopsided smile that she's probably thinking, *Sure, sure, that's what they all say.*

In an effort to be civil, Aurora says, "Geez, you seem like a nice girl Diana, what could you possibly have done to get yourself thrown in jail?" although she's not sure she really wants to know.

"Well, to start with, my family is from New York," she says sitting up in the bed excitedly. It's all too apparent that hers is a story she's bursting to tell. "My parent's marriage sucked, and when they divorced my mom and I moved to Florida."

Diana has a wistful look.

"While my mom was busy working - she's a nurse practitioner - I made friends with what she calls, A Fast Crowd."

She pauses, maybe thinking of the time that's past.

"They're good kids - no, really, but their idea of fun was to steal stuff out of unlocked cars at the beach."

Again, she pauses, reminiscing it seems.

"They figured out how to use the banking numbers off of check books and withdraw money electronically and I got pretty good at forging checks," Diana says. "I'm in here because the police were watching us, and they set a trap. We're all in jail now, but in different facilities. I'm in for two years pending early parole if I'm good."

Aurora can only stare at this fresh-faced girl in silent shock thinking, *Geez, this young woman has ruined her life.*

***

Diana's pants are rolled up to her knees and Aurora can't help but gawk at the deep purple gash pulling the skin on her leg.

"How did you get that?" Aurora asks pointing to the wound. "It looks like it's going to come open. Maybe you should get someone to look at it."

"Oh that - that's nothin'!" Diana says, and with an air of showing-off lifts the material up higher and unveils a bigger scar on her kneecap.

"Yeah, so, like, you know, my old boyfriend was pissed I didn't cut up the coke equally, so he shot me in the leg a couple of times."

"Oh, my," Aurora says shifting uncomfortably on the bed, waiting for the rest of the story.

Diana seems exuberant. She tips her head back and sighs for an impassive effect, then she hops off the bed and traipses over to the little mirror. She bends down to examine every angle of her face and wraps a springy coil of hair behind her ear.

"Man, I'm a wreck," she says. "This light makes me look like a rat; I hate rats," she says with a shiver. "Yeah, well, anyway, we hooked up to score eight balls of blow - you know - cocaine? We cut it, sold it at bars and made tons of cash. We didn't steal after that." Diana examines her teeth and lets out a deep sigh. "If we'd just stayed with that - it was so easy - everything would'a been cool."

Aurora watches Diana examining herself at the sink. Taking up the soap she says, "It's not that bad in here. I've made a lot of friends." She vigorously scrubs both hands, forearms and elbows, the water splashing everywhere. "I even have a new boyfriend," she says over her shoulder. "We've been passing notes under the door behind the basketball court." She dries her arms with the tiny towel and neatly hangs it on the back of the metal chair. "There's a lot of secret dating going on here because they don't allow the men and women to openly mingle. Leroy and I met during a fire drill last month when everyone was ushered out to the side yard. He says he loves me, but I'm not sure. Well, I'm pretty sure - yeah - I guess you could say that I'm pretty much in love with him." Diana's attention is fixed on her face in the mirror. She moves her head at different angles and runs a finger across her skin searching for blemishes and squeezes a few.

Aurora thinks to herself, *Love? How can this adolescent woman think it's love?* Aurora closes her eyes and shaking her head she prays, *Please God, help this girl.*

Diana reaches into her pocket and pulls out a folded sheet of paper. "Here - take a look -" she says showing Aurora a crude drawing. "He pushed it under the door the other day - he wanted to give me a present - he said he drew it himself."

Aurora shudders inwardly.

The sketch of a muscular man flexing his tattooed forearms in a disproportioned Popeye pose, looks menacing. Black penciled beady eyes are staring right out of the paper with a look of inflated defiance. Is Aurora's opinion a bit too harsh or is it that her intuitive radar is on high alert? Because the portrait to her, looks like a certified maniac. Suddenly, inexplicably, Aurora is very concerned and worried for this young woman.

"Doesn't he look great?" Diana asks giggling with pride; she's hopeful and happy. "We're making plans - where we'll go - what we'll do when we both get out. What do you think?"

Aurora shrugs her shoulders and says nothing, but she'd like to say, *Find out what the guy's in for before you run off with him.* Aurora thinks the girl's innocence has been stolen and beyond anything else, from now on her life will be hard. Diana may be resilient enough to sustain herself within these walls, but she has a record now. It won't be easy to find her way in the big world with that hanging over her head. Aurora isn't going to tell Diana that the idea of planning a life with this stranger, convicted of God-knows-what, is doomed.

She has no right to say anything, she doesn't even know the girl.

In actuality, Diana doesn't seem to want her opinion anyway. She's just talking, to hear herself speak.

Aurora lets the dialog lapse.

It's been mostly one-sided, so it easily fades into a quietude where Diana, deep in her own thoughts, doesn't notice.

Aurora closes her eyes; she can't even pretend to listen anymore.

Accountability

Images are spiraling in her head: Diana at the beach in a little floral sundress wandering through parking lots rattling car doors - Diana in an oversized t-shirt and cut-off jeans, her mangled leg propped up on a chair, a pile of white snow at a table with a guy standing over her with a gun in his hand - Diana dressed in a glittery gown, Popeye gripping her tightly as they run from the authorities - Diana screaming as a rat scurries across the floor of her cell.

***

Diana appears impervious to Aurora's withdrawal, her face animated, carrying on a quiet conversation with herself.

Aurora lifts her drowsy eyes a little. She can see Diana fussing, and hears a burping sound when Diana drops down to the rubber mattress. Aurora faintly hears Diana say, "I think I'll start a letter to Leroy," before she nods off.

Chapter Eight: Inmates

"Judith? Hey Judith - wait - wow - come back -" Diana shouts, rousing Aurora from a deep slumber.

Diana scrambles up from the floor, and dashes out the door.

Aurora pulls a pillow over her head, but she can still hear Diana chatting in the corridor.

"Yes - of course - I do remember - I know - here two weeks ago - oh - is that so - brought in last night - for the same - oh man, Judith, you got another DUI? Everyone knows that a second offense for Driving Under the Influence is automatic jail time," Diana says with a sympathetic whine. "No - yes - I'm still waiting - no, no word yet where they'll send me - yes - this cell now - yes - moved me - come in - tell me what the heck happened - what did you do? How long do you have this time?"

Diana leads a tall, strawberry blonde-haired woman into the room, and helps her lay down on the rubber bed. "Aurora, this is Judith," Diana says over her shoulder.

The sullen solemn woman casts an indifferent shrug toward Aurora and groans stretching out on the air mattress.

Diana kneels and gently tends to her friend smoothing her hair, laying her arms across her chest, as if preparing her for burial.

"How's that - better? Is your back still bothering you, Judith?" Diana asks, but the woman doesn't reply.

Accountability

Judith stares into space zombie-like; her mouth twitching in a nonverbal dialog with no one in particular.

"I'll stay for a while if that's okay?" Judith finally whispers in Diana's direction.

"Of course, no problem. Ok Aurora?" Diana says looking at Aurora with imploring eyes.

"I guess so," Aurora replies. "Is it legal? I mean, is she allowed to be here in our cell?"

"Yes, well, I don't see why not - all the doors are open," Diana says in an optimistic tone.

Aurora rouses herself and tiptoes around the lounging woman to splash some cold water on her face, but she eyes the damp little wash cloth and wonders how she would dry herself. Instead, she unwraps the little toothbrush and cleans her teeth, rinsing once and then doing it again, depleting the tube of toothpaste. Running her fingers through her hair, she avoids looking at herself in the lopsided mirror; afraid of what she looks like. She stands facing the women feeling like an intruder - but wait - isn't this her cell? She swiftly sits back on the bed.

"So, what happened?" Diana asks Judith as she wedges next to the reclining woman.

"Man, I still can't believe it," Judith begins scratching her head, coming out of her fog. "Last night I was out partying with friends having fun." She sits up more alert, and looks around the room. She focuses on Diana and continues. "After 'last call' we tried to go to another place," Judith says getting up from the mattress, starting to pace. "But all the bars were closing so we got in my car and headed to my house."

The cramped space hampers her stride, which seems to frustrate Judith. She drops down onto the rubber bed with an exasperated sigh, sending Diana in a whoosh to the ground. The mattress makes a low, wheezing sound as Diana climbs back on.

"Then what happened?"

Diana anchors a foot on the floor so as not to slip off the motion-sensitive mattress again.

"Everything was peachy until I got nabbed going through a stop sign," Judith whines.

Wriggling to a sitting position, she wobbles and tries to gain some balance on the mattress.

"I swear, you couldn't have seen that friggin' stop sign even in the daytime."

"And then?" Diana asks, her eyes sparkling with anticipation.

"They ran my license," Judith says with a sigh. "My last DUI popped up and now I'm back in here."

Judith looks exhausted.

Aurora feels awkward, the odd man out. She wants to leave the room, but she's afraid that the communal area is too much to take on. She's oddly curious as to why Judith is so angry about the whole thing. She must have known what would happen.

Aurora waits. She's sure the story will unfold.

The skinny woman rolls to a crawling position and as she rises, Aurora can see that her legs are thin as twigs, her arms like long sticks as she thrusts her hands into her pockets and leans against the wall.

"I think my friends took my car - I called my mother to pick up my son - I hope she doesn't say too much - who knows what poison she'll fill his head with while I'm here."

Judith is a bit out of breath. "Hell, it's not easy raising a kid alone - I try to be a good mother - I love my boy - but it gets lonely - you know. I don't have a drinking problem - I could stop any time - I just like to unwind and chill out with a couple - know what I mean?"

She glares at Aurora and Diana.

"Yeah," Diana says automatically. She reaches out to take hold of Judith's hand, but Judith turns away.

Judith nods at Aurora, but Aurora has no reply.

She holds her tongue, partly because she's not inclined to get into the conversation, but mostly because she can't pretend to relate. She's so busy running around all day, that there's no time to *chill out*.

She and William used to party it up, but now her days are filled with so many tasks that getting some sleep is her only tonic at the end of the day.

Sure, it must be hard to raise a child alone, Aurora thinks, and she has a deeper appreciation for all that William does to help, but clearly Judith can't expect to break the law and get away with it.

"How long will you be in this time?" Diana asks.

"I need a cigarette. I've got to get out of here -" Judith says, and wanders out of the room.

Diana jumps up following her. "See you later Aurora," she waves over her shoulder, "I have to make sure Judith finds her way."

Aurora stares at the empty doorway and sighs.

She pictures Denial as a sneaky coercing ally to Judith, but it's cruel because the comfort it gives is fleeting.

She feels sad for the lost woman and prays, *Please God, help Judith find her way.*

***

Aurora is alone with nothing to do. She can't remember the last time she was really alone; she hasn't been by herself since her first child was born six years ago. Since then her life has been one hectic day after another; the purpose that drives her.

The responsibility of caring for William and the boys is a job Aurora relishes. Each and every menial task.

The thought of them brings tears to her eyes.

She wonders if William is keeping to their routine.

She knows exactly what they'd be doing at that moment and it pains her not to be there.

Being idle is torture for someone like Aurora who is normally very active.

With all this time on her hands, her worries are running rampant. She looks around the cell and decides that during her confinement she'll keep to herself and just rest.

Straightening the bedcover she lays down and thinks, *Maybe catching up on years of deprived sleep will do me good. What else can I do?*

***

An insistent woman is nudging Aurora, prodding with the strength of her chubby body for Aurora to scoot over on the bed.

The room suddenly has a bad smell; the woman has gas.

Aurora covers her nose in the crook of her elbow and looks at the woman with distaste.

"Oh, sorry - my stomach's a mess - it's the food in here -" She's crowding Aurora in an effort to gain more than half of the bed.

"I've had diarrhea since my first meal - uh, you're new right? I haven't seen you around - but, so many people come and go - you know - and I haven't been here that long - my name's Dawn, by the way."

"What - are - you - doing - here?" Aurora asks, slowly rising up on an elbow. "Where's Diana?" The edge in Aurora's voice is unmistakable, but Dawn's pleasant demeanor disregards it.

"Oh, she'll be back soon. She's watching a basketball game with Judith. You're Aurora, right? Diana told me. What are you in for?"

Dawn's bubbly personality makes Aurora's nerves stand on end.

She's annoyed at being invaded by this stranger and impatient to shoo the woman out.

Aurora has no intention of having a conversation with Dawn, but Dawn has another agenda.

"You won't believe it when I tell you what happened to *me*," Dawn says, tugging on her wavy, raven-colored hair.

"If I'd known that I'd be arrested and put in jail for talking to a man in a hotel room - well," she says with a sigh, "I would have stayed at the party with my husband."

Aurora pulls herself up to a sitting position, now too curious about the disconnected story to ask Dawn to leave. "Okay, I'll bite. Who was the man in the hotel room if not your husband?"

"Yes, well, you see, the man who picked me up hitch-hiking was the man in the hotel room."

"Wait a minute - you went to a hotel with a stranger who picked you up on the roadside?"

"Well, when you say it like that - it sounds wicked, but it wasn't. At the time anyway."

Dawn stands and waddles to the little mirror. She inspects her face and continues to talk to her image. "At first, I just wanted a ride home, but after we'd talked - he was nice then - Darren convinced me that a drink at his hotel would be just the thing to help me forget my troubles and end the day on a happier note. He was kind and he seemed quite harmless - the stinker."

***

As Aurora is thinking, *He was obviously looking for his own Happy Ending,* an image of a seedy hotel room, peeling striped wallpaper, and a faded floral bedspread pops into her head.

Aurora can see Dawn, decked out in a sparkly sequined top, her hair pinned up in a twist, sitting on the edge of the sagging bed, taking a filthy glass of amber liquid from the hand of a stout, balding man in a light blue polyester leisure suit who's smiling at her with lust in his eyes.

Aurora tries to push the picture from her mind.

Dawn goes to the sink, lets the faucet run, makes a cup with her hands, and drinks some water. "He was gracious in the beginning," she says wiping her chin with the back of her hand. "We had a drink and just talked - but now that I think about it - he did ask a lot of personal stuff - you know - like what kind of sex I liked - but it was only in conversation - it wasn't like we were going to *do* anything."

Dawn's pudgy hand dips into the pocket of her snuggly fitting orange pants and pulls out a bag of M&M's. "Want some?" she asks Aurora, simultaneously opening the bag, tilting her head back, and pouring the candy into her mouth.

"No - thanks anyway," Aurora says, watching Dawn chomp aggressively on the chocolate.

Dawn gestures for her to take what's left in the bag, but Aurora declines, shaking her head.

"Naturally, you can imagine my shock when out of the blue Darren flashed a police badge and said that he had enough evidence on tape to arrest me for prostitution - prostitution! He must have worn wires -" her eyes bulge as the light bulb goes on in her head. "*Yeah* - that's gotta be how he recorded everything and *tricked* me! He set me up - I mean - can you believe it?"

The story unfolded as Aurora thought it might; the plot easily figured out after the first few minutes like any dime store novel or low-grade movie.

Dawn was cast perfectly in her role too: the slightly dumb innocent victim easily coerced by the smooth-talking conniving conman.

"I think you need a good lawyer, Dawn," Aurora says to the pink-faced woman. "I don't know anything about the law, but it sounds like you may have a solid case for 'Entrapment'."

"How could he have mistaken our conversation for a come-on?" Dawn says softly licking her lips, folding the empty wrapper into a compact square, not hearing a word Aurora has said. "What kind of woman does he think I am?"

Dawn seems more concerned with her public image than looking into a case she may have against this policeman to rectify herself.

***

Though apprehensive about venturing out, Aurora feels a pull to leave the tiny room and get away from this woman.

She needs to move. Her body feels stiff; she's not used to being sedentary. It's claustrophobic in the windowless cell; the walls are closing in on her. She closes her eyes and breathes through her nose deeply. Muddled surreal scenes flash in her head: Diana, the pretty teenage rogue - Judith, the emaciated rag doll - and now Dawn, the inadvertent hussy.

Walking seems like dragging an anvil across the room.

"Come on Dawn," Aurora coaxes, "let's take a walk down the hall. We can shake our legs - what do you say?"

Aurora stands at the doorway waiting for her to get up.

Dawn seems stuck; lost in the forum of a silent debate.

Even though she desperately wants to go, Aurora doesn't want to go out alone. "Hey -" she calls loudly, "Come *on*! Let's go look for Diana and Judith - you said that they're watching a basketball game. How about you take me there?"

***

The community area is like a blank, grey canvas with abstract splashes of orange.

Just as Aurora is thinking that it must be hard keeping a slew of caged individuals in order, she hears a woman in the room bellow, "Yo - bitch - that's my spot - get your ass up -"

"Now Gloria, that's no way to talk to your friend," Aurora hears the guard nearby say.

***

Dawn and Aurora walk over to where Judith is leaning on the glass wall at the basketball court.

Judith nods at them and Dawn touches her arm. "Hey, are you okay? You look kind of sick -"

Judith frowns at Dawn and turns away.

"I don't know what I'll say to my son," Judith says, keeping her eyes on the game.

The women are not just playing ball, they're battling; screaming at each other.

"I promised him, no more drinking, no more trouble. I can't stand it; he's going to be so mad at me." Judith puts her hands on the wall and bowing her head lets out a slow agonizing moan. "The worst part is that child welfare will definitely take him if I'm in here a long time."

Dawn, who seems to have little interest in Judith, shrugs her shoulders, and walks away.

Aurora stays. She remains with Judith but she's unable to utter any words of solace.

Judith's shoulders sag as she sighs and gnaws at her already worn-to-the nibs nails. "I did this to myself. And to my boy. What a mess I'm in, just for a good time."

"I'm sorry Judith," Aurora says, finally. "I hope it all works out for you."

She wants to slip away and let the woman be, but she feels compelled to stay with her.

A rescuing voice calls, "Aurora -"

It's Diana waving. "I'm headed back to our room to meet my friend Ann - come on, you'll like her - she's a real pisser."

Aurora touches Judith's arm sympathetically, but the troubled woman doesn't notice.

***

A tiny wisp of a woman is talking with Dawn in Aurora's cell when she returns with Diana.

"Aurora, this is Ann, and you know Dawn. We were all on the upper level together," Diana says with a tone of self-importance being allied with this group of women. Her grin is sincere; she seems thrilled to be with the 'In Crowd'. "We're gonna hang in here 'til lunch, okay?"

Aurora nods at Ann who is hovering near the air mattress. She nods with a slight frown at Dawn who is lounging on her appointed bed, and nods indulgently at Diana who is perched on top of the desk. The little room is now so crowded she can only take a seat on the metal chair.

Accountability

The character in the movie, 'Coal Miners Daughter' comes to Aurora's mind looking at Ann. She has auburn colored hair cropped short in the front, puffed out and trailing down the back. Ann pulls the collar up on her shirt in a recognized attempt to cover the purple and yellow splotches dotted around her neck, but the lapel falls flat.

"Sheeit, I done told yous before, he only beats me," Ann is saying, following up her conversation with Dawn, "when I don't get my shit done; when I don't bring it on home."

Aurora has only heard that little bit of the conversation, but she thinks, *Oh Please, I can't hear another story.*

***

Ann scans the faces in the room to see if they're really interested to hear more. Dawn has her eyes brightly fixed on Ann. Diana has the eager expression of please-please-please more, but Aurora looks away hoping she won't continue.

Not to be deterred, Ann continues, and by her own definition she explains that her *job* is to make seed money by soliciting 'Johns'.

"My old man's job," Ann tells the three gaping mouthed women whose eyes are now fixed on her, "is to git buyers. We gotta good source for the crack. Gnarly shit. Then we cut it up, sell it for the goin' rate, and split the little bit a pure stuff we keep for us. If he did *his* job - I wouldn't have to turn tricks - I'd be home right now; not in this shit-hole."

Aurora is shocked silent as she thinks, *Whoa, the husband is a dealer, and the wife is a prostitute - for drugs?*

Aurora inhales deeply wishing they'd all leave, but Ann has more to say.

"Yeah, I can see it sounds brutal to you prissy bitches," she says looking directly at Aurora. "And if any a ya happen ta be Narcs -" her eyes steadily appraising Aurora, "I'll deny everithin'- but sometimes man, sacrifices gotta be made. What I do ain't so bad," she says straightening her collar again. "It's gettin' cheated out of my cut that sucks ass."

Ann pats down the puff of hair on her head and yawns.

"I didn't know your husband worked with you at Home Depot," Dawn says.

"He don't," Ann replies.

"Who works at Home Depot?" Diana asks.

"I used ta ," Ann says with a sigh. "Before the accident we were sittin' pretty good. We even had money socked away. I did good at that 'do it yourself' store. It was a pretty decent job," she says with a faraway look of reminiscence. "Then my old man Bob was crippled by a drunk driver - too bad it didn't kill him - some bad shit started after that." She sighs while playing with her long hair and twisting it into a coil. "He was in the hospital a hell-of-a long time. We had insurance then, but the rates went up so high, we couldn't pay. After that, everything started to go to shit."

Ann walks over to the wall and examines herself in the little mirror. She turns the water on and leans down to drink from the faucet. After many gulps, she wipes her mouth on her sleeve and slowly kneels down onto the mattress. "When his meds ran out, Bob's friends got him weed and alcohol, but his pain was so bad - man - he whined all the time - he found the way to oblivion - smokin' crack."

Aurora isn't sure what crack is, and she doesn't want to ask, but from the conversation she gathers its affect is short term so it's an expensive habit.

Diana and Dawn seem impassive about Ann's story, but maybe they've heard it before. Aurora, though, sits up on the metal chair, her pulse racing. She's never heard a personal account of what is often written in books or acted out in films or plastered brutally in the media. *My God*, she thinks, *This stuff is real. And it's not a pretty picture.*

Aurora watches Ann shift position on the rubber bed, extending her feet in front of her. She reaches out to touch the tips of her shoes. "Because of his friggin' *need,* we lost it all," she says angrily. "We used to have a house; almost paid for too. Now we cayn't barely pay at the trailer park. It got so bad, I had ta git out and make us some more money."

Ann crisscrosses her legs; the mattress barely registers the movement. "I only do crack to be with 'the cripple'," she says trying to switch her position. The air bed seems to be tricky for any-one who tries to inhabit it. Ann gets up and starts to pace. Her strides are short, taking mini steps from one end of the tight cavity to the other.

"I got a system now," she says. "Down to Ybor City late - walk around til 'bout two or three - then hit the bars at closing time. Lots a times I'm lucky and get the same tricks."

"But it must be dangerous - don't you worry about getting a depraved guy?" Diana asks.

"No," Ann says flatly, shaking her head. "Well, there was this one time -" she starts to say more, but stops, "but - hey I'm still here, ain't I?"

Ann holds up a hand to end the conversation. "This shit - my life - ain't never gonna change."

"You know Ann," Aurora boldly interjects, "you could transform your whole life if you really wanted to - get out and make it on your own." She pauses thinking of safe houses and drug programs she's heard of on television. "There are places, shelters, help getting a job, and help with the drug problem too."

Aurora is parroting information she's heard second hand; she has no idea what this woman would really need to do to free herself from the chains binding her to the life she's described.

I should shut up - I sound like a commercial, Aurora says to herself. Aurora wants to be helpful, but she can see by Ann's defiant expression that any proposal, from any source, would fall on deaf ears.

Ann stops in the middle of the room with her hands on her hips. "What can I do?" the little woman cries. "I got no edjacation - I cayn't do anythin' else. Plus, man, that trailer's all we got now; it's our home. I cayn't leave the cripple - he needs me. So I gotta make money - somehow -"

Aurora smiles meekly and the dialog between her and Ann fizzles out.

The other women continue talking, asking more questions, but Aurora feels a rumble in her stomach and steps to the doorway to see if there is a clock anywhere. She leans out looking to the left; nothing. Just as she twists to turn her head to the right, she collides with an officer who catches her by the arm right at the moment Aurora begins to totter, thwarting an imminent fall.

"Oh, thank you," Aurora says.

The tidy-looking official nods a 'you're welcome', straightens her jacket and adjusts her tilted cap. She peers into the cell. "What's going on here? Oh, no - everyone disperse - Now! This section isn't going to be penalized because of you fools - we could lose ten whole points for having too many people in one cell!"

The officer waits with one hand resting on her hip, the other arm extended, pointing the way to insure that the errant inmates make a swift departure out of the room.

Chapter Nine: A day in the Life

The line to the cafeteria is extensive.

The trail of orange bodies wraps around the corner. Other hues seem more vivid and pronounced to Aurora as she inches along with the others. Pigments of color are popping out in every direction. The red box over a glass door indicating an emergency exit, glows. The metal security bar that reads 'EMMERGENCY USE ONLY' is a vibrant yellow. Ceiling sensors blink incessantly neon green. Workers wearing cherry and white striped aprons in the back of the canteen, swirl like candy cane poles.

Aurora notices a stripe of vibrant sapphire on a tall, slender woman with long black tresses and a puff of pink on the cropped hair of an inmate with olive skin.

The film, 'Pleasantville' pops into her head as the various shades create an Impressionist's watercolor painting. The movie's theme seems to fit right in with Aurora's surroundings. She silently recites: *Dull is the world in black and white, but life in color alters the universe completely.*

**

As she gets to the dining area, Aurora calculates that the room could accommodate at least one hundred fifty people.

The open-working kitchen behind the service line is setup like a lot of the kitchens she's worked in.

Mighty grills, gas ranges and ovens, walk-in refrigerators and freezers, a dish washer with a conveyer belt big enough to wash a small car, a staff of at least twenty; Aurora has done all that and more.

The atmosphere triggers thoughts of the Air Force base in Germany where she'd worked and attended culinary school when William was in the Army overseas. For two years Aurora was the kitchen manager at the Air Force Base Officer's Club.

Moving on in the queue, she reaches for a tray and utensils at a station that precedes the steam tables. The service personal are busy getting ready to dish out the meal of the day.

Aurora thinks, *I wonder what menu plan they implement here,* and she has a flash back of the 'O' Club.

***

The building's worn exterior was being restored. The inside though, had a grandiose splendor in its regal setting. The high-pitched cathedral ceilings with glossy mahogany arches, the magnificent gold-plated crystal chandeliers, and the floor to ceiling cream-colored damask draperies with rich, gold braided trim that framed the massive dining room, were spectacular.

Aurora recalls the plush, royal blue air force insignia patterned carpet and remembers how luxurious it felt when she'd slipped off her shoes for a quick feel. She'd been perched primly on the edge of a red velvet Queen Anne chair, waiting to find out why she'd been summoned.

"We've heard a lot about you Mrs. Sabel," the elderly manager had said to Aurora.

She remembers studying the stout man's ruddy face; his wide mouth housed chunky sugar-white teeth that flashed in his broad welcoming grin. She couldn't help but smile back.

"What you did at our German-American Community Club has the higher-ups buzzing."

Accountability

The manager pulled out a thick manilla folder with Aurora's name on it.

As he'd opened it, and scanned the top sheet, Aurora remembers feeling a bit shaky that they'd had a file on her.

"I see here that you interviewed for a bartender's job, but your questions about inventory, menu planning, and service landed you in the manager's seat. There's a notation here about a multi-cultural menu; yes, on Wednesday's you do a Mexican night, right?"

Aurora recalls her tight-lipped nod; she'd been in awe of how much he knew about her.

"Well, young lady, our menu has been status quo for about thirty years, but with this face lift, we need you to create an innovative dining experience to go with our brand-new look."

Aurora reminisces, still proud of the menu she'd designed for the newly renovated facility.

***

Behind the serving line she observes a heavyset man with a five o'clock shadow taking lids off the chafing dishes. With a side-ways glance, Aurora watches the woman next to her place utensils on her tray and continuously rearrange the plastic cutlery on her napkin.

Aurora looks away from the obsessive display, closes her eyes for a second, and sees the face of the bushy-mustached bigwig who often came into her kitchen before events.

"Sho' smells good in here, Aurora. How 'bout you give an ole dog a bone and let me taste a bit of that steam ship round 'for those grubby hounds get their paws on it?" the good-natured general would say, his voice a smooth, deep southern drawl.

Aurora smiles remembering her sauciness and the playful banter she'd had with the Commander.

"Stop picking at the crispy parts, Sir," she'd always said, swatting his hand.

"When I'm ready to cut it General, I'll save an end for you. Now, out of my kitchen, I have work to do."

She can almost smell the aromatic juices of the mammoth mounds of meat that her team roasted for big events. It was a challenge and an accomplishment to oversee all the intricate preparations for over twelve hundred service members, the official balls, and ceremonies.

Aurora holds her tray up to receive the day's meal and notes that it looks nothing like anything she's ever made.

***

Diana is seated at a table with a pair of pregnant women.

Aurora takes the empty chair across from Diana and pushes her tray to the middle of the table. She doesn't look directly at anyone as she shyly makes her proposal. "I was given a portion of everything they're serving today, but I have no appetite. Would any of you like to have some of this food?"

Without comment the offering is a piecemeal as the women simultaneously take shares.

"Aurora, this is Rebecca. I know her from my last cell," Diana says touching the arm of the sallow-looking woman on her right.

Rebecca gazes at Aurora but doesn't extend a salutation. She grabs the roll off the plate cautiously; a wary expression as if she's expecting a protest.

The other gal abruptly nabs the apple on the tray, seemingly determined to get something.

"And this is Missy," Diana says nodding to her left.

Missy smiles biting into the fruit.

"How far along are you Rebecca?" Aurora asks, averting her eyes. She's alarmed by Rebecca thinking, *My God, what is she ailing from? She should be in a hospital not in a jail.*

"Too far if you know what I mean. Lucky me, I turned twenty-nine yesterday and today I hit seven months," Rebecca says as she rubs her belly and sighs.

Accountability

"This baby is sitting wrong; I'm in pain all the time. I had no trouble with the other two."

Rebecca labors to cut her food and put it into her mouth.

Aurora has to restrain herself from taking the fork out of the woman's hand and feeding her.

The dark veins on Rebecca's emaciated hands are so pronounced that they look like an old woman's.

It seems to Aurora that the sickness causing Rebecca's body to deteriorate is turning her into a living corpse.

She thinks to herself, *What about the baby? I hope it's okay.*

Rebecca touches the deep creases around her mouth and spies Aurora.

Aurora slowly turns her head and tries nonchalantly, to look away.

Rebecca keeps an eye on Aurora the whole time.

As Aurora's gaze, like a magnet, pulls her focus back on Rebecca, the frail-looking young woman sighs and says, "I know - I look like shit. Man - please stop looking at me. I know what you're thinkin' - I can see it in your eyes. You're thinkin' - 'Goddamn, what happened to this girl?' Well, Heroin did this. But, hey, it's okay. I'm on meth now."

"What's meth? Do you mean methadone?" Diana asks.

Aurora is interested to know too, but she looks away so no one sees that she's curious.

"It's a synthetic drug to fool the body into thinking we don't need heroin," Missy says, tying her bottle-blonde hair up, the brittle strands stiff like straw from so much bleach.

"You, too?" Diana asks.

"Yeah," Missy says glancing at Rebecca. "That's another reason why the powers-to-be put us together. So we could take our meds at the same time."

They nod and smile at each other.

Rebecca slowly shifts in her seat.

She lifts her belly and the little round mound sways from side to side.

Rebecca can't find a comfortable spot.

"Man, I can't get rid of this load fast enough," she complains sourly. "Once this kid's out of me, I'm havin' my tubes tied. There ain't no way I'd go through this again."

Rebecca changes position and her stomach rolls like a wave; the baby's very active.

"I've been livin' in Hell - you can see - and it almost sucked the life right out of me."

Rebecca, stiff-lipped, stares defiantly at Aurora, almost challenging her to look away.

Willing herself not to look away, Aurora uses all her might and holds the woman's gaze with a sympathetic expression.

"I'd take it all back if I could - you know - but what I don't regret - not for a second - is having my kids. God - I love them. I'd be *nothing* without them; they saved me." Rebecca looks down at her tummy and rubs the moving mass in a gentle swirling motion.

"Even this one - if he doesn't end up being the death of me."

Aurora can only smile weakly and offer Rebecca her orange juice.

Missy takes the plate of what looks like a hockey puck sitting in a puddle of grey colored gravy, a hardened tennis-ball-shaped heap of rice and wilted brown green beans. "Well, if no one's going to eat this -" she says grabbing a fork and starting in on the food.

Missy is an attractive teenager, even with the splotchy run of pimples on her face. Her ocean-blue eyes are like Rebecca's in color, but Missy's face isn't shadowed by dark circles.

"How old are you Missy?" Aurora quietly asks. "I just wondered - I don't mean to pry -"

She has no intention of asking either of them why they're in jail, and so far, neither have offered to tell.

"Hey - no problem - I've got nothing to hide. So - first question - right - I'm eighteen -" she giggles, "but I can't say that I've never been kissed -"

Missy pats her belly and smiles. Her brightened face looks even younger when she smiles.

"I'll bet your next question is, how far along am I? Five months. She'll be born right before my nineteenth birthday. And the final quiz answer is, it's my second bambini."

Aurora goes to the counter where a huge steel urn holds coffee and pours herself a cup. When she returns to the table, the conversation has hit a dead end and she's relieved that everyone is keeping their own counsel. She can't bear to hear any more 'True Confessions'.

The tragedy of all these fractured women and their unfortunate circumstances is a reality way out of Aurora's league.

***

Diana suggests a game of cards.

The table gets cleared, and another one is dragged over to make room for more players. A game of Spades commences.

Rebecca starts turning green at the end of the first round. "Could someone call a guard?" she asks breathing fast, seizing her chest.

Aurora shoves her chair back, but Diana's faster. She jumps up and runs to fetch a guard.

"I've got you Becca -" the official says scooping Rebecca up like she weighs nothing. He nods at the group and whisks Rebecca out of the room.

A few minutes later, Missy looks unwell.

"I'm tired. I'm going to take my meth now and lay down. Let me know who wins," she says getting up from the table.

Missy protests when Diana and Aurora pop up at the same time. "I'm okay - don't bother - I can get back on my own," she says waving them off and waddling away.

With two spots open, Diana calls out to Ann and motions for another woman to come, sit down, and join in.

"Mona here is our resident scholar," Diana says to Aurora. "She's twenty-one. She's in *college*."

Diana is eyeing Mona with what Aurora can see is pure envy. She openly gapes at her movie-star-like idol's every move, changing her deportment, trying to emulate Mona.

Aurora gives Diana's hand a motherly squeeze and turns her attention to the pretty woman.

Mona has an air of self-assurance that Aurora instantly recognizes as traits of the affluent. She maintains a posture Aurora can identify: the subtle exhibition of boredom at the mundane that comes from being born into a privileged life. Aurora knows the type from her own social circle. Mona is poised and appears relaxed. She crosses her legs, looks intently at her issued cards, and begins sorting the suits in her hand.

"What are you studying Mona?" Aurora asks.

"Criminal Law, but I may change my major to International Finance and Marketing." Mona puts her cards face down on the table and takes a drink of the soda she brought to the table. "If all this nonsense didn't set me back a month, I'd be taking my finals this week."

Aurora is intrigued by Mona.

She's managed to make the orange uniform look semi-chic by folding the sleeves of the shirt neatly above her elbow, flipping up the collar and cuffing the wide-legged pants to swing at the ankle, sailor-style. She seems to be completely at ease, regardless of her surroundings.

"What happened to you?" Aurora asks, interested to learn more about her.

"Well, it's my fault entirely - I admit it. No excuses. I knew better."

Mona slowly runs a well-manicured hand through her stylish hairdo. Her brown eyes shine as she recounts the day that she found herself at a stop sign with a police car behind her.

"I was fully aware that I was driving with an expired license. I'm embarrassed to say that I also had a cracked windshield - totally illegal - and, to fully confess - expired license plates."

She looks at the others with a bashful grin.

"I know, I know, you must be thinking, 'What an idiot'. But I've had zero time to address these issues because right now school is, and has to be, my top priority."

Mona laughs modestly and brushes long bangs off her forehead in an automatic gesture.

"I knew I was doomed when I saw the police car behind me. I was stopped three months ago for the expired driver's license, but they only gave me a warning. When I was snagged for the windshield - that was two days in jail. Then I was arrested a second time last month for continuing to drive with an expired license and expired plates - that was one week in jail."

Switching one shapely leg over the other, Mona smiles sheepishly in Aurora's direction. Involuntarily Aurora smiles back. Mona seems to know her charm is effective. She looks at her audience cordially and continues her discourse.

"It was a colossal show when the police apprehended me - my fault again, I'm afraid. Instead of acquiescing to the call of the siren, I started to drive. And I kept on driving. I don't know what compelled me to be so obnoxious, I simply didn't want to stop. When two more police cars arrived, I pulled into a gas station to surrender. Once all three cars surrounded me, the officers drew their guns and shouted, 'Step away from the car and put your hands up!' They seized me, cuffed me, and read me my rights. I've been here a week, as of today. I have another three weeks to go."

Mona sighs and folds her hands in her lap smiling benignly at everyone. "I wish it had happened after finals, but I'll pick up more classes in the summer."

She scoops up her cards, looks intently at their order, and rearranges them. "So, who's up for finishing the game?"

Chapter Ten: Court

The overhead lights in the facility automatically dim as nightfall approaches.

Aurora is leaning against the wall outside her doorway. She watches a matronly female officer stroll down the hall toward her; her sturdy body moves with assurance. She looks into each cell and nods at the inhabitants. She smiles warmly as she approaches Aurora, giving Aurora the feeling that they're not strangers.

As if she knows Aurora's habits, the woman says, "The bell will ring soon. If you'd like something to read, there's a bookshelf in the common area."

Aurora's voice catches in her throat. "Oh, yes, I appreciate that, thank you," she squeaks.

***

Women shuffle slowly to their cells like automatons as Aurora passes them in the corridor.

Faint groans echo in the halls.

A small band of inmates are huddled in a corner carrying on an intense conversation. Aurora thinks that their crafty glances make them look sneaky, like they're worried someone will hear their plan of escape.

Aurora says, *Good luck,* under her breath.

She's exhausted.

She notices the scuffed and teetering bookshelf and meanders toward it in search of reading material. Among torn books and dated magazines she finds a worn Agatha Christie novel. Deciding that it will do, she heads back to her cell calling it a night.

It's seven thirty.

***

Diana's prattling away while primping for her date. She's telling Aurora that the meeting point is on the far side of the courtyard. "It's kind of romantic - you know - we have to peek through the doorframe just to make out each other's eyes. We'll talk until they say lights out." Between slight twists and half turns eyeing herself in the dysfunctional mirror Diana squints and asks, "So - how do I look?"

Aurora thinks, *What does it matter? You're both heading blindly down a dead-end road* - "You look lovely Diana, really," Aurora says with a sigh. "I hope you have a great time."

Diana grins from ear to ear and prances out the door.

***

Turning down the wool blanket and settling herself in, Aurora starts to unravel.

When she thinks about the previous day's events, a rush of tears roll down her cheeks.

She closes her eyes and faces bounce around her head: William standing dejected in the doorway shaking his head. Officer Manning's anxious sincerity in warning her to watch out for herself. Bluebeard's awful cackling disdain.

She can see the Jamaican guard's benevolent smile and her eyes well up again at the thought of Kenny.

Oh, Kenny.

Thinking about Ann and Judith, Aurora can only shake her head.

She sighs sadly, seeing Diana's bright-eyed exuberance about her future, and recalling the self-assured persona of Mona makes Aurora smile wryly, but her face contorts, and she frowns when she thinks of that rotund, clueless imbecile, Dawn.

They all chatter at once; the buzzing noise lulling Aurora like a sleeping potion, to a weighted inertia. She's emptied out; once a wellspring of energy, depleted. Not a drop left.

***

Aurora wakes with a start; the bell for breakfast is ringing loudly.

Diana is sitting calmly on the air bed staring up at her. "Welcome back to the world of the living," she says smiling.

Aurora sits up and waits for Diana to speak; her mouth is twitching like she's rehearsing what she's going to say.

"Now listen up Aurora," she says in a pointed tone, "you've got to get this straight. Those who are to be prosecuted and released will be taken to a closed courtroom within the facility. A judge on close circuit TV will sit in and rule from another county courtroom."

Diana seems impatient for it to register with Aurora, nodding her head encouragingly.

"The session will pan out by the court's order - sometimes it goes fast and other times - well - they'll let you know - just go with the flow and everything will be okay. Okay?"

Before Aurora has time to ask Diana to explain what she means by a judge on a television, the loudspeaker summons her. And just as she hears her name being called, a heavily made-up guard appears in the doorway.

Her hair is pinned up with cascading curls. Her makeup is like a plastic coating, abundantly applied.

Geez, another odd character - Aurora thinks lowering her eyes. She can't look at the woman even though she's no longer disturbed by the strangeness of things in this half-world.

Accountability

When other inmates pass by the dolled-up official they smile but cover their mouths and snigger.

The guard is oblivious and pleasant in her greeting.

"Good morning, good morning," she calls out making it her business to be cheery. "Mrs. Sabel? You ready? Okay, let's go." She extends her arm in a gesture of commencement and they proceed down the corridor. "Wait right here until further instructions," she says with a more formal air, motioning for Aurora to stand against the wall of a long hallway that's already occupied by many women. With a satisfactory nod at Aurora, the guard pats down her hair, turns, and dashes away.

***

The hallway is a melting pot of jiggling orange.

People are stirring restlessly trying to maintain their law-enforced positions in the line.

Aurora doesn't engage with anyone because too many questions are racing through her head: *What happens now? What will they do to me? How will William know where to find me?*

***

When the group of women is shuttled into another section of the facility they approach a trainline of men leaning on the opposite wall preceding the entrance doors to the courtroom.

As the female guards prod the women inmates down the lengthy passageway, Aurora anxiously searches the crowd. Further on she sees the back of his head and his frame. He's talking to a short guy who's casually looking in her direction; they're chuckling.

Aurora waves to the little man who's eyes perk up in surprise and Kenny turns around to see what he's looking at. He smiles in acknowledgement and raises his big arm in a greeting.

Aurora feels a rush of emotion and her breath catches.

In a desperate hurry she leaves her spot and moves along the corridor cautiously elbowing people out of her way.

"Excuse me, excuse me," she says trying to be polite, but her voice is lost in the mingled dialog in the corridor.

Kenny pats his comrade on the shoulder and ambles toward Aurora.

The people on both sides, move aside for him.

A bald-headed guy Kenny passes snorts as he sees what's going on, "Go ahead - pop that cork big guy -"

A heavy older woman looks crossly at Aurora barking, "What chu tink yer doin' chicky?"

Ignoring the onlookers, Aurora reaches Kenny and lays her hands on his muscular arms. Breaking down she hiccups and cries, "What's going to happen now? What should I do?"

Kenny looks tired; like he hasn't slept at all.

He bends down, leveling his gaze to meet Aurora's. His eyes twinkle as he smiles at her. He looks down the hall and back at Aurora. "Have faith. It's what I've been tellin' you."

Before Aurora can protest and question him further, he turns and heads quickly back to his spot.

***

Male guards corral the men, and they move like a herd of restless cattle into the courtroom. The male inmates are crude and hostile, making sick jokes at the women as they pass them in the hallway.

They're placed by reversed alphabetical order starting from the last row in the back.

When Kenny is seated, he's five pews up, concluding the lineup of the men's group.

After the men have been seated, the guards deliver the women inmates; seating them in the same reversed alphabetical order.

As Aurora makes her way down to her section, she sees that her location's starting point is one row ahead of the men.

As she moves across the pew, she finds herself sitting directly in front of Kenny.

She doesn't turn around, but her panic eases when she hears him behind her breathing.

She starts to count the rhythm of his steady, one deep inhale, two slow exhale, one deep inhale, two slow exhale.

His being there, right there, calms her, a bit.

***

The room is filling up to capacity.

The barrage of eccentricities; people with blue or pink hair, cornrows or afro, skinheads or punks and the eclectic buzz of different languages shouting for attention, bombard her senses giving Aurora a dreadful headache.

Tentatively looking about, she sees faces tattooed with apprehension.

***

A blaring announcement in surround sound blasts, "Attention, attention. Due to technical difficulties there will be a slight delay. Proceedings will commence shortly. Please stay calm and remain in your seats."

A thundering roar of disquiet gains momentum, rising to a precariously aggressive level.

"Fucking hell -" a lady one row in front of Aurora screeches. "I gotta go to the bathroom -"

A man behind her shouts, "Let's get this going already - I've got to get back to work -"

The authorities have assumed falsely that these individuals will sit still because the aggressive force gathering into the possibility of a full-blown riot appears to think otherwise.

Aurora wants to hold it together, but her hands start to shake, and her pulse starts racing.

Everyone in the room looks like they're ready for a fight.

Aurora can almost see sparks of an electric current like little silver lightning bolts bouncing off of the vexed faces around her. She starts to turn so she can have a quick word with Kenny, but the inmate next to her gently elbows her in the side.

"Don't try it -" she says, "no one's allowed to talk - they'll pull you out of the courtroom."

Aurora nods at the inmate as they see an angry-looking officer rushing up the aisle; her hand raised, shaking a finger in their direction. Aurora sighs and quietly thanks the inmate.

***

Within a few minutes the loudspeaker blares, "Please rise for the honorable judge -"

The whole room promptly stands facing the front of the courtroom.

Eyes scan the dais for the judge, but all they see is a man in black robes in a television set. The box is propped on a podium above the high platform where a real judge would sit.

The crowd watches the judge gather his files, stack them in neat piles on his desk, and raise his hand to initiate proceedings.

A foreman calls out in a forthright manner, "Please take your seats. Court is in session."

A rush of adrenalin makes Aurora's body break into a cold sweat. *And so it begins,* she thinks with trepidation.

***

One by one, by alphabetical order, the cases for various crimes are assessed and charged.

First to be called are the women. Petty theft, soliciting, unlawful entry.

The men in the back rows make vulgar and indecent comments every chance they get. "Yeah, baby, I'll enter *you* unlawfully!"

Accountability

When the men are called to the podium to be charged with crimes like third-degree murder or manslaughter or rape or drug dealing, not one person in the waiting area makes a comment.

Processing everyone through the legal system takes quite a while, no stopping for a break.

Domestic violence cases are a secondary part of the proceedings.

Hours later, the crowd has diminished by more than half; those remaining, primarily men.

The judge motions for the room to be quiet. "Today we will be implementing a new ruling on domestic violence disputes. It is imperative that you understand this clearly," he says raising his voice above the growing moans and whines. "Renewed access to the home will not be granted and all parties with a domestic violence charge will be issued restraining orders."

The judge waits for order, but the infuriated group will not be subdued easily.

Guards pace the aisles pointing at rowdy individuals. "Restrain yourself or you will be removed from the courtroom," they call out to the crowd.

Aurora is stunned speechless; the judge's statement seeping into her brain, paralyzing her.

The judge continues. "As the accused will not be allowed to return to the home, they will need to make other arrangements once they are released."

The grumbling of unrest is so loud it makes the walls vibrate, but the judge continues as if he doesn't hear it. "The restraining order assigned to anyone charged with domestic violence means zero access to the victim in any way whatsoever. This is the Zero Tolerance Act, and this district's ruling on the issue."

Gaping mouths gasp in awful dread as the indisputable finality of the new ruling sinks in.

The judge's words envelop her, and Aurora feels like she's been stabbed in the heart.

She cries out in an anguish of pain.

The shrieking sound makes everyone around her flinch with irritation. They all turn and stare. Even the guards turn and look at her, smirking with disgust.

Before one of the officials reaches Aurora demanding quiet, Kenny leans forward and lays a hand on her shoulder.

She slumps on the seat letting out a body-wrenching wail.

Kenny bends down until his lips are brushing against her ear; his breath hot on her neck, and he whispers, "Listen girl, you're gonna be okay, do ya hear me? It's gonna be all right, you're going home - *listen to me.*"

Nope, she isn't listening.

She's shaking uncontrollably with disbelief.

The judge is saying no one will be allowed to go home.

Aurora wants to scream, really *scream* out loud.

She wants to demand that the judge to take it all back. She wants to yell at God for turning His back on her.

Aurora crumbles into the pew like falling down into a deep, dark, bottomless hole. Dazed and in shock, she shuts her eyes and rocks back and forth; completely overwhelmed.

The judge hits a gravel on his high platform commanding the assembly to quiet down.

The collective moans of mutinous voices lesson and finally the racket begins to abate.

The woman who has been wedged against Aurora throughout the whole session tries in a kind gesture, to put her hand over Aurora's clenched fists, but Aurora pushes it away.

"NO!" she wails.

Kenny leans forward and tries to say something more to her, but the guard standing at the end of the pew motions for him to sit back.

Aurora lowers her head, clamps her hands tightly over her mouth, and silently screams.

***

Accountability

The judge hears the dramatic accounts of every incident and morbid story. It's a terribly depressing stint of time. Once the ruling is given, restraining orders are issued, and the inmates are led out of the room.

When they call her name, Aurora stands up grabbing the bench in front of her for support. She slowly wobbles to the front of the courtroom; her breathing is short and strained.

She's crying.

She can't stop hiccupping.

She's afraid she's going to be sick.

Pounding in her head she's thinking, *This can't be happening. What did I do to deserve this?*

She's making quite a scene.

William is on the television standing near the judge. He's a wreck too, saying something directly into the camera with a distraught look on his face.

"William -" Aurora mumbles wordlessly, pointing at the television.

"Aurora -"

She thinks she hears her name, but William's face disappears from the screen.

Even without high definition, the judge's pinched face is clear.

"Madam, please control yourself and state your name," he sternly orders.

But Aurora cannot control herself or state her name.

The judge looks impatient.

He consigns himself to stating her name for her.

"Are you Aurora Sabel?" he asks, his tone implying that he expects it to be.

Aurora nods, silently pulling out her shirttail, wiping her eyes, blowing her nose, and tucking the soggy corner of fabric back into her pants.

William conveys something in earnest to the judge, but Aurora can't hear what he says.

Her head is throbbing, her ears are ringing, and she is so tongue-tied she can't utter a word.

The judge is looking weary; like he could use a break.

He loosens his skinny black tie, unbuttons the collar of his shirt, slowly runs a hand through his thick silver hair, and sighs.

"Return to your seats, both of you. We'll get to the bottom of this at the end of the session - and Mrs. Sabel, it is by recommendation of this court that you pull yourself together by then."

***

There is a steady flow of hectic activity as inmates are called up to the judge to hear their orders, acknowledge their obligations, and then swiftly be ushered out of the courtroom.

The room empties out.

Aurora sits alone in her torment stewing over the new ruling, trying to figure out how and where she's going to live without her family.

Did she see Kenny before he left? Didn't she feel someone touch her on the shoulder?

Aurora jumps when she hears the judge's booming voice call her name. "Mrs. Sabel, please come forward."

Aurora thinks, *It's so strange to be beckoned from a television set* - as she scrambles awkwardly up the aisle. When she gets up front she sees William on the television screen standing near the judge's bench.

The judge, who appears to be looking directly into her eyes, gets right down to business. "Well, now that I've read your file thoroughly Mrs. Sabel, I have a better understanding of what I'm dealing with. You both appear to be more composed now and able to conduct a rational conversation, so let me ask you, how long have you been married?"

"Eleven years, sir," Aurora whimpers.

"And has anything like this ever happened in your marriage before?"

"No sir, never!"

"I see on the report that no weapons, drugs or alcohol were involved." He hesitates. "So what threatening act was so prevalent as to give the police cause to arrest you Mrs. Sabel?"

"NOTHING HAPPENED SIR!"

"Why this is absurd."

He takes off his glasses and wipes them with a cloth.

"Some kind of violence must have been committed."

He sets the glasses back on his face.

"It states here that both parties were calm."

He turns to William, then he seems to look right through the television at Aurora.

"Whatever happened here - whatever misuse of - this case will be duly noted - so in such scenarios - misjudgment won't happen again. Is that clear?"

"Yes sir - I mean no sir - that is - oh my!" Aurora cries out, racked with uncertainty.

The judge looks contemplative for a moment, then he speaks to William.

"Mr. Sabel, as there seems to be no threat to you what-so-ever, are you still inclined to press charges against your wife?"

"CHARGES?"

William and Aurora both blurt out the word 'Charges' so abruptly that it causes the judge to hold up his hand.

He looks questioningly at the ceiling, jots something down in the file on his desk, and sighs.

"Sir, I never signed a statement pressing charges," William respectfully tells the judge.

The judge looks at the file with a keen interest, averting eye contact.

Aurora is gripping the edge of the pew taking deep breaths trying not to lose her balance.

The judge is quiet for another moment and then he speaks.

"First let me say that I have never seen, throughout my entire career, anyone so physically shaken, so inconsolably distraught as the two of you."

The judge shakes his head, and in a tone laced with disgust continues.

"This kind of thing shouldn't have happened to people like you."

Penetrating eyes shoot through the screen so stunning Aurora that she can't move or speak.

He pauses for seemingly interminable seconds, then the authoritative voice states, "Mr. Sabel I suggest you go to the county jail, pick up your wife, and take her home."

Aurora hears William thanking the judge profusely. She looks at the female officer standing next to her and asks, "What - did - he - say?" breathless with confusion.

As if he's read her mind, the judge clarifies the order. "Mrs. Sabel, I recommend that you be released - you may return to your home - but you will need to make arrangements - to get some kind of professional help - don't let whatever caused this altercation to become worse."

Aurora sees on the television screen, the judge collecting his paperwork, and stepping down from his podium. She sees him take off his glasses, rub them with the edge of his robe, and sigh.

She hears him say to the clerk he's handing the pile of files to, "Man, what a day. Let's all go home."

There isn't time for Aurora to thank the judge or talk to William before the TV goes black.

Chapter Eleven: Release

When she gets back to her cell, Aurora goes straight to the tiny sink and starts to retch. She hasn't eaten anything in two days so there's nothing coming out but sour yellow bile. She hugs the porcelain, trying to steady herself. After she splashes her face with water, she uses the little white towel, and screams noiselessly into it.

Unbelievable, she thinks. Feeling shaky, she stumbles to the bed, grabs the pillow, and hugs it tight. *Thank God this is finally over,* she says to herself. She lays down on the bed, closes her eyes and thinks about Kenny.

"You're going home," he'd said. He had been so steadfast in his conviction, so certain of her release.

She wonders, *How could he possibly have known that?*

Aurora feels that she always tries to pray for things of significance with a faith-filled core. Prayers that will be truly deserving of His ear. And yet it's never felt like God is listening when she prays for herself.

But like a twitch or an itch or a tingle or a warm fuzzy feeling, she's sure she's felt something pulling her through the labyrinth of the last two days.

And Kenny is as likely an angel as anyone could be, as far as she can tell.

And a pretty big angel at that - she thinks, wishing she could see the smirky grin on his face one more time, and hear him say, *"I told you!"*

Aurora knows that her encounter with the unusual man is one of those unexplainable things. No one would probably understand it, or believe it. She isn't even sure *she* believes it.

Judith and Mona peer in at Aurora's open doorway. "Oh, you're here!" they say at once.

"How are you doing?" Judith asks.

"How did it turn out?" Mona asks. "You're back so much later than everyone else."

Dawn walks in and Aurora asks them all to sit down.

"You're not going to believe it - I can barely believe it myself," she says gawking at them. "The judge released me - *me* - and no one else. I'm going home - yes - *home* -"

"But we heard all about the judge's new ruling - bad news travels fast," Mona says.

"I know, I watched everyone go -"Aurora says panting, "I was the last person to see the judge - he read my file - asked me some questions, and told my husband to come and take me home. I told you my story - you know what a terrible mistake it was - well, now they're releasing me - they're letting me go home."

"Good for you. I can't believe the system didn't suck you in like the rest of us," Judith says shrugging her shoulders. She thrusts her hands in her pockets and walks out the door.

Mona hugs Aurora and smiles at her warmly. "Justice prevails and the innocent will be redeemed, etc., etc., etc."

A guard comes by and brakes up their conversation, so they say quick, tearless good-byes. The sullen faced officer barks in a voice saturated with scorn, "Stay put, Mrs. Sabel. Don't go wandering around now. Be ready. Someone will come for you very soon."

Aurora is hoping to talk to Diana, but she hasn't come back to the cell.

While the thought of Diana's future weighs heavily on her mind, and she waits impatiently, anxiously hoping to have a few last words with the girl, Ann pops in.

"Diana was moved again, but she left this for you - asked me to give it to you with a hug -" she says hugging Aurora.

The note reads:
Aurora, I wish you luck in whatever you do.
I'm glad we met you're a wonderful person. (I'm sorry we met here) I hope we stay in touch, you're a great friend.
Take care, Diana

The letter is written in a school girl's big, loopy flair; exactly like her.

***

It's very late in the afternoon before a guard comes to get Aurora. She hasn't left the cell at all; fear racking her that maybe the judge had lied. He'd felt sorry for them, but then remembered that a ruling is a ruling.

She's so relieved when a guard pops her head into the cell and says in a hurried, annoyed command, "Come on Sabel, let's go already!"

***

The compound is larger than Aurora imagined.

She's dropped off in an access garage; placed with a dozen or so women who are awaiting transport to another part of the complex as well. "Wait here," is all the female officer says before walking off.

A big white van advances slowly into the garage and stops within inches of their spot.

A heavyset male guard in a white jumpsuit slides off of the driver's seat, opens the sliding door, and says in a friendly tone, "All aboard!"

The women load into a van with padding on the walls and vinyl benches around the perimeter. They sit across from each other like in a cargo plane, strapping themselves in with the belts hanging from above.

It's stiflingly hot in the van until they start moving, then gusts of frosty steam rush through the vents so fast, they're all freezing within a minute.

The shrugging of shoulders, grimacing, and complaints against the cold-air assault ushers forth a communal dialog of grievances.

"I went through Anger Management last time this happened to me. You just do the time and get it over with," says an olive-skinned woman of medium build, with a heavy accent to the woman next to her. Her sleeves are rolled up past her elbow; the name 'Alex' is etched in thick black script on her upper right arm. "All it is," she gripes, "is a bunch of mumbo jumbo about personal rights and mutual respect. If you get through the assessment without killing anyone, they take the charges off your record."

Aurora keeps her head down. She doesn't know what they're talking about, but she's reluctant to ask anyone to explain.

"My boyfriend had to do it too. He said it was a load of crap," says a woman with long black braids and an air of sarcasm.

Aurora wonders if she should get involved but stays quiet. She ponders asking the nice-looking woman sitting next to her what it's all about, because she has the least amount of hostility written on her face, but she can't rouse herself to speak.

Kathryn, seemingly aware of Aurora's furtive glances, kindly nods and introduces herself.

"It's a program called Diversion," she says answering Aurora's silent questioning eyes.

"Instead of being prosecuted for domestic violence, giving you a record," she explains, "the program, officially called, Domestic Violence Intervention, offers state-authorized counselling anywhere from eight to twenty-six weeks - depending - so you avoid the criminal record."

"Who would have to do this program?" Aurora asks, timid but alert, sitting up in her seat.

"*Everyone* has to do this program. You'll find out. You'll see. They'll fix you up good when you go to court," says an exhausted-looking woman whose cold eyes tear into Aurora.

Accountability

"Come on Pamela," Kathryn chides, "don't be so mean. She doesn't know any of this, okay?"

"Wait - No – I was in court, here, today, and the judge let me go home," Aurora says quietly. "I'm done. There isn't - there can't be - I most certainly *won't* be coming back!"

"You're going *home*?" asks Kathryn incredulously. "I had to call my friend to fetch me and she'll have to go to my place to get my stuff. I can't go anywhere near there!"

"Were *you* in the courtroom today?" Aurora asks shyly with a chill of embarrassment.

"Yes," she says angrily, "and I couldn't believe it when he said that we all had to find other living arrangements when we were released."

"I was there too," says Pamela rubbing her dry eyes. "This sucks. My mom's coming for me with my kids and the four of us have to stay with her for a while. She'll have to go to my house to get what we can get by with until we figure things out. I only defended myself, and now I'm banned from my own home."

She sighs weaving a strand of long black hair behind her ear.

"What sucks the most is that my no-good husband can stay in the house. He's abused me for years - but he's not judged - while I'm treated like a *criminal* and have to go back to my mother and suffer under her authority again."

The other women nod; sympathetically acknowledging how hard it would be to go backwards like that.

Kathryn leans forward and checks Aurora out.

"*Hey* - you were the one in the courtroom who cried out - right?"

The entire group shivering in the van turn to stare as Kathryn accuses Aurora, intensely studying her face. Everyone glowers with curiosity and rising clarity.

Before Aurora can speak, defend herself, or otherwise explain, she hears someone shout above the noisy fans, "Oh yeah, that's her - that's the woman who lost it in court today!"

The van stops in front of a gray paint-peeling three-story building. The women get out and go up two flights of stairs into a huge open area with beds lined up in rows dormitory-style. There are a few round tables filled with women playing cards. Along the right side of the room are toilets and showers. Women are mulling around everywhere.

An officer sits at a school-sized metal desk and calls out names from a list issuing papers to fill out. "When you bring them back, you should find a quiet spot to wait. You'll be called when it's time to be released," says the tired-looking woman with stringy grey hair and a smile like daggers on her pinched face.

Filling out the forms is easy, but finding a place that won't bother anyone proves to be more difficult. Aurora has to move many times. Each time she sits in a chair or leans against a wall, some woman comes up and tells Aurora that she's in her spot and has to move. She wanders around for a while, finds Kathryn and Pamela, and the three of them take a little corner table.

With detached curiosity they watch two dislocated women who've assigned themselves a purpose. They patrol the room with an air of authority ordering the meek who will let them, as time inches along pathetically slow.

Aurora turns her attention to her tablemates, listening more attentively to the conversation.

Kathryn is at the beginning of her story. "I guess I'd been living with Ned for a little over six months when things started to change. Our fleeting romance had lost its spark and we were aggravated with each other," she's saying. "We really didn't have much in common beyond sexual attraction, so we didn't do things together."

Kathryn seems reflective. "About three months ago we had a huge fight and he got really rough with me. It scared me so much that I called 911."

She straightens her posture and sits up in the chair. "The police came, heard my account, and took Ned away. He was in jail for twenty-four hours on domestic violence charges.

Accountability

We were both sorry and made solemn promises to make a new start, but -"

"But you can't change a leopards' spots," Pamela says shaking her head as if she knows.

Kathryn nods at Pamela.

"Yes, you're right, but everything has been good for the last few months. Just recently we started to argue again. The other night I said I've had enough - that I can't do it anymore. We went at it - you know - yelling at each other - he went crazy and came at me shouting, "You can't do this to me - I'll get you - no one walks out on me!"

Kathryn smooths her hair and sighs in recollection of the episode. "He pushed me and grabbed the phone. He waved it in my face and then with a sneer, he dialed 911. I ran from him, locked myself in the bedroom, and hurried to throw some things into a bag. I just wanted to get out of there, but I stayed in my room because I knew the police would come on a 911 call. They arrived alright. They knocked on my bedroom door and asked me to come out, assuring me that Ned was being detained in the kitchen. They questioned us separately, but Ned's statement was that I'd attacked him. Although he showed no physical evidence of being assaulted, the police, after stating the new law, cuffed me and took me in."

"So, they didn't listen to you - and they didn't listen to me try to explain either," Pamela says flatly.

Kathryn nods at Pamela again and they smile consolingly at each other.

"What baffles me the most is that the authorities had the records showing the previous altercation with Ned, but they said that any prior incident had no bearing on this episode. Without further inquiry the judge issued the restraining order. So, because of his lies," Kathryn says with a groan, "my whole world is upside-down. Now I have to finagle getting my clothes and my stuff out of our apartment when he's not there. I'm afraid he's already done something vindictive like cut them to pieces, or burned them."

She sighs.

"I knew he was trouble. I should've left for good the first time around."

Aurora and Pamela shake their heads in commiseration; there's nothing more to say.

Finally, a guard calls all their names, and they walk out together.

Kathryn has to decide what to do.

Aurora asks her if she can help.

"No thanks, a girlfriend is picking me up. I'll probably stay with her for a while."

Kathryn asks if either of them would like to join her for a drink.

Pamela shakes her head, "No, no thanks, I'm sure that my mom's outside with the kids. If nothing else, my mother is punctual."

Kathryn looks at Aurora hopefully.

"Oh - no, I couldn't possibly," Aurora says breathlessly. "My husband is coming. I've got to get back to my children; I've never been away from them this long."

Pamela sighs with acute envy, "God, you're going home. Some people have all the luck."

"I won't believe it until I'm in the car, leaving this place," Aurora says quietly.

As they head silently to the Items Room, they come upon a few grease-balls who are loitering in the hallway.

The men, still in orange uniforms, glare at the women. While rubbing their crotches and swaying their hips, they call out, "Hey Chickies, jew want some a 'dis?"

Aurora wants to say something harsh, but she has no energy.

The women lower their heads and walk faster trying to ignore their jeers as they pass them, but it only excites the men into more feverish calls.

"Aw, come on - ya know ya wan eet -" they taunt.

Pamela turns around to protest, but Kathryn takes hold of her arm and moves her aside.

"Hey! Hey assholes - What do you think this is your own personal playground? Beat it or I'll scream, and you'll be back inside quicker than you can shake your -"

Just as Kathryn is about to finish her spicy reproach a door opens, and they're waved away from the goons; given a timely escape route through the passageway.

The room is empty except in the far corner a woman is standing behind the opening of a cutout, framed window. After receiving their papers, the unsmiling woman has them sign a release form and gives them their brown paper bags. Another female officer pops in and takes them down to the lavatories to change.

***

Aurora feels a little better being back in her own clothes, even though the items she neatly folded are wrinkled from being crammed on a shelf for two days. She's the first one in the hall. Pamela apparently, has dressed and dashed. She's nowhere to be seen.

Kathryn comes out clad in a tailored black blazer with an A-line pinstriped skirt. The two dressed up women smile and nod at each other.

Kathryn scrutinizes Aurora's face. "Oh my - you have make-up. I left all my stuff on the bathroom sink at home. Can I borrow your lipstick? I've looked a fright for two days."

Aurora smiles shyly, retrieves the little make-up bag from her purse, and offers it to Kathryn.

Kathryn dabs her lips with lipstick and beams at Aurora. "Hey - maybe we should exchange numbers - just in case." She rips a bit of paper from her leather datebook, finds a pen from her bag and presses them into Aurora's hand. "You can't talk about this stuff with just anyone."

"I can't imagine talking about this to anyone at *all*," Aurora says emphatically.

She quickly jots her number down and gives it to Kathryn.

They walk amiably back to the Items Room and return the uniforms to the dreary-looking guard in the booth.

Kathryn seems a little giddy prancing in her shoes. "I'd forgotten how uncomfortable these new heels are - maybe I should ask for a parting gift and get a pair of those plastics jobs, eh?"

"That'll be $14.95 if you really want a pair Ma'am," says the guard before announcing to the two of them; "Be aware ladies, you'll be getting information in the mail about the follow up hearing."

Aurora wonders, *What kind of follow up hearing?*

She reassures herself; *I Don't have to worry about that - it doesn't concern me.*

***

When it's finally time to walk out the door, Aurora can't do it.

She can't move.

She can see William pacing outside with an anxious look on his face. Nervous and uncertain, she looks over at Kathryn.

Kathryn twirls a loop with her hand and says, "Okeydokey - let's blow this pop-stand -" as she pushes on the metal cross bar forcing the entry to swing open, and steps through the doorway.

Aurora vacillates, and then with her head down, shoulders sagging, she follows behind Kathryn.

William nods at Kathryn and rushes toward Aurora with a welcoming smile but he stops abruptly when he sees her drawn face. He frowns in disappointment seeing that Aurora is stiff and guarded. It looks like there's a spiky fence around her meaning no trespassing, Do-Not-Enter.

Although she's pined for him, dreamed about him coming to save her, ached for his arms around her, at this very moment she's only frustrated and furious thinking that he's to blame for everything that's happened to her.

Her high hopes of having a happy reunion, and all of the loving feelings and words she's stored up to share with William, have vanished.

Now she can't even look at him.

She's forgotten the long soul searching talks she had with God. The prayers and promises she made in earnest to be a better person.

Now she's stuck.

She can't go forward, and she can't go back.

Caught in this quandary not knowing what to do, she drops her arms, bows her head, closes her eyes, and just stands there.

After the briefest hesitation, William walks steadily up to her, reaches out, and lovingly takes Aurora's hand.

Laura Strobel

The Wallet Photos

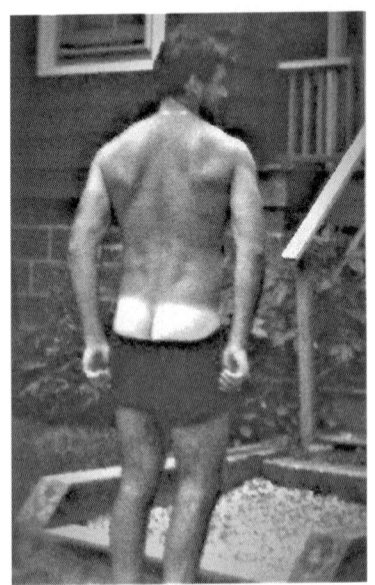

The boys at the beach and the showoff.

Part Two: Denial

Chapter Twelve: Home

The silence hung between them like a dark shroud.

William stole a few glances at Aurora, while going the short distance to his parent's house to pick up the children.

Aurora remained withdrawn and aloof, fidgeting with her hands. Without looking at him, she said, "I'll just stay in the car and wait for the boys to come out. I can't talk to anyone. You understand, don't you?"

William rubbed his forehead, and with a despondent sigh he got out of the car and said, "Yeah, sure, of course. I understand."

Aurora rolled the window down and stared intently at the bristly dry patches on the lawn. The shrubs and palms that should have been green and flourishing were brown and corroded. Even the other lawns were ravaged. Everywhere, the essence and spirit of life, were in decay. She wanted to cry; her little life had shattered, and with one gust, she'd been blown away.

When the door opened, she looked up hoping to see her little boys rush out, but instead it was her father-in-law. He seemed chipper albeit a bit wobbly on the uneven lawn waving. "Hello - how - are - you?" he called out with a broad smile, stepping gingerly down the front lawn.

Aurora watched him moving slowly toward her, her jaw tight in a grimace. "My gosh Barry, what're you doing? You can hardly walk - you shouldn't be out of bed - should you?

You could have fallen and broken your neck on that hill - where is everybody?"

He leaned into the car, kissed her cheek lightly, and said, "I just wanted to see for myself that you're okay, Aurora. You had us pretty worried."

Seemingly dejected, he turned to walk away.

Aurora took a deep breath and contemplated her manners. "Wait - I'm sorry Barry, I'm not myself - how are you? Have you started the meals I made you? You seem stronger - feeling better now?" She wanted to be kind, feeling badly that she'd been surly to the genuinely sweet man.

"Yes, yes," he replied looking relieved that Aurora was interacting. "The meals are great - but I'm starving all the time - Nancy's a strict commander - I only have fruit to eat - she found all my stashes - not a bite of sweets anywhere," he said chuckling. "The boys will be out in a moment - Nancy's gathering their things - we didn't say anything - tell them where you were or anything - that's for you and William to do." He touched her arm. "Call us if you need anything Aurora - anything at all." He smiled kindly before heading slowly back up the hill.

As she watched Barry getting to the door, a rush of nausea overwhelmed her, and Aurora thought she was going to be sick. She pushed open the car door and leaned out just as the boys came bustling out of the house shouting, "Mama, Mama!" as they ran down the hill to her.

Aurora got out of the car just in time to be encased in their arms. She dropped to her knees, pulled them in, and buried her face against their soft little bodies. A babble of words and gestures flowed of what they had been doing without her as she clung to them fiercely. She kissed their faces as they tried to talk, laughing at everything they said, not hearing what they had done, just drinking them up. "Oh, how I've missed you! Have you both grown in only two days?"

She couldn't believe that in barely forty-eight hours everything seemed so alien, that the world she knew was not the same. Not the same at all.

Accountability

William joined them and looked amused, but after a moment he said, "Okay guys, that's enough. All this noise is too much for Mama. Give her a little breathing room. We don't want to wear her out."

Aurora stared at her husband in disbelief.

She wanted to shriek, *Too much noise? Wear me out? And when did I ever need breathing room!* but instead she gaped at him, open-mouthed while he pried the boys from her grasp, took them to the car, and buckled them in.

When they were all in the car Aurora heard William say to the children, "Listen up boys, when we get home, I want you to let Mama rest while I make dinner. So go straight to your room and play quietly, okay?"

With building resentment Aurora thought, *Rest while you make dinner? You've never made dinner!*

Her cheeks began to flush as she fumed while fastening her seatbelt.

She was thinking, *And, uh, when do I need to rest? I never rest –*

She wanted to scream at him, *Why are you doing this? I need them close to me - to get past that nightmare -*

But she didn't.

Aurora wasn't about to start an argument, so she smoldered, and dug herself into a deep seat of bitterness.

William, looking tired and bleary-eyed, put on some soft music, eased the car out of the driveway, and they drove back to their home.

***

The boys unbuckled themselves and bolted to the house.

William got out and went to the mailbox to get the mail.

Aurora hesitated before leaving the security of the car, then disembarked, and ambled toward the open front door; not completely wanting to go inside.

She took her time looking around the neat, clean house as if it were someone else's home.

William scooted around her like she was a foreign object that got put in the wrong place, an obstacle in his path that he needed to dodge, and called for the children to come and get the shoes that they'd kicked off and left in front hallway.

At that moment Aurora thought, *So, life has gone on without me.*

All of a sudden, the full weight of what she had been through hit Aurora and she felt terribly drained and exhausted. Every bone in her body felt like lead, and it hurt. She decided that William was right, she needed to rest. He had everything under control; she could see that.

Clearly.

While the boys scampered to their room, the novelty of their mother being back already yesterday's news, Aurora slipped quietly away to her bedroom, and closed the door.

***

William made dinner and washed up.

Aurora stayed in her room but opened the door to listen to the typical prattle of her family as William bathed the boys, dressed them in PJs, and settled them down to read a book in bed.

She walked slowly down the hall on her way to kiss them good night, enjoying listening to their giggling rebuffs at their father's antics. "No Papa, that's not the way the story goes, tell it the right way," she heard one of them say as she entered their room. "Mama, Mama!" they called when they saw her standing there. "Where were you Mama?"

She wasn't sure what to say, so she evaded the question by attacking them with kisses; big sloppy, smoochy kisses. They cooed squealing with delight and the inquiry was forgotten.

After prayers and I Love Yous, out went the lights.

William had already retreated to the living room; he was changing channels; the sound of cut-off dialogs, like a Short-wave radio, could be heard coming from the television.

Not wanting to confront him, or go back to bed, Aurora snuck out to the patio. She still hadn't looked him in the eye.

Later on, William came outside with the phone. Covering the mouthpiece, he said, "Sorry Love, it's Karly. When she called Monday night, I said that you couldn't talk, but when she called this morning and I said the same thing, she made it clear that she had to talk to you."

Foregoing the usual, 'Hi, how are you', Karly launched into an onslaught of questions. "Where have you been? Why didn't you call me back? Why was William home when I called this morning? Do you realize that I've been trying to reach you for the last two days?"

At first, Aurora tried to be light with her cousin. "I've just been busy," she said coolly.

"Wrong answer," Karly chided. "Come on - what's up? I know you, and I know your voice. This is not *you,* and that is *not* your normal voice. So, tell me what's going on? And why was William at home all day?"

Aurora was hit with the reality that she couldn't avoid it.

She knew she'd have to talk about what happened to someone, and Karly was family; their grandmothers being sisters.

Though they talked sporadically, they genuinely liked and understood each other.

So spending seconds thinking it through, Aurora said, "Okay Karly listen, before I say anything, you have to swear that you won't tell a single soul what I'm about to tell you - really Karly, I mean it - you have to promise - this is serious - you can't tell Jedd - or your mother - oh God, she'd tell my mother - please - not a word to *anyone!*"

"Come on, Aurora, now you're scaring me - what is it? Tell me - what the hell's going on!"

So Aurora told her.

Everything.

Aurora poured out the entire, ludicrous tale.

She'd almost finished describing the details of prison life when her cousin burst out laughing.

"My God," Karly exclaimed, "of all the impossible things in the world, it's crazy that this happened to you!"

Holding the phone out, still able to hear her cousin snorting with laughter, Aurora shuddered. She was stifled and muted; painfully aware of how much of herself she had exposed.

Karly tried to console Aurora. "I'm so sorry this happened to you -" but she couldn't stop laughing. She said between chuckles, "I've never heard such an outrageous story in all my life."

Aurora wondered how to escape. Karly's cackling was giving her a throbbing headache. She speculated if hanging up on her would be too rude. She hesitated, the remote humming with Karly's voice, and almost hit the 'off' button. She sighed heavily and noiselessly withdrew.

Not noticing that Aurora had gone silent, Karly asked, "Well, is that the last of this nonsense?"

"I thought so," Aurora said, looking out at the pool, "but the last official I spoke to said there'd be something coming in the mail - maybe I have to go back and talk to them again - let's hope not."

Aurora leaned forward in the chair and looked out into the darkened pool area. "I'm in a daze. William's done everything. I can't seem to move. I'm numb; exhausted but anxious and awake. I don't know what to do with myself. I can't even decide whether to get up and go into the house or stay outside," she said wearily.

Hearing the unmistakable suffering and despair in Aurora's voice, Karly apologized for laughing at what she finally acknowledged must have been a horrible ordeal. In a take-control tone she said, "Aurora, go have a bath and a cup of tea or something stronger and get into bed. Now that you're home everything will be good as new; just let it all go."

Karly was right; Aurora should let it all go and everything would be good as new.

Right.

"I'll call you at the end of the week," Karly said. "Don't worry; try not to worry, okay?"

They said good-bye and Aurora was left with an empty feeling, setting the dead phone down.

She dropped her face in her hands.

Dear God - she screamed in her head, *help me! I need to get my life back!*

Sadly, she could tell that God wasn't listening; she knew He was off helping someone else.

***

Eventually Aurora went to the kitchen, sat on a stool at the open counter, and looked at the mail. Most were just advertisements; nothing too important, but then she found a letter from the state of Florida addressed to her.

She frowned when she read that the post date was the day after her arrest. She tried to peel the official stamp off, but it was glued on too tight. She turned the document over in her hand but couldn't bring herself to open it.

"Well, it certainly isn't confirmation that I've just won the lottery, so it must be some dreadful continuance of this nightmare," she said as she threw the notice at William when he came into the room.

He watched the document fall to the floor, leaned down, picked it up, and sat down quietly next to Aurora.

Aurora snatched the letter from William's hand and opened the envelope. It was an official notification for Aurora to appear in court. It read:

YOU ARE HEREBY NOTIFIED TO APPEAR IN PERSON BEFORE THE HONORABLE JUDGE - OF THE COUNTY COURT OF HILLSBOROUGH COUNTY, FLORIDA.
YOUR FAILURE TO APPEAR AT THIS TIME AND DATE WILL RESULT IN AN ARREST WARRANT BEING ISSUED BY ORDER OF THE COURT.

A certification stamp of the circuit court seal was in the right-hand upper corner above a crooked pre-stamped message in smudged red ink that read:

PROPER ATTIRE REQUIRED:
NO SHORTS OR TANK TOPS.

At the very bottom of the page was a number to call to verify the information and to obtain directions for the 'Diversion Section'.

Aurora dropped the sheet on the counter, and without a glance or a word to William, she went to the sink, got herself a glass of water, and left the room.

In her bathroom she brushed her teeth, washed her face, and peered at herself in the mirror thinking, *Why won't this end? How much more do I have to do?*

Aurora groaned bitterly.

She pulled down the covers and slipped into bed.

Nothing will ever be the same again, she thought.

***

Aurora was despondent because the belief she'd had in God as a savior, was now to her, a disillusionment.

She'd always counted on her faith in His power as her abiding judge, but now she felt abandoned. She felt the cruelty, as harsh as being told you are no longer loved, that she was very much alone.

***

In the dark of the night, while tossing and turning, troubled and inconsolable, Aurora slowly inched across the bed to nestle up to William. She got very close to him, but didn't touch his warm body.

William rolled over and wrapped his arms around Aurora.

She relaxed in his embrace and sighed heavily.

She thought about the disgrace and humiliation of the last few days and started to cry.

William caressed her in a comforting way.

They kissed and - no need to go into all that.

They made their way back to that solid, fixed place where the heart of the matter is not what will be, but what is.

Chapter Thirteen: Real Court

Aurora was up early as usual.

"Come on boys - breakfast!" she called, feeling much more like herself after a deep sleep in her own bed.

With her mind on the day's chores, Aurora had little time to ponder who'd be calling at seven-thirty in the morning, when the telephone rang.

"Hello?" she answered absently as she poured orange juice into two small glasses.

A deep, business-like voice inquired, "Hello, may I speak to Aurora Sabel, please?"

"Yes, uh, this is Aurora," she replied catching the spoon full of oatmeal that was dropping onto the counter instead of going into her toddler's mouth.

"My name is John Dower. I'm a lawyer with Smithton and Browne. I would like to talk to you about possible representation. May I have a few minutes of your time?"

Aurora was balancing the phone between her shoulder and her ear as she was trying to help her little boy feed himself. She almost dropped the device on the floor when her knees buckled in mid swipe, trying to think.

Juggling the phone, she slipped and hit her elbow on the counter.

In a hushed voice as if she were planning a secret rendezvous, she whispered, "No! Not now. Can you call back in thirty minutes?"

She hoped that it would not be a good time for Mr. Dower to call back, but he answered in a congenial voice, "Okay, fine, talk to you then."

When they hung up, Aurora thought, *Don't think about any of that now* - She raced around getting her kindergartener's backpack together so he could run to the bus stop. She pulled out her young aspiring artist's half-finished artwork to complete. When she had time to take a breath, Aurora wondered, *Okay - so - what did he say? But I don't need representation - Why do I need representation? I don't have to go to court again - this is another mistake - I'm not going back - I'm done with this whole mess.*

***

Mr. Dower called back promptly, and immediately offered to enlighten Aurora as to what was going on with her case.

"Well now, Mrs. Sabel, to start, if you haven't received it already, you will be getting a summons to appear in court," he said in a cordial but business-like tone.

"I have it in my hand as we speak," Aurora said trying not to sound as nervous as she was.

"Good. Let me explain step by step, what to expect. When you go to court, you'll be given an option to plead no contest, which you want to do. Then you'll be offered a program called Diversion, which you will want to take. Would you like to write any of this down? Yes? Good. Are you ready? Okay. Then you'll have to go through a drug and alcohol screening to determine what kind of classes you will attend. Before you do this, you must go to the county clerk's office and get a copy of the police report to take to the screening office. After you are evaluated, you have to make an appointment to meet with your probation officer who will tell you about the monthly check-ins and the monthly payments. Any questions so far?"

Drug and alcohol screening? Probation officer? Monthly payments? It was all too much for Aurora to process.

She'd tried to write it down, but her pen ran out of ink and the little note pad wasn't large enough. Everything she'd scribbled was a garbled mess.

"Excuse me, who are you again?" she asked in a voice laced with acid, "and why are you calling me?"

Apparently, Mr. Dower wasn't fazed by her abrasiveness because smoothly, as if he were reading from a script, he began his speech. "I am with the Smithton and Browne law firm Ma'am, and we would like to represent you. We feel that it's in your best interest to have expert legal counsel. We can save you a lot of time and expense if you have us on your side," he said, quite confidently.

"But why do I need your services?" Aurora asked boldly, her voice rising to a pitch close to hysteria. "This is all a terrible mistake. The judge told me to go home. I don't think I'm supposed to go back to court. I was already *in* court - now I'm done. It's got to be a mistake."

"I'm sorry Mrs. Sabel, I realize this is upsetting to you," he said patiently, "but you have to understand that this is clearly not a mistake, and you *do* have to go back to court. If you do not comply, the authorities will put out a warrant for your arrest. It's that simple."

Whoa.

All she got was the last part. If she didn't go, they'd arrest her again!

My God, what next - more jail time too? she cried to herself.

She felt dizzy, and had to sit down.

Neither spoke for a moment.

"I need to understand this better," she said in a softer, more demure, acquiescing tone. "Could you please tell me, what it is exactly that I need representation for?"

"Mrs. Sabel, having professional legal counsel is very important. We can be with you in the courtroom when your case comes up. We can get your fees reduced, and the time in the Diversion program reduced, possibly eliminated altogether, " said the lawyer in a level tone.

"We can speak to the judge on your behalf, and be the mediator in your case. You would benefit greatly, by having us there."

Aurora paused, taking it all in.

"What would happen if you were *not* there to represent me, Mr. Dower?" Aurora asked in a high-pitched voice.

Mr. Dower hesitated and Aurora suddenly had to ask, "Mr. Dower, how do you know all of this about me? How did you get my information?"

"It would be impossible to say what would happen if we were not there to speak for you," said the man calmly, "but believe me, you don't want to find out. We get our information for prospective clients through the public records department at the county jail. Your report, your case, is unrestricted; accessible to anyone."

"You mean anyone, *anyone*, can look up my case?"

"Yes, and *we* take these cases hoping to assist people through what can be a difficult time."

Notwithstanding an assured way to make a buck, Aurora thought sourly.

"How much does it cost to be represented by your firm, Mr. Dower?"

"Well," he said slowly, "first we'll meet and go over the details. Then we come up with a good defense. Then we -"

"But sir," Aurora interrupted, "what will all this cost me?"

"For us to do a thorough job and all but guarantee your complete freedom would be about, oh, somewhere in the ballpark of, well, uh, the fee would be twenty-five hundred dollars."

"Twenty-five hundred dollars? Oh, my, I can't see us coming up with twenty-five hundred dollars this fast. What happens if I don't have representation?"

"Well, then," he said, with a reproachful sigh, "you'll have to take your chances with the court. They may inflict the maximum on you for everything, just to make a point, or you may get off lightly, depending on what judge you get, and whether this is your first offense or not."

He sighed saying, "In either case, you'd be taking a risk."

Mr. Dower concluded his sales pitch saying, "I admit that we can't guarantee anything, Mrs. Sabel, but we can up the odds for a reduced sentence, considerably."

"Do I have to make a decision now?" Aurora asked, bowled over by so much information. "Can I talk to my husband first? I can't commit to anything until I've talked to my husband."

"Why don't you take my name and our number, talk to your husband, and get back to me."

Aurora found a workable pen and scribbled down the essentials.

She thanked Mr. Dower for his time and overlooking its cradle, set the phone down on her son's dish of half-eaten scrambled eggs while thinking, *Man-oh-man - okay, if I don't go to court, the police will put out a warrant. If his firm doesn't represent me, I could get the maximum. Their cost is twenty-five hundred dollars. I would be better off with representation for my case.*

My case?

Aurora started to cry because it was all too much.

She closed her eyes and had a terrible vision.

She was standing in a glass-cracked, graffiti-splashed payphone on the corner of a filthy narrow street calling a number on a tattered business card.

She was instructed to walk through a dark alleyway, up a dingy staircase, for the meeting in a seedy, rundown room.

A big, fat, ugly cigar-smoking dick with a scowl and a scruffy five o'clock shadow would say in a raspy voice, "Do you have the money?"

She'd hand over the twenty-five hundred dollars, stuffed in a brown paper bag.

She'd pay the ransom required to obtain her innocence.

Beep - beep - beep - the phone needed to be set back in its rightful place.

Aurora wished someone would set her back in her rightful place.

William had gotten up and out of the house early that morning. So as not to disturb her sleep, he'd gotten his own breakfast, and left her with warm kisses, loving caresses, and kind words about having a good day.

He was in Tampa when she called.

"You are not going to believe what's going on now," Aurora said, between sniffles. She gave him a full account of the conversation with the lawyer, and all its frightening prospects for her future. The outcome, no matter which way it went, looked grim. "William I'm going nuts - I can't do this alone - I need you - come home - *now* -" she demanded pathetically. "Can't you tell your boss that I'm sick and you have to go home?"

"Sorry Love, but I can't leave right now; I have a lot of work to do. Try not to worry - let it go - get it out of your head and we'll talk it all over when I get home - okay?"

Aurora breathed deeply and looked over at her little boy who was waiting with brush in hand to start painting again. She smiled at him as he waved anxiously summoning her to join him. "I'm so edgy. I can't *not* think about all this coming at me," she said bitterly.

"Come on Aurora, get busy - you always have a ton of things going on - when you're busy you'll forget all about this stuff. Don't worry, everything's going to be okay - Okay? Listen I'm sorry it's crazy here - I've got to go - Have a good day - I love you - Bye -"

Of course, William was right. She just wanted, *needed,* to hear from *him* that everything would indeed be okay.

For the rest of the day she didn't think about all that scary stuff. Between the boys and the house, the garden, the pool, and the dogs, she was too busy keeping busy to think about court orders, legal jargons, and jails.

The following day Aurora called to tell the attorney that she didn't need his services.

She and William had discussed everything the night before and decided that whatever was going to happen, would happen, lawyer or no lawyer.

They figured that if Mr. Dower were right about the course the events were going to take, they would have to pay something to the court anyway, so why not try to cut expenses and keep a lawyer's fee out of it.

Aurora thanked the clearly disappointed man, who, at not being able to take *No* for an answer, continued profusely, to expound on his very necessary virtues for her defense. Aurora thanked him loudly through his insistent dialog and hung up the phone while he was still talking.

***

Aurora went to court on the first of November.

She and William walked up to the second floor where the Diversion Section was located.

The building was new, the carpeted area plush with oversized chairs in colors of mauve and hunter green. Fake palms in wicker baskets with Spanish moss were scattered around the open waiting area; it looked like the lobby of an upscale hotel.

William took a seat and picked up a magazine while Aurora walked around the room looking at the large landscape prints on the walls; she could not sit down.

Finally, after waiting the entire morning, Aurora's name was called.

She left William and went into a room where two men stood at a long metal table with three metal chairs.

There wasn't another thing in the room; nothing on the walls, not even a window.

Just them.

They got right to the point.

"We're here, from the State Attorney's Office, Mrs. Sabel, to advise and guide you through the judicial process. We'd like to offer you a Diversion Program, run by the state, for all parties involved in a domestic violence dispute," said a tall, heavyset man in a charcoal gray suit.

Aurora stared at the floor, and waited to hear more.

"You fit the criteria, and it would be in your best interest if when you go into court, you plead no contest when the judge asks you," said the bearded Santa Claus look-a-like, whose rotund belly was bulging out of his three-piece suit.

Aurora looked at both men, trying to comprehend.

"We have the paperwork already filled out and ready for you to sign, then we'll get it initialed and submitted and you can be on your way to the courtroom."

He handed Aurora the Agreement, and they left the room.

She scanned the document which said:

THE COUNTY COURTHOUSE OF THE THIRTEENTH JUDICIAL CIRCUIT FOR HILLSBOROUGH COUNTY CRIMINAL JUSTICE DOMESTIC VIOLENCE DIVISION FOR THE STATE OF FLORIDA VS AURORA B. SABEL DOMESTIC VIOLENCE DIVERSION PROGRAM AGREEMENT

HARRY LEE COE III; STATE ATTORNEY; thirteenth Judicial Circuit by and through his undersigned Assistant, hereby warrants and agrees that, should the Defendant meet the terms and conditions of this Agreement as determined by said State Attorney, the pending charges in this case shall be dismissed.

THIS AGREEMENT, entered into this first day of November nineteen, ninety-nine, by and between Aurora Sabel, the Defendant (which was blank), **the Attorney for the Defendant** (which was also blank), **and HARRY LEE COE III; STATE ATTORNEY; thirteenth Judicial Circuit of Florida, by and through his undersigned Assistant.**

1. It is agreed that the Defendant meets the criteria and qualifications for admission to the Domestic Violence Diversion Program and Defendant's Attorney, having fully investigated the case and fully advised the Defendant's best interest to enter into this Agreement.

2. It is agreed that the Defendant shall participate in the Domestic Violence Diversion Program for a period of up to twelve (12) months and shall report in person each month on an assigned date to the Domestic Violence Counselor unless otherwise directed. The Defendant agrees to pay the supervision fee of forty-five ($45.00) dollars per month for the period of this Agreement.

3. The Defendant may be submitted to early termination upon completion of all conditions of his/her Agreement. Under no circumstances will this program period be less than ninety (90) days. The Defendant agrees to make restitution in this case to the victim, - in the amount of - payable as follows:
The Defendant stipulates and agrees that, in consideration for entering into this Agreement, the Defendant waives his/her right to invoke the statute of limitations applicable in the prosecution of the case.

4. The Defendant stipulates and agrees that he/she will keep the Domestic Violence Counselor advised of his/her current address throughout the entire program. The Defendant further stipulates and agrees that if the address placed on this contract and/or subsequent addresses change, it must be presented in writing for the Defendant to receive further notifications of subsequent court hearings if prosecution is reinstated as discussed in paragraph nine (9). The Defendant further stipulates that notice sent to the address shall be sufficient notice to the Defendant to appear and that failure to appear after said notice is provided, may result in the issuance of a warrant for the arrest of the Defendant.

5. The Defendant agrees to an evaluation to assess any potential for future violence and/or drug and/or alcohol abuse. The Defendant further agrees that the cost of such an evaluation shall be his/her responsibility.

6. The Defendant agrees to attend any counseling sessions recommended based upon the assessment.

7. The State Attorney's office stipulates that all information the Defendant may give during evaluation or counseling, shall be given the same level of confidentiality as found in the Psychotherapist-Patient Privilege in Florida Statutes (F.S.90.503).

8. The Defendant shall take no action or engage in any conduct which may endanger the safety of the victim or witnesses or family members of the victim or witnesses and shall be completely law-abiding during the term of this Agreement.

9. The parties stipulate and agree that the Agreement shall in no way operate as a contract for immunity from prosecution for the charge pending in this case, and further, should the Defendant fail to meet the terms and conditions of this Agreement, the Agreement, shall be deemed void at the discretion of the State Attorney, without notice, and prosecution may then be reinstated.

10. It is stipulated and agreed that the State Attorney's decision regarding full compliance in this regard shall be final and shall not be reviewable by the court.

Lines below the contract were for her signature, full address, and the date.

Another space was for the Attorney for the Defendant, which would remain blank.

It was a shock to read; this was serious stuff.

It would not be over any time soon seeing as she'd have to attend some sort of rehabilitation classes. It would be costly too, and she couldn't get out of any of it.

The part of the contract agreement that upset her the most was number eight.

When Aurora reread that part, she became incensed thinking, *This is too much - I am not a threat to anyone - I've been a law-abiding citizen my whole life.* She huffed and thought with a sardonic smirk, *Oh yeah - like I could really endanger a man whose over a foot taller and almost a hundred pounds heavier than me -*

***

The men in suits returned.

They watched Aurora sign the document with solemn faces, nodding their approval. Then they led her out of the room and down a long hall to a small carpeted courtroom where she was cordially placed in a pew.

They smiled neutrally at Aurora before walking away.

***

The judicial process is a well-run organization until human error muddles it. An official had misplaced a witness, so court was delayed until that person was found.

While professionals, clerks and people were talking and planning, Aurora took the opportunity to scan the room.

It wasn't at all like the courtrooms she'd seen in the movies, with heavy dark wood benches for the jury, a booth for the witness, and a high throne for the judge. It was set up like a debating forum.

The judge's seat was on the right side of the room, next to a large chalkboard with the day's events and schedule written on it. In the forefront was a carpeted, round platform where the accused would stand.

To the left of the defendant's side was a jury box that stood empty and Aurora thought, *Too bad, maybe I'd have a better chance if a jury of my peers were here to judge me.*

All the legal counsel and clerks were dressed in uniforms or business attire.

All the other unfortunates were dressed for a picnic.

Accountability

One woman wore a multi-colored muumuu, and as Aurora nodded at her she thought, *So much for the dress code.*

Aurora wore her 'Little House on the Prairie' outfit: a long, pastel flowered dress with a white cardigan sweater and a simple string of pearls.

She had high hopes that she would look so modest, so demure and unthreatening, that the judge would be moved to say, "Here, here, we've made a grave error in judgement, and put this innocent woman through a terrible ordeal. Please accept our apologies Mrs. Sabel, and just GO HOME!"

But that did not happen.

"Please rise for the honorable judge -"

Here we go again - Aurora thought as she stood hoping for a speedy acquittal.

After the morning announcements were made, and everyone was seated, the proceedings began. It was a long, arduous task, weaving through the tangled webs of each case.

Aurora fiddled with her hands in her lap and waited her turn; waited to be called up for judgment.

Unlike the others, her fate was decided within minutes of stepping onto the carpet.

Without even glancing up in her general direction, the judge, concentrating on the information on the sheet in front of her, addressed Aurora. "I see by your file here, Mrs. Sabel, that this is your first offense."

"Yes, Ma'am, but -"

"And I see here that you have had been offered the Diversion Program."

"Yes, Ma'am, but -"

"Well, this will be the road to a new beginning for you, Mrs. Sabel. You may enter into the program after your evaluation. Have a good day."

"Thank you, Ma'am, but -"

Standing on the podium flabbergasted with her mouth gaping open, her eyebrows arched in anticipation hoping to say a few more words, Aurora couldn't believe how swiftly her case had been opened, and shut.

A large guard approached her, took her by the elbow, and escorted Aurora from the center mound.

Aurora had seen from the start that the judge wasn't paying attention; she hadn't looked up once during the whole sixty seconds allotted to the case. She wouldn't have been able to give a description of Aurora, or pick her out of a line up. Aurora felt defeated that her case was of no consequence to this higher authority.

She was now committed to a program for domestic violence prevention. A program meant for people who needed help with anger and control issues.

At that moment Aurora was so furious, she had an uncontrollable urge to smash something.

Chapter Fourteen: Rules and Regulations

Before Aurora left the courthouse with William who'd been sitting in the same spot with the same magazine for hours, she was given an important piece of paper. It read:

DIVERSION PROGRAM

The State Attorney's office is offering a Diversion Program for Domestic Violence defendants. In order to avail yourself of this program, the following steps need to be taken:

1. Meet and obtain paperwork from the Salvation Army Court Representative in the courtroom.

2. Report to the Salvation Army's Domestic Violence Division within 48 hours of this court hearing to sign the Domestic Violence Diversion Contract. At this meeting, the Counselor will contact the Spring Family Violence Intervention Program and set up an appointment for an assessment.

3. After the assessment by the Spring, report back to the Salvation Army Domestic Violence Division to select and schedule an appointment with one of the listed court-approved program providers.

This appointment will be scheduled as soon as possible.

4. **Maintain contact as required by the Salvation Army Domestic Violence Diversion Counselor and attend all program appointments.**

5. **Commit no further acts of violence.**

6. **Follow any special instructions listed in the D.V.D Contract.**

7. **Attend any future court hearings which may be scheduled.**

8. **Make all payments to the program provider and the Salvation Army Domestic Violence Division.**

Aurora looked over the paper as they were walking out of the building, and she began to cry.

William tried to put an arm around her, but she dashed on ahead pushing through the double doors. She stopped abruptly, turned, put her hands on her hips, and shouted at William. "All this is happening to me because of a *slap*? This is a ridiculous and cruel injustice - I don't even come close to the kind of people that live in this type of world - the people I met in jail were really messed up lost souls - they didn't have God in their lives, or the drive to make their lives better - the fact that I've been lassoed into this, is just too much to believe!"

She bolted down the walkway as fast as she could. When she slowed down to catch her breath, she caught site of number five on the sheet, and read it out loud, "Commit no further acts of violence."

Commit no further acts of violence! she thought bitterly, *I am not violent! I may be loud, emotional, and quick-tempered - but I am not violent!*

Aurora felt thoroughly beaten and walked the rest of the way to the car in a trance.

***

When Aurora called the Salvation Army Correctional Services office and made an appointment for the following day, she stated that her two young children were in her care and asked if she was allowed to bring them along.

The friendly voice on the other end of the phone said, "Oh, please do!" as if they were joining her for a walk in the park.

***

They arrived early and made a niche for themselves in the long narrow waiting room. Sitting on a threadbare couch they looked up at the unusually high windows facing the street.

"Look Mama, there's bars on those windows," her older boy declared. The calico curtains with little red and blue flowers couldn't camouflage the iron grate over the dirt-smudged glass.

"Yes, I see that sweetheart." Aurora made room on the seat so that both of her boys could sit closer to her. "That's to keep out the - the birds that may try to fly in," she said hoping they didn't notice the metal grille on the door as well.

A jumble of toys were crammed in a purple plastic crate; they were dirty, scuffed, menacing-looking things that Aurora asked her boys not to touch.

"Come on guys, let's play with these instead," she said, pulling some of their things out of her large canvas bag.

She closed her eyes hoping to expunge the disturbing impressions in her head. She pictured abandoned houses hiding drug-addicted persons, ratty tattered mattresses on wood-bare floors, brown stained sinks, and toilets, cracked windows and exposed light bulbs, dangling on wires from plaster-peeling ceilings.

This is a safe place - I've seen too many movies.
Aurora sighed, exhaling slowly.

When her name was called a staff member directed the group down a long hallway with offices on either side. Midway on the left was a barn-style door; the top part hung open, the bottom had a little ledge, perfect for resting an elbow.

Aurora peered in and sitting at a desk inside the little cubicle was a stout woman in a yellow dress.

Straining to see over the shelf, the children stared mesmerized as the service worker wiggled out of her chair to greet them.

Eyeing the woman, Aurora put her hand to her mouth and thought, *Oh gosh, I hope he doesn't say anything this time.*

Aurora worried remembering William telling her about their three-year-old parroting the book, 'One Fish Two Fish', by Dr. Seuss when he'd seen a big woman in the post office with a yellow hat. "Look Papa, the fat one has a yellow hat!" the innocent child had exclaimed, and the lady had heard.

Dr. Seuss certainly would have had a good chuckle, but Aurora didn't think the lady here would enjoy the humor.

While Aurora signed and initialed forms, the disarming woman cooed at the boys and gave them each a colorful sticker, becoming fast friends. Aurora was thankful that she had the insight to do such a simple thing to put them at ease.

With the niceties out of the way, the clerk shifted gears, went into receptionist mode, and got down to business. "Now, Mrs. Sabel, do you understand the terms of your agreement?" she asked in a patient, genial manner.

"Well, I know I have to make payments of some kind, but I don't know how much or for how long," Aurora said in a pitiful voice, angry at herself for sounding meek and vulnerable.

"Don't worry my dear," she said with motherly-minded kindness, "your P.O, Counselor Stone, will go over everything after we're finished. Let's get you checked in, then you can talk with her."

She smiled and winked at the boys.

"I see here that you're in the Diversion Program. You'll have to pay forty-five dollars every month when you come for your check-in. Can you make todays payment?"

"Yes, I was told to bring a money order when I made the appointment," Aurora answered handing the cashier's check to the woman.

Stamping a pink receipt, the secretary handed the slip of paper to Aurora.

Aurora gasped as she read the last payment date with the remaining balance. "Good God, I'm going to have to pay five hundred forty dollars, total!"

Seeing Aurora physically shaken, the sympathetic lady apologized. "I'm sorry this is happening to you Mrs. Sabel. I can see that you're a fish out of water, so to speak. The whole situation seems incongruous with who you appear to be."

The clerk got up and pushed through the half-door. She took each boy by the hand and escorted them all down the hall to the threshold of an office.

She cordially wished them a good day singing happily, "Take care - see you next month!"

***

An authoritative looking figure was busy at an oversized desk; she didn't look up as they entered the office. The individual clad in a starched white shirt, her bowed head crowned with short tight cornrows, was working on a stack of files with determined earnest.

Aurora gathered a child onto each knee after taking a seat and watched the woman expectantly. While they were waiting, Aurora observed that all around the cramped workspace were pictures of a cute little boy posing with a woman. Aurora was vexed with dismay that the pleasant image represented in bright colored dresses was undoubtedly the same foreboding character who sat before them.

Finally, an unfriendly face looked up as if she'd come out of a stupor and scrutinized Aurora with narrowing eyes.

"Sabel, right? Sharlee Stone. So, have you committed any further acts of violence recently?"

The official stared at Aurora waiting for an answer. She rubbed the deep lines creasing her forehead ignoring the children.

"*What?*"

Aurora was stunned by the weight of the words as a mental picture of violent acts flashed in her head. She shifted the boys on her lap, confused for a second.

"Uh, excuse me, but do you have to ask a question like that in front of my children?" she hissed quietly, trying hard to control her temper.

Sharlee Stone snapped her head back as though Aurora had spit the words in her face. Then she glared at the three of them.

"Yes, as a matter of fact, I do have to ask you that question, every time you come here, Mrs. Sabel. If it's too sensitive for them to be exposed to, you may want to make other arrangements before you come in every month."

The official looked smug and self-righteous.

She licked her lips as if she savored her authority and the tasty morsel of berating a person within her control.

She seemed to enjoy Aurora's discomfort.

***

From the start, the probation officer had rubbed Aurora the wrong way.

Maybe it was her hostile disinterest. Perhaps like many officials who process criminals, any measure of cordiality had corroded over time, severing their humanness. Mostly though, it was that Aurora felt ostracized for the first time in her life.

The official's lack of common courtesy had the effect of totally stripping Aurora of her dignity.

Accountability

Sharlee Stone's countenance was vacant, devoid of any semblance of emotion. She was, as her name suggested, stone cold. The kind of ice freezing hell over kind of cold.

"To answer your question," Aurora huffed as she sat up in the chair and shielded her boy's ears, practically smothering them, "No, of course not. I'm not violent."

"Good. I hope it stays that way. But I have to ask."

Silence fell on the little room.

Counselor Stone sorted her papers.

Aurora sat fuming.

"Do you have any stickers for us?" Aurora's older boy asked tilting his head with a hopeful, cajoling smile.

"Oh, no sweetheart - she wouldn't -" Aurora whispered protectively, smoothing her boy's hair, and pulling him close.

The officer eyed the child stony-faced.

"NO," she said looking away. "Move the kids off your lap Mrs. Sabel, so we can go over your terms of agreement," she commanded.

Aurora put the boys down on the carpet, gave them each a bag of sliced apples, and put a book in their hands to keep them occupied.

Officer Stone handed Aurora a copy of the document. "First," she said, setting the top sheet between them so they could read it together, "we have to go over your probation conditions, then we'll talk about the screening process and where to get your police report."

Poised with a red pen they went line by line through the list and the Counselor circled the conditions applicable to Aurora.

It read:

CONDITIONS OF YOUR PROBATION

Listed below are the conditions of your probation. Please read them carefully and be sure you understand each one.

1. You will not change your residence or employment or leave the Tampa Bay Area and/or the county of your residence without first procuring the consent of your Probation Counselor.

2. You will report in person each month, on an assigned date, to the Correctional Services Office unless otherwise directed by your Probation Counselor.

3. You will neither possess, carry, or own any weapons or firearms without first securing the consent of your Probation Counselor.

4. You will live and remain at liberty without violating any law. A conviction in a court of law shall not be necessary in order for such a violation to constitute a violation of your probation.

5. You will not use intoxicants to excess nor will you visit places where intoxicants, drugs or other dangerous substances are sold, dispensed, or used unlawfully.

6. You will work diligently at a lawful occupation and support any dependents to the best of your ability, as directed by your Probation Counselor.

7. You will promptly and truthfully answer all inquiries directed to you by the Court or the Probation Counselor, and allow the Counselor to visit your home, at your employment or elsewhere, and you will comply with all instructions he/she may give you.

8. You will pay the following to the Salvation Army Correctional Services:
(a) Forty-five dollars (45.00$) per month to cover the cost of this supervision and rehabilitation beginning on the date of the court order.

Accountability

ALL PAYMENTS MUST BE MADE BY MONEY ORDER, PAYABLE TO THE SALVATION ARMY CORRECTIONAL SERVICES.

9. You will be responsible for the following conditions set by the presiding judge: Complete the following community service:

Hours with the Community Restitution Program.

She did not circle this.

Hours with the Hillsborough County Sheriff's Work Program.

This also wasn't circled; and none of the other work programs were circled either. Skipping down:

Obtain Domestic Violence Assessment within 14 days and attend counseling as recommended.

No violent contact / No contact with the victim.

No contact with the victim, was crossed out with her pen.

10. Can supervision terminate early?

Yes, was circled.

I have been advised of and understand the conditions of probation as described above.
Signed - Date –

Sharlee Stone signed the deed and pushed it towards Aurora who let it sit on the desk, making no effort to comply. Taking no notice of Aurora's obstinacy, the official stoically proceeded.

"I'm going to make a call now for the screening at The Spring. As this states, you must go within the next fourteen days." She tapped the sheet that still needed to be signed and picked up the phone to make the appointment.

"Fine," Aurora said, making no move to sign the form. She let it lie, and looked away.

Aurora sat silently infuriated at having had no choice but to submit to the whole program.

***

As she waited for Ms. Stone to schedule her, Aurora read the general information brief:

INDIGENT SCREENING UNIT:

Bring two copies of two recent pay statements of the person in the house-hold, an Award letter or a Warrant for AFDC / SSI / SSA disability, unemployment / workman's comp benefits or a notarized statement if you have no income and are being helped by a relative / friend or any other instructions given at the time of the screening. Your application cannot be processed without this information.

"Take this to the Sheriff's office to obtain your police report," said the probation officer sternly as she tossed the slip of paper on top of the unsigned Probation Conditions sheet. It read:

THE SPRING OF TAMPA BAY:
RESTORING PEACE TO VIOLENT FAMILIES

The person who holds this letter is :

Aurora's name was in the box.

Accountability

Case number: xxxx is court-ordered to our program for an evaluation and is required by us to bring a complete police report pertaining to the incident in question. Please release a copy of that report to him / her.
Thank you. Ms. Stone's initials were in red.

Aurora was given directions to the Family Violence Intervention Offices. The probation officer's name was highlighted in yellow with the assessment date and time: **November 15th, 1 PM.**

The last paragraph before a hand-drawn street map said:

Please do not bring children with you to the assessment appointment; it is not appropriate for them to be at the interview and we do not have childcare available.

Oh, I can certainly comply with that - Aurora thought to herself, letting the air out of her lungs slowly.

A calendar was consulted, and Aurora's next check-in date was set for December second.

"Could we possibly schedule January's check-in now as well?" Aurora asked controlling her voice to sound less frosty.

Aurora needed that date set; her plans depended on it.

"It would be so helpful to have that arranged - you know - what with the chaos of the holidays and all."

The probation officer frowned at Aurora.

"There's no reason to make that appointment before you've had your first class. It will probably be in mid-January. Until then we can't schedule anything."

Counselor Stone stacked the papers and eyed Aurora carefully before continuing.

"I think you understand the conditions of your agreement Mrs. Sabel, but be aware that I can insist on any grounds to come to your home and evaluate you," she threatened with a twisted smile.

Rising from her chair Ms. Stone cleared her throat and said, "I'll see you with payment next month."

She walked to the doorway and stood there, stiff as a board; chin up, not looking at anyone, as the little troop started to depart.

Aurora solemnly took the papers and maps off the desk, corralled her children, and walked with them past the probation officer's tight-faced rigid body.

The conditions document remained unsigned.

Chapter Fifteen: Spring Assessment

"Well, I guess I can't go then," cried Aurora. "It says in the regulations that I can't leave the *county* without informing the authorities - I'm sure they won't allow me to go to *Germany*!"

Aurora showed William the 'Conditions of Probation' sheet. "See, it states right there in number one: 'You will not change your residence or employment or leave the Tampa Bay Area and/or the county of your residence without first procuring the consent of your Probation Counselor.' God knows what would happen to me if they found out. I can't take that chance."

"You don't have to tell them a thing Aurora. After the December second check-in you have no other obligations until January. Didn't the probation officer say that you'd probably start classes in mid-January? Well, we'll be home way before then." William sipped his coffee and tried to comfort his wife. "You shouldn't worry, it's not like you're leaving the country for good."

Aurora wished that she were.

***

They were set to travel to Germany in December to celebrate the millennium new year. The tickets for their trip had been purchased in June. Everything was set.

They'd rented an apartment overlooking their friend's cozy little town where they could entertain and watch the fireworks. The sweet high school girl was procured to come along as a nanny to care for the boys so Aurora could have a vacation as well. She even had the menu organized for the special dinner party.

Aurora wondered, *Should I tell the authorities I'm leaving the country?* She despaired thinking, *Who would I tell? My charming probation officer? God, no.* Aurora decided to postpone alerting anyone of her intentions until after the assessment. Then she'd know where she stood.

***

November fifteenth arrived.

The day of the big evaluation.

I can pull this off, Aurora thought, taking a deep breath.

She'd practiced facial expressions in the mirror all morning, lowering her eyes acquiescingly.

She talked to herself, *No, sir, I'm not aggressive - Oh no Ma'am, there'll be no more acts of violence* - coaching herself.

She pulled her hair into a tight bun causing her head to ache, so she undid it and let it hang long down her back with a clip.

She changed outfits many times, finally settling on a simple dress and jacket. Only her wedding ring and gold watch adorned the ensemble. She figured less show would be more appropriate.

Over and over she told herself, *Just get through this cross-examination and make a good impression.*

The agreement stated that the length of time an individual must attend the classes was determined after the evaluation. It was a minimum term of eight weeks, a maximum of twenty-six weeks.

Aurora wanted the absolute bare minimum.

She'd laid awake all night praying for it.

With the police report in hand, Aurora arrived at what looked like, a deserted warehouse.

A few windows were knocked out; the broken panes easy access for derelicts seeking a place to hide. It could have been the stage set for an action movie.

Instantly she created a scene: S.W.A.T. vans surround the dilapidated building - the felon they're hunting is cornered at the reception desk holding a knife to his hostage's throat.

"Come out with your hands up!" the police shout.

"Don't say a word," the criminal whispers, imploring the frightened woman with the tip of the blade, *"or I'll slit your throat!"*

***

Aurora hit the buzzer panel on the office building, nervously.

She walked up the two flights of stairs not wanting to try the rickety-looking elevator.

She nodded at a tall pointy bearded man in rolled-up overalls washing the floor with a stringy mop, and approached a door with the title, **The Spring of Tampa Bay**, painted in black Italics on the glass.

She turned the knob and the hinges moaned.

She peeked in and thought, *Oh please let there be humane, human life in here.*

Seated behind a glass partition, was a tiny old woman with huge eyes. "Hello, hello, come in young lady, come in," she said waving a hand encouragingly.

"I may be a bit early," Aurora said approaching the window. "My name's Aurora Sabel. I'm here for the interview - I mean the evaluation - I mean the assessment - here's the money order. Do you want the police report as well?"

Aurora was tongue-tied over the woman's bulging orbs; they looked like they were about to pop their sockets as the receptionist bobbed her head and smiled brightly at her.

"No, no, that's not necessary, I only take the money," the woman said putting on spectacles that made her eyeballs look even larger. "Keep it for the examiner, she'll need to see it."

She blinked twice slowly, her eyelids covering only the upper half of her eyes. "Take a spot and I'll call you when it's time to go in. You're up next."

Aurora thanked the woman and found herself a seat.

Gazing around the room, Aurora took in the eclectic furnishings. The lime-green tweed couch and pink and purple floral chairs made her a bit dizzy, but it was the additional blue and white striped curtains that really stung Aurora's eyes. *No wonder the woman's bug-eyed,* she thought, *having to look at these conflicting patterns all day.*

Aurora glanced shyly at the two men sitting opposite her, draped her jacket across the back of her chair before sitting, smoothed her dress, and laid the police report on her lap.

She was apprehensive. *What if Sergeant Rafferty and Officer Manning fudged the details and made it out to be more dramatic than it was?*

Curiosity seized her.

Aurora broke the seal and opened the envelope. The description and comments of the incident were brief. The report said:

Type of Incident: BATTERY
Location Type: Residence
Type of Weapon: Hands / Fist / Feet

Drug Type:
There was a slash across that line indicating that there were *none.*

Skipping down past names and addresses was the report. The Synopsis read:

On 09-26-99 at approximately 21:11 hrs. I responded to the above-listed location; reference to a 911 call.

Accountability

I arrived and made contact with William Sabel (#13 victim) and his wife (#15 arrestee), they were in the same vehicle getting ready to leave. I noticed a small cut on William Sabel's lip. William Sabel wrote out a written statement. As a result of my investigation and the interviews, I arrested Aurora Sabel and transported her to central booking.

The interview with William Sabel said:

William Sabel (#13 victim) stated Aurora Sabel was his wife. He stated he was disciplining their son and Aurora Sabel was angry with him for doing it. Aurora Sabel struck William Sabel in the face, cutting his lip. William Sabel explained that he grabbed Aurora Sabel's arms and held her down until she calmed down. William Sabel had no further information.

The interview with Aurora Sabel said:

Aurora Sabel (#15 arrestee) stated that her husband, William Sabel, became angry with their son and he disciplined their son, by striking him. She jumped up and yelled at William Sabel, and then she struck him in the face. Aurora Sabel stated William Sabel was just correcting their son, and he never hit her. Aurora Sabel stated this was the first time anything like this has happened. Aurora Sabel had no further information. NOTE: Aurora Sabel stated William Sabel did not strike their son hard. He struck him with an open hand along the backside.

The Domestic Violence Information Sheet said:

Type of Incident:
Battery - Domestic Violence - misdemeanor
#13 Victim: - calm

Injury: abrasion
Medical Treatment: not needed
Statement: written
#15 Arrested: calm
Injury / Medical Treatment: none
Statement: oral
Children: present
Photographs of victim taken.

At the bottom of the page were two boxes, each with a drawing of a human figure:

Male 6'4 - 245 lb. was documented in the victim box.

Female 5'3 - 140 lb. was written in the other box.

Aurora moaned silently, the words on the paper fusing with her anguish. *Okay, so they didn't exaggerate - but still, I can't see how a cut on the lip of a 245-pound man would warrant an arrest. This proves it was all a lot of nothing - I was arrested for nothing! How can this to be, when people are out there killing each other?*

***

Aurora folded the report, slipped it back into its envelope, and looked up to see a rotund woman obviously in the last stage of her pregnancy bustling through the glass double doors.

"Mrs. Sabel?" asked the flushed faced blonde bobbing in the passageway breathlessly. She waddled toward Aurora extending her hand.

"I'm Mrs. Hubbard. Come on, let's get started - my time is short."

She tucked the pocket watch dangling from a chain into her bulging red vest and swiveled back toward her office but swung around too fast and started to teeter.

Accountability

Aurora sprang from her chair and caught the woman by the elbow. "You shouldn't move so fast," Aurora said, "you'll topple over like a bowling pin with all that extra weight."

"Thanks Mrs. Sabel, you rescued me just in time."

I hope you'll rescue me, Aurora thought, smiling shyly.

They entered an office crammed with boxes, steel crates, and large rolls of paper stacked in a corner. Olive green potted spider plants capped three metal filing cabinets. Books haphazardly leaned on the long warped wooden shelves mounted floor to ceiling, and files were piled precariously on a bureau threatening to slip off the edge.

Aurora took a seat while the harried-looking woman set Aurora's folder on her desk. There amongst the chaos was an old wooden radio.

"Oh, what a beautiful antique," Aurora said running her fingertips appreciatively along the curved bell-shape.

Mrs. Hubbard eased herself into the chair by Aurora and patted the device. "Yes, it was here when I transferred to this building. I find it so pleasing to look at."

She rested her arms across her belly.

"It's good to have something well-built and solid to remind me that in this crazy life, everything has balance. Old and new. Good and bad. Real and unreal."

She looked directly at Aurora for the first time since they'd sat down together.

"I've seen a lot of unreal things come through those doors."

She started to say more, but then hastened to start the screening.

"I see here on the police report, Mrs. Sabel, that you and your husband were both calm at the scene of the assault? Will you explain to me what happened?"

Now, finally, my chance to set the record straight - Aurora thought, and measured her words carefully.

"Before we begin, I must tell you Ma'am, that this whole thing was all a big mistake - I -"

"Hold on Mrs. Sabel. Regardless that you feel it was a mistake - you were arrested for domestic violence, then you were offered the Diversion Program and the court ordered this evaluation."

"Yes, that's true, but I need you to understand *why* this is, was, a mistake. I was hoping - I want to tell you, about William and me." Aurora held her tongue, and waited.

The examiner looked over the file. "Alright, go ahead," she said, and made a little notation on the top sheet.

"We met in 1986 -" Aurora began, taking a deep breath. "William had just finished his first Army tour in Germany. He'd come from his grandfather's funeral in California, where he's from, and was staying at his sister's place in Connecticut, where I'm from. We were just friends at first, but it got serious rather quickly. So when he decided to go back for another tour, he asked me to join him in Germany. We flew back in '88 to get married in Connecticut. Then we lived in Germany for a total of five years - am I talking too much? Am I boring you?"

"No, it's interesting, but what has this to do with your incident?" She yawned covertly, reset herself in the chair, and shaking her head gestured with a hand for Aurora to continue.

"Well, during the years in Germany, I tried and tried to get pregnant, but it was always a disappointment. Month after month. Then finally it happened, and we were thrilled. We went back to the states because I wanted to be near my mom. We started to get settled, and then I miscarried. Then I got pregnant again and miscarried again. We were heartbroken."

Aurora had to stop.

She took out a tissue and wiped her eyes.

"To make a long story short, God has blessed us. In '93 we had our first child and in '96 we had our second boy - is this your first?"

The examiner sipped from a water bottle, nodded slowly, and scribbled again in her notes.

Accountability

"Ma'am, I wanted to make you understand that we're married eleven years now and we love our hard-won family. It's absurd that the fight we had, and that my striking William, would even be considered an assault. It was nothing. I just got a little crazy when he spanked our little boy."

Aurora quickly clamped her hand over her mouth to stop herself from saying anything more.

Heaving a sigh, Mrs. Hubbard rubbed her bump and looked contemplative.

"Thank you for giving me a clearer picture of your relationship with your husband, Mrs. Sabel. I'm sure you feel very fortunate to have overcome those difficulties. Let's move on, shall we?"

Mrs. Hubbard shifted in her chair and said, "So then, in the course of your day - or rather - well - when do you - when was the last time you had a drink, Mrs. Sabel?"

"A drink?" Aurora asked surprised. "You mean an alcoholic drink, right? Hmm, that's a hard one. Uhh, I really can't remember. We don't have alcohol at home, and we don't go out. I've never left my boys with a sitter - I don't trust anyone but my mom to watch them - Ah, we did celebrate our tenth anniversary with some sparkling wine - but that was in February -"

The evaluator's eyebrows raised with a look of skepticism that inferred, 'Are you for real?'

Mrs. Hubbard looked as though she didn't know how to proceed.

She squinted and said, "Do you mean that the last time you had a drink was last February? What about drugs?"

"Ma'am, I don't drink, and I don't do drugs - there's no room in my life for any of that."

With a puzzled gaze the examiner leaned on her elbow and studied Aurora.

She opened her mouth and started to say something but stopped herself and only mumbled, "Hmm."

Aurora smiled warmheartedly at the woman.

"When your little one arrives, you'll understand what I'm talking about. I'm so busy all day - cooking, washing, cleaning, and running after my boys that when the chores are done, I'm pooped. *I'm* ready for bed when I put them down."

The mother-to-be chuckled bearing perfectly straight white teeth.

Apparently, Aurora's explanation concluded any further discussion because she grabbed a thick blue pen and drew a line diagonally down the page headed: **Drugs and Alcohol Assessment and Screening**.

"Now, Mrs. Sabel, let me explain what this screening is about," she said handing Aurora a pamphlet.

"We evaluate you to put you in the right group for the maximum effectiveness."

She took a sip of water, sighed, and continued.

"If counseling were needed for drugs or alcohol, we'd put you in that kind of group. If it were a matter of rape, we'd place you appropriately."

She picked up the folder with her notes and set it back down on her desk.

"After reading your file and hearing your testimony, it seems to me that you needn't go through any of that."

"Oh my gosh, thank you!"

Aurora was so relieved that she wanted to jump up and hug the woman.

"*But*," the examiner cautioned while busying herself shuffling papers, "I do feel that the tension that's risen between you and your husband could, at a later time, become dangerous."

Aurora's mouth dropped open. "But you said -"

Disregarding Aurora's accusing tone Mrs. Hubbard replied, "I said that I didn't feel that it was necessary for you to do any of the *other* programs we offer.

By no means can you get out of the DVP program Mrs. Sabel, you were ordered by the court to go through it. Now it's just a matter of assigning the duration of weeks that you'll be attending the sessions."

Accountability

Mrs. Hubbard looked resolved but seemed restless.

Aurora followed her movements as she stood up and began to pace the room straightening and rearranging things.

"Ma'am," Aurora said softening her tone considerably, "about the classes - I understand there are terms - and since I have to attend," she frowned a little, "I was hoping to do the minimum amount because - well - uh - we're struggling financially. My husband gives me a set amount of money every month and the fee for the classes will have to come out of that. So could I just have -"

Mrs. Hubbard's body jerked like someone had pricked her. "What do you mean your husband *gives* you money? Don't you have access to your money jointly?" she asked with a reproachful air.

Aurora was immediately stunned silent thinking, *Uh oh, what did I say that was wrong?*

The examiner knitted her brows and her eyes narrowed. "Mrs. Sabel, if you and your husband have control issues, this program will benefit you greatly," she said with renewed authority.

"Mrs. Hubbard, what I meant was," Aurora answered with a sinking feeling, "we *discuss* the finances *together* and decide how much money I need each week for household supplies."

"But you can't take money out of your account without asking him first?"

"I *don't* take money out without *talking* to him about it first."

"Ah," was all she said.

Oh no - why can't I keep my big mouth shut - Aurora thought, sick with worry as she squirmed in her seat.

Mrs. Hubbard wobbled back to her desk and eased herself into her chair. Avoiding eye contact, she looked intently over Aurora's report and said, "Don't fret, Mrs. Sabel we'll get this sorted out. Why don't you take a seat in the outer room. I'll have a look at the program outline and let you know when I've made my decision."

Aurora rose from her seat slowly.

Her shoulders sagged, her head dropped down; she felt shattered that the evaluation had taken such a downward turn. Sitting in the empty waiting room with a dreadful foreboding, she felt sure that she'd hung herself by her own account.

***

"Please come in and sit down Mrs. Sabel."

Mrs. Hubbard seemed downcast as she rearranged the already neat piles of paper on her desk.

She averted her eyes as Aurora stepped into the room and took a seat across from her.

"Mrs. Sabel, your case has not been an easy one to evaluate. On the one hand, your relationship with your husband is strong, but on the other side, you clearly have control issues that need to be addressed. I've reviewed everything, and unavoidably, I believe it would be in your best interest - what I mean to say is - I've decided that you must attend the full twenty-six-week course."

Mrs. Hubbard seemed to be out of breath and genuinely distressed as she looked away rubbing her stomach.

Aurora stared at the woman not believing what she was hearing. She'd thought that the evaluation had gone well.

Numbers buzzed in Aurora's head as she quickly calculated twenty dollars times twenty-six weeks.

"Oh my gosh," she whined. "That's going to cost me five hundred twenty dollars!"

Mrs. Hubbard's eyes widened seeing Aurora's reaction.

Losing the restraint she'd tried so hard to maintain, Aurora scooted to the edge of her chair, pressed her hands on the desk, leaned in and shouted, "Why is all of this happening to me? I did *nothing* to deserve any of this!"

Aurora took a breath and yelled, "This whole thing is a farce! I wasn't violent. I am not violent!"

Aurora sat back in her seat, bowed her head, and clenched her fists in the folds of her dress.

She was fuming, but then she put her hand to her mouth on the verge of tears thinking, *Oh, no - What have I done?*

Mrs. Hubbard calmly ignored Aurora's fierce explosion and spoke in a tone geared to console her. "Mrs. Sabel, in my opinion doing the program in its entirety is of great value."

The examiner pulled out a calendar with a tropical island motif and consulted January.

"Since this term will end soon, I'll send your transcripts over to Mr. Thera's office and register you for after the holidays. Classes resume on January tenth."

Well, at least that will work, Aurora sighed heavily.

***

Aurora studied the photo of the month; it looked so tranquil and appealing. *God, I wish I were sitting on that island*, she thought longing for an escape.

Mrs. Hubbard pushed a flyer across her desk and motioned for Aurora to take it. "Let's go over the conditions," she said with a timid nod opening her copy of the pamphlet. "Number one: You will report to class once a week. Number two: You will pay twenty dollars at each visit." She waited for Aurora to find the spot on the page. "Number three: There may be no absences without a doctor's written excuse."

Aurora shook her head, her eyes lowered in defeat.

Mrs. Hubbard set the pamphlet down on the desk and sighed. She gave Aurora a sheepish grin, and tried to offer some positive reinforcement. "You'll be in a group with women of similar backgrounds and similar issues Mrs. Sabel. This program will be a meaningful experience for you. Believe me. You'll see."

"*You* may think so, Ma'am, but I sincerely doubt it."

With a pinched, sour face, Aurora unenthusiastically folded the paper and tucked it into her purse. Too irritated to look the examiner in the eye, Aurora simply set her jaw, and walked out of the office.

Chapter Sixteen: Diversion Class 101

January tenth, four forty-five pm. Orientation.

Leaving the country had been easier than Aurora thought it would be.

There was only one troublesome moment when they'd gotten to the counter to show their passports and get their boarding passes. She was sure there'd be a pop-up on the agent's computer screen of her face among the 'most wanted' persons.

But there wasn't.

Aurora sighed a huge breath of relief when the friendly-faced attendant handed her back her passport, smiled at all of them, and said, "You're all set - have a great trip!"

They'd had a wonderful vacation; slipped away and came back with no one the wiser, although there was a moment going through the police control gate at customs when Aurora thought for sure a uniformed official would grab her by the arm and say, "Excuse me Ma'am, do you really think you're going to get away with this?"

But no one did.

***

Winter in Germany is always cold. Snowcapped villages and ice shingled roof tops, but that rainy Florida evening, Aurora felt chilled to the bone.

Accountability

The frostiness had more to do with where she stood than the weather.

She shivered apprehensively outside the gated front door of the counseling center. Aurora looked up at the raindrops falling off of the cement awning that was unevenly mounted over the entrance, and became oddly enthralled with the goings on across the street.

In one of the connected shops along the mini-strip-mall, a sign flashed, 'Write Back Tattoo' in neon pink letters. The capital letter, 'T' flickered on and off. The second, 't' was cut off at the top, so the display read, 'Write Back atyoo'.

Two bearded bikers in leather jackets laughed loudly as they passed a brown-bagged bottle. They were leaning on a rack of bikes and motorcycles that were chained up outside of a pawn shop named, 'Don't Yawn, Come Pawn'; the bold gold lettering, in an old-time saloon style.

Aurora could see off to the side of a boarded-up storefront adjacent to a Seven-Eleven, a band of young teenage boys hanging out. Their attempt to covertly share lit cigarettes, was blatantly apparent.

Aurora considered that whatever was inside the facility, had to be less creepy than what was going on outside on the street, and pushed open the stiff heavy door.

She entered a room that was packed full of people. The pitch of their chattering was almost deafening.

Aurora's heart thumped as she shook off her raincoat and wiped her boots on the mat.

A prickly sort of heat hit the back of her neck as she realized that everyone seemed to have stopped talking.

She looked down at the faded black lettering on the bristled straw rug and felt it was apropos that the word, '**Welcome**' had been worn away. There wasn't a 'welcome' feeling in this place at all.

Overloaded with garments, the portable metal stand creaked and leaned to the right as Aurora tried to hang up her soggy jacket, so she draped it on a vacant chair and sat down quickly.

Afraid of looking directly at anyone, Aurora tried to study the wallpaper, but the pattern of tiny dots in pastel colors irked her, so she consigned herself to bow her head and just stare at the floor.

Talking resumed, the volume increasing, so that Aurora felt like all the oxygen was being sucked out of the room and that she was going to suffocate.

***

The desk clerk with a banal expression, called out in a curt tone, motioning to Aurora, "Ma'am -Yes *you* - get over here - come on - quick now - sign in and pay - or you'll be marked absent - and you surely don't want *that*."

Aurora was handed a long, cloth-bound clerical journal. After she jotted her name on line 282 and furnished the twenty dollars, the secretary retrieved the book and issued a receipt.

"Hurry - back to your seat now - the bells about to ring and then the action'll really begin - you'll see." The woman wasn't being surly, she just seemed nervous.

Aurora swirled back to her seat, grabbed a magazine, opened it to a random page, and hid behind it. To alleviate the unnerving sense of being in for a full-on assault, she listened, incognito, to the subsequent conversation.

"I got twelve more weeks, and I'm outta here. Can't be over soon enough for me," said a tired-looking woman swiping spiky magenta bangs off her forehead with a veined forehead.

"The damn thing's bogus," said a chubby teen in a skin-tight t-shirt and cut-off jean shorts, spitting out the words. "I gotta do *this,* and my boyfriend don't gotta do *nothin'*."

A woman wearing a white nurse's uniform with the name 'Regional Hospital' embroidered above the breast pocket set her duffel bag down and complained, "Ya know, I'll have to leave work and pay a sitter in the middle of the day to do this at eleven am. I can't come at night - my kids would be alone.

Accountability

I've got eleven weeks to go. Gosh, I wish it weren't so long."

"My old man should be doing this; *he's* the one with the *anger* problem," said a sickly-looking woman with a waxy yellow complexion.

Aurora moaned silently, *And I thought two days in jail was depressing. I'll have twenty-six weeks of this.*

***

At four-fifty-nine a small Indian man came through the front door, panting slightly.

"Hello, hello, sorry I was delayed ladies," he apologized shaking out his umbrella. "So, it's only fair that I don't penalize anyone if we start a bit late today."

"You can't get off that easy Lancel," said a very large Hispanic woman, her voice fierce with mockery. "How many times have *we* been threatened with an unexcused absence if *we* were late?"

"Yeah," said an older woman with short hair and a curled lip. "I was almost turned away last month, just for being *one minute* late due to traffic! What about *you* being *accountable*?"

"Alright ladies, we can discuss that later. Let's go in now," said the olive-skinned man.

With a cacophony of moans, the women gathered their belongings and moved in a jumbled mass, bumping elbows, down a narrow hallway. The human traffic jam forged into a room with rows of metal chairs. Bodies jostled the folding table stacked with papers and the large white board almost tipped over as they hurried to grab one of the quite desperately coveted seats.

Luckily, Aurora was able to nab a spot in the last row, against the wall, at the back of the room.

The crowded space filled up fast. Those at the end of the herd had to stand or sit on the carpet.

The slender little man stood at the front of the class and calmly observed the scene.

"It's good to see that you're all settled in now. Before we begin, please take some refreshment," bid the Counselor warmly. "You can serve yourselves. Coffee is free, beverages cost fifty cents."

Some women went to the mini fridge, dropped a few coins into a tin can marked, 'Change' and took a drink. Most of them went for the free coffee in the little kitchen across the hall.

The throngs heavy tread reverberated under Aurora's feet.

The place started to smell like a locker room.

***

The Counselor set an overly-stuffed brown leather bag on the table. The skinny metal legs wobbled as he opened it, pulled out a stack of papers, and set them gently alongside the bottle of water he'd bought for himself.

The class sat silently observing his every move.

Mr. Thera took a few moments to smile at the group. "Good evening ladies, I'm Lancel Thera. Welcome to the Domestic Violence Prevention Program."

The women watched him intently. For the time being, not one of them had a word to say.

"Have a good holiday Lancel?" A woman asked as if they were familiar acquaintances.

The Counselor smiled but didn't answer.

"I know that some of you are here after Drug and Alcohol classes, and some have to finish the remainder of your agreement from work service. Although each one of you has a different agenda, how much you get out of *this* program, will depend on what you do for *yourself*," said Mr. Thera as he handed out papers. "These guidelines, are your map to a successful journey. Your weekly assessment will reflect your willingness to listen, understand, and act as a group. Hopefully, you'll all get something out of these sessions."

Aurora sensed there was tremendous discontent amongst the women, but Mr. Thera seemed keen to ignore it.

"Let's go over the terms of the agreement and get started down this new path."

He pressed on, unaffected by the gripes.

"Please take a look at the first sheet as I read out loud:"

I (name), understand the following rules and regulations will be expected from me when I begin my Domestic Violence Program at Brandon Psychiatric Associates:
I will refrain from using any form of violence.
My goal will be to learn nonviolent ways of problem solving.

A few women started to protest that they weren't violent, when one woman shouted, "If I think they need a whipping, they sure as hell must deserve it!"

I will refrain from using language that is disrespectful of a person's sex, race, religion, or orientation.

Everyone nodded approvingly on this point.

I will wear appropriate attire.
Clothing that has sexually suggestive content, derogatory comments, and slogans that promote the use of alcohol, cigarettes and drugs is inappropriate.
I will not be permitted to attend groups if I am dressed in such attire.

Heads turned to consider people's attire with a short burst of prattle.

I will attend the sessions free and clear of the effects of alcohol.
I will not be permitted to attend group the first time I violate this condition.
Should I do so a second time, I will be terminated.

The room fell silent; the gravity of this rule was evident.

I will arrive at Brandon Psychiatric Associates at least ten minutes before time.
If I get here after group begins, I will not be permitted to join the group. This will count as an unexcused absence.

Mr. Thera took some flak for his tardiness again.

I understand that the Attendance Policy is as follows: Judge Vogel requires that those individuals who are under her jurisdiction have zero absences during the twenty-six weeks of group.
Exceptions will be made for those who have an excused absence i.e. death in the family, illness, being in jail. Documentation will be required to permit the excuse.
If a participant has an unexcused absence, Judge Vogel wants the individual to report to her in court.

Judge Ober permits those individuals, who are under her jurisdiction, two absences during the twenty-six weeks of group.
The individual would be required to attend a total of twenty-six groups.
In case I have a directive from the court that says, "No misses", I am to follow that order.
   Please Note - Brandon Psychiatric Associates is also required to enforce the attendance policy established by Court Operations of the Thirteenth Judicial Circuit, which is:
If a third unexcused absence occurs between two.
If a third unexcused absence occurs between fourteen through twenty-six, I will be sent back to group fourteen.
No refund will be made for sessions that were forfeited.
I will be required to clear any outstanding balance on sessions forfeited as a part of fulfilling my financial obligations.

Accountability

I will turn off my telephone and / or beeper during group.

"I'm an on-call nurse, what can I do?" asked a woman wrinkling fretting eyebrows.

"Please tell your staff that they need to make other arrangements while you're out of the office because the hour that you're here, you're unavailable," said Mr. Thera.

I will get started on the assigned date.
If I am unable to do so, I will be responsible for contacting Brandon Psychiatric Associates to advise them of when I can start.
If I neglect to reschedule a start date, I will be terminated due to non-compliance.

Aurora raised her hand shyly and asked, "Must we sign up for either the day or the night class?"

Before the Counselor could answer the woman next to Aurora said, "You can choose any class, they just need to see that you signed in once a week."

I understand that payment is expected at the time of service.
If I am unable to make a payment, I will not be permitted to attend group.
I understand that I am required to keep my outstanding balance below sixty dollars.

No one commented on this.

I need to have my outstanding balance paid in full before my last session.
I will not be permitted to attend the last session if I cannot fulfill this obligation.

"How about reduced sessions for good behavior?" asked a lady in the back row hopefully.

"Sorry," Mr. Thera said shaking his head, "all court orders must be completed in full."

The last paragraph stated the starting date, the approved fee for individuals with financial difficulties, and a place for the therapist and the patient to sign.

Mr. Thera didn't ask for the sheet back, so no one signed it or returned it.

***

A rumble of grumbling groans filled the room of bridled women and Aurora knew why.

Mr. Thera raised his voice louder than theirs.

"Here's an interesting fact ladies, it's reported that eighty-five percent of people who are killed, are killed by the hand of a loved one."

He paused and appeared to linger for a reaction, but no one responded or questioned him.

"You all know the O.J Simpson trial -" he continued, "it's national attention has incited the Zero Tolerance Act and that policy is being implemented state by state now, for all domestic violence incidents."

"What exactly does that mean?" asked a few women at once.

"Zero Tolerance," he began to explain as he leaned on the edge of the table, "is a new law wherein any call to 911 must be followed up, investigated, and reported. If there's been an attempt to harm a victim by any degree, even a slap, the assailant will be taken into custody."

Aurora's face reddened.

She blushed and thought, *He's read my file.* She could have sworn he'd looked right at her.

"And," he stated further, "if drugs or alcohol are involved, often both parties are arrested."

"You know, I've always been a passive person," said the nurse, "but the one time I lashed out, in my own defense, my husband called the authorities and here I am."

"I know what you mean," huffed an older woman. "I'm here because I hit back too - my boyfriend clobbered me - the cops saw I was badly beat up - look, I had to get stitches -" The woman lifted her hair and above her left eyebrow was a row of purple X's. "He called to spite me - ooh, I got chills - he held me by the throat - had this crazy grin - told the cop on the phone *I* was trying to kill *him* -"

She sniffed.

"I told them he was drunk, but they didn't listen to me."

"I'm sorry that such a terrible thing happened to you," Mr. Thera said walking toward the lady who was fixing her bangs back over the scar on her forehead. "Marcia isn't it? I hope you'll let me help you, Marcia."

He turned around to the whole class.

"I want to show all of you a better way to handle situations like that."

"You probably expect us to be deaf, dumb and blind - take whatever's dished out," said the Hispanic gal whose voice was rising. "I'll bet you want us to just lay down like a dog and-"

"No Ma'am. I don't want that at all," Mr. Thera assured her. "What I would like, is to introduce to all of you, a way to see things in a different light."

He hesitated to take a sip of water, wipe his mouth with a handkerchief, and exhale deeply.

"Everyone's here because of a conflict that got out of hand. You all have your own stories. The cycle of this program, the idea of these sessions, is to enable you to stop confrontations before they explode."

He waited for comments, but the class was poised, intent on listening, so he continued.

"I'm hoping that you'll learn to disengage and defuse a situation before it becomes a deadly encounter."

"I always give in," said a woman in response. "But it doesn't matter, he's always pissed off anyway."

Moving oppressively, as thick as a dense fog, a grey melancholy seeped into the mood in the room.

"Let me tell you all a story," said the teacher adeptly. "The famous Jackie Kennedy's life was very troubled. She was at times, under dressed, without makeup, showing little care of her appearance; lacking her legendary luster, her personal *presence*. She was seen at formal affairs in this state; an elegant lady who often looked, out of sorts.

At an event where she was talking to a pilot who'd trained her son, Onassis joined her, sneering, 'Ah, here you are. Christ, you look like something the cat dragged in.'

He'd openly insulted his wife and many people had heard.

It was a tense moment, but Jackie held herself.

'Sorry to be unsuitably dressed,' she'd said lightly. 'I didn't think formal attire was required in the company of friends.'

She thanked the pilot for his kindness and excused herself. She didn't argue with her husband in public. She didn't retaliate with harsh words, but kept her dignity, and showed self-respect by ignoring his hostility and removing herself from the situation. She was graceful, and above reproach."

The Counselor waited patiently.

"Is that a true story, or did you make that up, Lancel?" asked someone from the back row.

"It's a true story. Even through troubled times, the woman was skillfully sophisticated."

"She wasn't so-phis-ti-cated - she was stu-pid. If my old man'd done that to me, I'd've given it to him - right in front of everybody," a woman behind Aurora bellowed. "I don't take no crap from nobody - and if you think you can make me see otherwise - you're stupid too!"

Mr. Thera didn't react to the outburst.

The woman's nostrils flared. She folded her arms over her chest. She huffed and blew out what could have been steam; her expression unadulterated, merely tightly bottled, rage.

"I've tried to stand up for myself, but I found it makes him meaner," said another woman who was small and slight, with beady-eyes that darted from person to person, not settling anywhere.

Accountability

"I think what Jackie did was admirable," said the nurse calmly. "It'd be terrible to be ridiculed by your husband in public, but to hold yourself, take the higher ground, must be a powerful feeling. I'd like to be that way."

She sighed and folded her hands in her lap.

Solemn faces gave the impression of contemplation, then a burst of dialogue followed.

Aurora was amazed. She saw that most of the women couldn't 'Let It Go' and move on. Most of the women in the group wanted someone's head to roll. They seemed to want their mean angry husbands or deadbeat boyfriends to suffer and pay on all accounts for their abuse. It seemed that nothing less would satisfy these brutalized women.

It was impressive when the teacher hushed the class.

"I'm sure you've all been through a lot," he said. "I only ask that you start by being gentle on yourselves. Think of how you want to be treated as a person, and think of what you would say to your partner if you could -"

"I'd say, 'Get The Hell Out' if I could pay the bills myself," said the same loud woman.

The whole group laughed, and their heavy load seemed to lighten somewhat. Like most women who have the natural propensity to be optimistic, these ladies were finding a little humor in the midst of some dreary realities.

An easier dialog lifted their spirits as they turned to their neighbors with casual greetings until a few minutes before the session was due to be over.

Mr. Thera watched the women mingle, smiling with his arms rested across his chest.

"Ladies, I think this is the beginning of a beautiful friendship - quoting my favorite movie, 'Casa Blanca'."

He collected his papers, slipped them into his leather bag, and snapped it shut. Smiling at the group he said, "I wish you a healthy journey until next week - don't be late!"

The clock struck six.

Everyone grabbed their things, dumped their trash, and ran.

Chapter Seventeen: Power and Control

Aurora was always awake with the sun's rise.

Most days she prayed, *Thank you God, for this wonderful life. Thank you for William and the boys - thank you for this glorious joy.*

But these days she moaned, *Please God, help me get there on time.*

Her routine started very early, beginning with kitchen duty: making breakfast, assembling lunch, and prepping for dinner.

Every day Aurora cooked ahead.

The day before she'd prepared a spinach and feta quiche that William had eaten for breakfast that morning. He'd taken beef and bean burritos, saffron rice, and a fresh green salad to work for his lunch.

That night they'd eat Chicken Cacciatore; it would go into the oven at five pm.

Her varied chores continued throughout the day, but most were done before anyone else had gotten up.

The second load of laundry was in the dryer, the first batch in a basket already folded. Two big jugs of chlorine had been poured around the circumference of the pool. Leaves had been scooped out and the sides brushed down while the boys had still snoozed in their beds.

After she'd kissed William goodbye and he'd left for Tampa, she'd fed the dogs and let them out as well.

Accountability

Aurora had to hurry.

Coordinating everyone to assemble their belongings and get to their destinations was a never-ending challenge.

To begin with, her first-grader had to catch the bus.

"Have you got everything?" Aurora asked knowing his Spider Man backpack was full of books, a whole grain sandwich, a granola bar, sliced apples, and a bottle of water. "Now don't forget to look both ways before you cross - and remember your route number - 2A - and keep a watch out the window for your stop on the way home - we'll be outside waiting for you - have a good day!"

The second task was getting her three-year-old ready to go to her in-law's house.

Having her father-in-law watch the boy was convenient, but worrying if he would stay alert to supervise the child, troubled her.

"Have you packed everything you want to bring to Grandpa's?" Aurora asked even though she'd helped her son pack fruit and snacks, plastic dinosaurs, workbooks, and markers.

When he started to whine that he didn't want to go Aurora said sweetly, "Oh sweetheart," taking him in her arms, "it'll be fun at Grandpa's house, you'll see - and I won't be long - but please don't watch TV okay? We'll set you up at the little table so you can practice your numbers instead - and we'll ask Grandpa to read a book to you again - and we'll lay a blanket down outside so that you and Grandpa can have a picnic!"

Aurora felt a terrible lump in her throat as she waved an overly breezy goodbye to her arms-over-the-chest, tight-lipped boy who was leaning against the doorway with a 'How-Dare-You-Leave-Me-Here' look on his face.

***

The forty-five minute drive to her in-law's had taken an hour due to heavy morning traffic.

The ten minutes it should have taken from their house to the counseling center took a little under half an hour because Aurora had the bad timing of hitting every red light.

Although she arrived in plenty of time, her heart still raced wildly like she had been running a marathon.

***

"The rule of thumb," said the Counselor holding his thumb up at the second meeting, "was a term used at the turn of the century. It meant that it was legally acceptable for a man to use a stick, no thicker than a thumb, any length, as an instrument of discipline upon his wife."

"*Whaaaat?*"

A roar of antagonism shook the little room.

Mr. Thera held his hands up.

"Hold on, there's more."

The morning group of women looked exasperated.

It looked like they were jogging in place, almost panting with a nervous type of energy; as if these sessions were only one of a million other burdens they were obligated to carry.

The Counselor tried to placate them with several statistics.

"Things started to change when women had to help with the war effort."

His level voice continued, "Because almost all of the men were gone, there was a need for women to enter the work force. They contributed a great deal at that time, and made a substantial difference. When the war ended, many women continued to work and serious conflicts became prevalent."

"Yeah, the king lost his crown!" a woman Aurora hadn't seen at the first meeting bellowed. "And all the kings' horses and all the kings' men, couldn't put him back together again, so he beat her, cheated her, and tried to knock her down -" she continued, looking swiftly around for acclamation.

The room echoed with low tense laughter, but the other women didn't verbally encourage her further.

Aurora was uncomfortable.

The concept of William using a stick on her or the children or trying to oppress her was unthinkable.

She bowed her head and stared at the grey carpet.

Though her body was stuck there, she zoned them all out.

She started to make lists of the days chores and thought, *I have to get more mulch for the yard - I need to pull the weeds around the queen palms - I'll mow the lawn this afternoon - it's time to change the linens.*

She decided the next day's menu and the shopping list; groping in her bag for a pen and scrap of paper to jot it all down. All the while ignoring the session.

Mr. Thera moved some papers on his desk, sat on the corner, and spoke loudly.

"Power and Control are serious issues in today's society.

"Let me tell you a story about a young woman whose parents were very strict. She wasn't allowed to go out unaccompanied or permitted to date until she was eighteen. When she comes of age, the girl gets a job. Soon the friend of a fellow worker asks her out, but she tells the young man, 'I'm sorry, but I don't think my parents will let me.'

"The man says, 'Don't worry, I'll take care of everything.' He phones and asks for a few minutes of the parent's time. 'Evening folks,' he says greeting them cordially. 'I wanted to introduce myself to you and to assure you that I'm from a good family, I'm almost finished with law school, and with your permission, I'd be honored to take your daughter out.' "

By the captivated look on the women's faces, it was plain to see that Mr. Thera had the class's full attention, so he carried on.

"The parents are thrilled, and the couple begins to date. After a short time the young man asks the parents if they can marry. The parents readily agree and make arrangements to organize a grand surprise engagement party.

"The man hasn't proposed; the young woman hasn't even thought about the possibility of marriage."

Mr. Thera paused to drink some water, and gazed with a look of anticipation at the group.

"I think I know where this is going Lancel, but go ahead, tell us more about the poor girl," said one woman.

"I hope she kills him, gets away with it, and starts a new life with the insurance money -" said another woman.

Oh, I hope it's not that melodramatic, Aurora worried silently.

Mr. Thera overlooked the outburst of comments and expounded on the story.

"The young woman is coaxed to the party for obscure reasons and everyone bombards her with congratulations on her engagement. The parents bring the man and their dumbfounded daughter to the front of the room and they make a toast announcing their happiness at their daughter's great 'catch'. The young woman is shocked hearing about this new development in her love life for the first time, but she submits to their well wishes and goes with the flow. The young man is charming to her and her family, so she's easily carried away with the whole idea."

Mr. Thera paused as his audience sat there, fidgeting.

Some women were fussing with their handbags. Some had to get up and move about the room. Most of the group sat quietly and waited to hear what would come next.

Aurora had the sensation of water seeping up through the floor with the intention of dragging her under.

No one spoke out, so he continued.

"They have their first sexual encounter in a field, in the dark, on the ground, rough and quick. She's ashamed about the non-loving act. This is the first sign that something is not right, but she puts it out of her mind. Weeks later, they go to her company's Christmas party where she's happy and proud to introduce him to everyone. When the young man sees her boss embrace her in congratulation, he becomes quiet and withdraws from her for the rest of the evening. During the car ride home, he stops the car, slaps her, and yells, 'I saw you - you slut - I know you've been screwing your boss - now everything's ruined and it's all your fault - the wedding's off.'"

Accountability

A couple of women gasped.

Most nodded and hissed with disgust that they knew it; they were sure what would happen.

Mr. Thera waited for them to quiet down and pressed on.

"The young woman is appalled by his behavior. She tries to explain herself, but he won't listen. She's afraid that he'll hit her again, so she quickly apologizes and begs him for forgiveness, pleading with him for another chance. He wavers a bit and then relents, but he warns her, aggressively tapping his finger on her face, to watch her step.

"She's really afraid for the first time.

"The wedding comes off as scheduled and things go well at first. He gets a good job; she has a baby. He moves up in the company; she has another baby. She's a dutiful wife, but he controls everything; where she goes, who she sees, what she buys.

"She's gone from her parent's strict authority to her husband's strict set of rules."

One woman said, "My husband's just like that. Puts on a nice front to the outside world, but he's a real monster to us at home."

While most of the women had a glazed look in their eyes, the woman who'd spoken prior, shook her head and said, "I still say she kills him in the end." Her frowning face was smug nodding at the other women.

"Ladies, this story has a point, let me get to it," the Counselor said, not unkindly. "The now middle-aged man starts to drink and when he drinks, he becomes mean. He criticizes her all the time. 'This house is a mess - Why can't you control the children? What do you do all day?'

"The marriage deteriorates from verbal abuse to physical abuse. He strikes her without provocation.

"She never knows what he'll be like from day to day.

"He's cruel.

"She's scared and submissive.

"The woman's marriage, her life, has become a jail sentence."

At the end of the narrative, a few women pulled out tissues and blew their noses.

Mr. Thera asked quietly, "Can any of you relate to this?"

"You could be talking about my life," said a woman with tired eyes. "I had parents like that. I have a husband like that, and my life, every day is like that. I wish I had the nerve to leave, but I got my kids to think about."

"My real dad left us when I was a baby," said the chubby teen from the week prior. "I've got a step-father as mean as that guy. He's a monster to my mom.

"I left when he tried to rape me. Been on my own since I was thirteen, but I made the same mistake. My boyfriend treats me like a slave - while he lays around and does nothing but criticize the world - and me."

***

Aurora was getting a headache.

These were true stories; horrible, real, and mind-blowing.

In all of her life, Aurora had never heard the likes of any of this madness before.

***

Mr. Thera handed out a paper.
The illustration was like a wheel.
An inner circle had the words:
POWER AND CONTROL.
The top spaces said:
ISOLATION and **EMOTIONAL ABUSE.**
The middle sections said:
INTIMIDATION and **ECONOMIC ABUSE, USING MALE PRIVILEGE** and **SEXUAL ABUSE.**
The bottom sections said:
THREATS and **USING CHILDREN**.

The group studied the sheet with interest.

After giving everyone a few minutes, Mr. Thera started with the top headline and began reading the text.

"A person who has always used power and control or violence as a form of problem solving, will not be able to address any given problem *without* using power and control or violence."

"Does it mean we can't escape abuse, 'cause my husband can't help doing what he does?" asked a small, middle-aged woman with tight, honey-colored corn rows.
"You know, I never hit another human being before my old man started threatening me and beating my kids."
The woman fidgeted in her chair, seemingly awkward at having revealed so much personal information.
"That's not quite what it means," answered Mr. Thera.
He walked around the room and said calmly, "Violence has become *normalized*. Let's look at the first box,"
ISOLATION:
It says here that:

"Controlling what she does, who she sees and talks to, where she goes, is a form of power and control."

Mr. Thera solemnly scanned the faces staring back at him asking, "Would anyone care to share their feelings? Are any of you ladies isolated or controlled in this manner?"
"I grew up with that," said a pimply-faced young woman wearing a lot of makeup. She looked like a painted doll.
"My father made me feel like shit about myself – he always said that I was fat and ugly - wow - it's right here on the sheet where it says:
EMOTIONAL ABUSE:

"When someone puts you down and tries to make you feel bad about yourself."

"You'd think I'd know better than to pick a guy like that, but my boyfriend's the same way. He humiliates me in front of our friends all the time and -"

"God damn girls - you're still young - you can leave those losers and find a better man," cried a heavyset woman standing with her hands on her hips. "I got four kids and bills to pay. My job's hard enough, but do you think I'd get any help from *him*? Oh no, he makes me do everything; says I'm worthless; but he's the lump laying around, outta work."

A low hum grew to a louder roar as the group reached out to each other in commiseration. The class appeared to be forming a deeper kinship based on their comparable circumstances.

Aurora was shocked to hear of such despondent situations in all their terrible realities. She couldn't fathom living a day to day life trapped in that kind of abuse. She wanted to tell the group that they all deserved better than that, but wondered why they didn't see it themselves.

"I have another story to tell you," said Mr. Thera gently. "It's about a high school girl whose family was very poor. Both parents worked and the girl had a job after school, but still there was never enough money.

"In her sophomore year, she confided to her mother that she'd been invited to the prom. They secretly planned to save up a portion of the household money for a new dress.

"The evening arrived, and the girl got all made up.

"When she posed for her father, he spat at her, 'What's on your face? Makeup? You look like a Ho - I know what you've done - you think you're off to a dance - no way - take that dress off - we'll get the money back."

Mr. Thera didn't pause.

"Shocked and humiliated, the girl ran to her room crying.

"The mother pleaded with her husband, but he yelled, 'You should know better than to use hard earned money on such worthless things.'

"He struck his wife and stormed out of the house."

The room fell silent.

Aurora bowed her head feeling her pulse pounding at her temples.

The teacher read the next section on the sheet:

"Making someone feel like they are bad or crazy is unacceptable behavior. Playing mind games is unacceptable. No exceptions. No justifiable reasons. No one should be entitled to control, by force, another person."

Before anyone could or would comment, Mr. Thera said, "Here's a quick story about a four-year-old boy who was playing dress-up in his big sister's high heels.

"The father came home to find his son parading around saying, 'Look at me' while shaking his hips, showing off. Assuming it was homosexual behavior the father angrily grabbed the child and dragged him down the corridor of their apartment complex shouting, 'Look everyone, here's my fagot son!'

"The child was confused and frightened by his father's rage. He didn't know what he'd done, but he knew that he had done something wrong."

Mr. Thera paused long enough to catch his breath.

"Please look at the next box:
INTIMIDATION: It states that:"

"Putting her in fear by using looks, actions, gestures, a loud voice, smashing things or destroying her property is another form of control. This form of intimidation goes from subtle control to outward violence for control."

He looked out amongst the group and said quietly, "These fathers shamed their children so they could retain control."

"Assholes," blurted out an angry-looking woman sitting forward. "Someone should take those degenerates to a deserted place and shoot them," she huffed before collapsing with a thud back into her chair.

"No Sarah," said Mr. Thera in a subdued voice, "that would be just as bad, or worse. We have to recognize that this behavior as entirely unacceptable. Then we have to find alternate ways to deal with these issues."

"But people like that don't ever change," said the woman with corn rows. Her face was smiling, but her jaw was set. "I know for a fact that they don't. I've tried every way possible, from being quiet to screaming, and it don't make no difference. If a man's mean and angry, he's always gonna be mean and angry."

Many women nodded in agreement.

So much disharmony, Aurora thought sadly.

Since she was a small child, she'd kneeled at her bedside and prayed the powerful words:

Our Father, who art in heaven, hallow be Thy name. Thy kingdom come, Thy will be done, on earth as it is in heaven. Give us this day our daily bread, and forgive us our trespasses, as we forgive those who trespass against us. And lead us not into temptation, but deliver us from evil, Amen.

Aurora couldn't imagine forgiving such terrible treatment. Nor could she understand why these women had helplessly endured it for as long as they had.

"I think a break would do everyone good," Mr. Thera announced. "Why don't we stretch our legs, get a beverage, and then we'll continue."

Aurora remained seated with the sheet in her hand.

The stories frightened her.

The other women could relate, right away they could relate. Aurora had found no parallels to associate herself with any of it, but she had felt an anxious quickening of her heart just the same.

For the millionth time she thought, *What am I doing here?*

***

The women returned to their places and all of them seemed to sigh in unison. It sounded like a slow, faint whistle of air being let out of a balloon.

Mr. Thera sighed as well, and resumed the session saying, "Now we have the issue of, "**ECONOMIC ABUSE**."

"Trying to keep her from getting or keeping a job. Making her ask for money, giving her an allowance, taking her money."

Before a discussion began, the statement screamed in Aurora's head. *For heavens' sake -* she realized, *that's why I'm here - it was about the money - but I explained it to her !*

Deep resentment seeped through Aurora as she silently moaned, *The system, in every way, has manipulated me!*

***

"Is anyone in a situation like this, where you are 'kept' in this way?" the Counselor asked.

Aurora raised her hand.

"I have a question Mr. Thera. How do you identify the difference between what may look like a control issue, but is actually a collaborating system?"

She took a deep breath and tried to hold back her indignation. "For example: if the monthly finances are discussed by the partners *together,* and the sum needed, *mutually* agreed upon, and that exact amount is dispersed to the person who runs the household, is that person being *controlled* ?"

Aurora felt the pressure of the group's eyes bearing down on her. *Who do you think you are*? they all seemed to say.

"Can you elaborate, Mrs. Sabel?" asked Mr. Thera before anyone else could remark.

Aurora raised her eyebrows alarmed that he'd known her name. "What I mean is," she said clearing her throat, "when husbands and wives talk things over before making decisions, and work together -"

"Girl, if it was that easy, I'd be president of my own company," interrupted the woman on Aurora's right with a mocking grin. "He don't even *sit* with me, let alone *talk* to me. If we could lay out a plan, we'd be sittin' pretty. For real, does your husband do that with you?"

Aurora was nervous because everyone was staring at her, waiting for her to answer.

"Well, yes," she said slowly. "We're on a tight budget because I'm home with the children. Living on one income makes it essential that we discuss how to cover everything. We have to be careful."

"I wish we did that. We're always fighting cause no one knows who paid what," the woman said with a sigh.

"It wouldn't be that hard to get things sorted out," Aurora encouraged. "If you start by writing out all the bills you have each month, you'll see how it looks on paper and -"

"Ladies," Mr. Thera interrupted, "let's get back to work. I recommend you talk later."

Aurora and the woman nodded and smiled at each other.

Well, isn't that something, thought Aurora suppressing a satisfied grin.

***

Mr. Thera proceeded.

"Okay, at the next box, we have a common occurrence with men:
USING MALE PRIVILEGE.
The statement below says,"

"Treating her like a servant. Making all the 'big' decisions. Acting like the 'master of the castle' ."

"Oh-ho, my man's like that," chimed a tall, bejeweled lady in business attire. "He thinks he's king, he does. Runs round tryin' to tell us all what to do, but we just ignore him."

A few women laughed.

"If he was half the man he thinks he is," she chided, "we'd being doin' fine, doin' great. But he comes by bad luck like a rash; always whinin' and moanin' 'bout how unfair his spoiled life is."

Her joke got a round of applause. The humor lightened the dismal atmosphere, considerably.

"That's a good one Tamara," commented Mr. Thera. "Except, anyone who puts demands on another individual, like a man who treats a woman like a slave, takes away her rights as a free person."

"Ain't that the livin' truth, but I could name a few guys like say, Mel Gibson, Denzel Washington or that gorgeous foreign guy from the James Bond movies, who I'd gladly be a slave to !" a woman in the back row shouted out, grinning.

Everyone laughed.

Aurora felt like part of the group - a little.

The teacher smiled and pushed on.

"Let's talk about this next box:
SEXUAL ABUSE is USING MALE PRIVILEGE.
We see the correlation between the two where it states that,"

"Making her do sexual things against her will. Physically attacking the sexual parts of her body. Treating her like a sex object."

Mr. Thera spoke softly, "These are ways of controlling using male privilege. When he controls her body, he controls her personal rights."

"No one has the right to take what isn't freely offered. Everyone has the right to say *NO if* they don't want to be touched."

"There is no fuzzy area about this," said Mr. Thera. "There is no tolerance for this kind of cruel abuse. Does anyone have a comment?"

No one did.

The room went silent.

No one was willing to participate in a discussion so personal.

The group seemed restless and busy adjusting their belongings, repositioning themselves in their seats.

The silence spoke volumes.

Obviously, no one wanted to take a trip down that dark alley.

Mr. Thera waited a few more minutes in case someone was inclined to speak out; bare their soul.

But no one did.

"If anyone wants to meet with me after this session or any other time, I'm available," he said amiably to the group of withdrawn women.

He advanced quietly, moved around the room, and said, "The bottom, left side box, states," **THREATS**.

"Making and/or carrying out threats to do something to hurt someone emotionally. Like threatening to take the children, or commit suicide, or report her to welfare or child services."

The teacher waited for a reaction, but none came.

Even the ladies who were previously loquacious were now stilled. Heads were down; lips tight shut. Obviously, these topics hit too close to home.

Aurora realized in that moment that the subject matter they were going over in class, was what many of these women were in fact, *living*. Nothing could have prepared her for this rude awakening.

"Okay, we can come back to that later if anyone wants to," said the soften spoken Counselor. "So, moving on, please take a look at the right hand box at the bottom of the sheet where it states," **USING CHILDREN**.

"Making the children the go-between to relay messages, cancelling visitation as a way to harass her."

"Yeah, my husband does stuff like that," confessed a woman breaking the silence.

"He'll tell the kids he's coming; they'll get ready and wait by the door, but he doesn't show up. By the time we realize HE'S NOT COMING, my plans are shot, and the kids are let down, again."

"I know what you mean," someone else chimed in. "It always happens when his visitation day comes around. I try to convince the kids that this time he *will* show, but it never fails that something comes up and he bails on them. His kids mean squat to him. He has no regard for anything but his own needs. That's why I left him a long time ago."

The walls seemed to vibrate as many of the women spoke about their grievances.

Once again there was a common denominator between them.

Once again, Aurora was on the outside, looking in.

***

These women had issues with most of the subjects written in the cycle of the wheel. Some of the topics could be freely expressed and their discord and their disappointments voiced. The other, more sensitive issues, the truly dysfunctional aspects of their lives, would remain hidden behind a forbidden door, where no one would venture to go.

At that point, there wasn't one topic in the program, save for the total misunderstanding about the money issue, that showed Aurora any parallels in her life. There'd never been any kind of parental abuse or childhood trauma that she could recall right then, or anything in her present home life that correlated with the subjects in the program so far.

The reality check to learn that this kind of unrest existed in the world was tough enough, but Aurora could not relate to any of it, at all.

It agitated her a great deal as she thought, *I can't believe that I have to be subjected to this, for the next six months.*

Chapter Eighteen: The Cycle

As Aurora hit the yellow knob on the side of the building and walked through the opening doors leading into the hospital, she reminisced about how she and Charlotte had first met.

The gym had been full that morning, three years prior. All the machines were occupied.

Aurora found a spot to do her sit-ups, free weights, and then a treadmill became available.

The woman next to Aurora had noticed that Aurora needed help, so she'd stopped her machine and trotted over to assist. "Look - you have to put in your speed, time and hit program."

"Ah." Aurora studied the control panel, tried to do it, but nothing happened. "Uh -"

"Here, I'll show you," Charlotte had said. She'd fixed Aurora up and resumed her workout. They'd jogged in unison for some thirty minutes.

Aurora had admired the woman's stamina. "I hope you don't mind me saying so, but you're very fit for your age." Aurora recalled that she had been drenched with sweat after her run, but the woman had only a glistening, flushed face.

"Not bad for seventy-one," she'd chuckled, wiping her brow with a fluffy pink towel. Her workout leggings were also pink. Shock pink to be exact, with black swirls down the left leg and the logo Adidas printed across her waist band.

Accountability

Charlotte was a small compactly built lady whose muscles hugged her body.

"I like to work out, although time doesn't often permit it," she'd said thrusting her hand out, introducing herself with an open, confident smile.

Her face was not beautiful, but her effervescence had an allure that was simply gorgeous. A high forehead rested above a perky celestial nose that wrinkled when she laughed hard. Her lips were always painted a deep cherry red, the only make-up she ever wore. Aside from a brilliant mop of silver hair, what really stood out from the balanced combination of her features, was her readable eyes. They could be the lightest color of an aqua Bahamas ocean if she were being mischievous or playful, or they could turn to a deep moss green when she was either angry or serious. She had never been angry at Aurora, and she wasn't often serious, but when she was, you saw it, right away in her eyes.

They'd met once a week at the gym, then finding out that they had much in common, they ventured to other places. Getting out together quickly became bi-weekly excursions.

Aurora remembered vividly the first time she'd gone to Charlotte's home. The house was on a sleepy little street, tucked behind a huge magnolia tree on the corner of a dead-end circle. The low shutters were painted dark green, the wood panels a crisp white. To get to the front door you had to walk along a terracotta brick-laid winding path, and all along that path was purple-leafed ground cover and marigolds - hundreds of marigolds.

Aurora had tentatively poked her head through the front door that had been left ajar. "Hello-oo-" she'd called out in a sing-song voice.

For a moment there was no answer. Aurora had hoped that she was at the right place because the directions, drawn like a cartoon road map, was to that spot.

"Come in - the doors open -" Charlotte had called out cheerily.

"Where are you?"

Aurora made her way past the living room with its rich, plush, beige carpet. She stopped to regard the honey-colored wicker and white linen couch and chairs. Then she dawdled in the hallway to admire the photos that hung in clusters along its entire length.

"Keep coming - I'm here -" Charlotte had coached.

Aurora went through the kitchen with shiny brass pots hanging from a wrought iron grid. She remembers smiling at the artsy whimsical chandelier of sparkling silverware. Forks, knives, and spoons dangled between the lights above the granite topped island in the center of the room.

But what she'll never forget was the smell. The wafting scent of butter and brown sugar will always be the pure essence of Charlotte. It infused the modest house, filling it with an energy that was all encompassing, like a loved one's warm embrace.

Charlotte was an exceptional cook. Her instincts for adding a little something extra to a recipe matched Aurora's ability to mix up traditional fare with a trendy flair. They never seemed to tire from sharing and comparing recipes. They also loved going to a gallery or a bookstore, but their all-time favorite was meeting at the old theatre to see a Retro film. Mostly though, they'd simply *talked*. The age difference was a numbers draw. They were equally given friends.

When Charlotte's second husband Nate was struck with cancer, it had been a tough time. Hospice came daily, but Charlotte was the twenty-four hour 'nurse' who had to care for him, and help him retain his dignity.

During that time Aurora went to see Charlotte often. She'd go to get her out of the house, just for a walk, to give her friend a reprieve from the 'death watch' she'd had to endure.

Nate rapidly declined and passed away. A year after Nate died, Charlotte was diagnosed with cancer as well. She was in the hospital for the third time when Aurora went to see her. The doctors weren't sure if she would go home.

Accountability

Living through someone slowly dying has got to be the worst kind of helplessness.

***

The scent of orange blossom coming from Charlotte's favorite cream, permeated the hospital room.

Aurora inhaled deeply, embracing the presence of her friend; letting Charlotte's true self wrap around her like a blanket warming her. She walked up to the bed.

Charlotte was resting serenely.

Aurora wanted to stroke her pretty silver-tinged hair. It was all but gone now; the hair that had been, like the woman, bright and shiny, and so full of life.

Charlotte had been a pioneer among women of her day. She had gotten a job in a hospital in the early forties as a clerk. It was not a job normally offered to women. The organization in those days was terrible. All supplies and medications were shelved without rhyme or reason.

Charlotte got to work and created order impressing her superiors. She rose in the company. When computers hailed the way of the future, Charlotte developed the data system for the hospital.

Charlotte had said that her first marriage of thirty-six years, had been like a fairy tale. "You could say we lived high on the hog," she'd told Aurora. "What with entertaining in high circles, traveling abroad every summer and winter; our life was filled with adventure."

When her beloved husband David had been gone a few years, Charlotte got together with Nate. He and his recently deceased wife had been part of their social circle.

Nate and Charlotte had always been comfortable with each other, so after a brief interval, they decided it would be both practical and companionable if they married and lived under one roof.

Money wasn't an issue. They had their own estates; separate accounts, which stayed divided.

Sadly, their seemingly easy relationship went south shortly after their wedding day.

Nate was a man who praised high, but criticized harshly as well. Charlotte hadn't noticed how critical he was, until they lived together. She never knew what kind of mood he'd be in, and she became wary when they had guests over because he could tear her apart with an underhanded remark.

Nate was like a finicky day that showed signs of the warm sun peeking through, only to recede with the chill of a darkening cloud.

Charlotte disregarded Nate's turbulent moods and went about her days; she was a blooming happy person. A thorn of Nate's nature, could not whither that.

When Aurora and Charlotte had talked about life and men, their combined opinion was that all men are relatively the same.

In varying degrees, they are all overcome by and in need of, their own power and control.

The two women theorized about this stuff, even with a bit of levity, long before Aurora had been thrown into the wild world of domestic violence classes.

***

"Hi," Aurora whispered, sitting down on the bed, and laying her hand on Charlotte's bony shoulder. As she was opening her drug-droopy eyes, Aurora asked, "How're you feeling?"

"Hungry. I could go for some of that yummy Monk's bread we had - where was that place? Oh, yes, that little health food store with the cute café - remember?"

Charlotte tried to sit up in the bed, rested back down and shook her head weakly.

"I'll try to smuggle some in," Aurora said, touching Charlotte's arm and squeezing it gently.

"Hmm, that'd be great, but better not, they'll just take it away."

Charlotte chuckled, "You know, I had this craving earlier. I could almost taste your Mulligatawny soup - or I could go for some of that Ratatouille you make so well. Hmm, that stuff is so good, but I can't eat anything now, nothing at all."

"Oh Charlotte," Aurora whispered as she'd started to cry. "Why? You can't - this can't be -"

Charlotte rested her hand, as light as a wisp of silk, on Aurora's arm, and spoke in her, 'I'm-Gonna-Tell-You-Something-Important' voice.

"You know Aurora, I'll tell you this, when I was forty, I quit smoking. David and I were of a generation that had a libation every evening. And with that, went smoking. Oh, we all smoked at social functions. I smoked for twenty years and then gave it up hoping that I'd defy the Gods and escape this kind of end. But here I am, thirty-four years later, answering for my sins and dying like all mortals!"

Charlotte chuckled, and then she had a mild coughing fit.

Aurora's eyes teared up and she cried out, "Oh Charlotte, this isn't fair - I need more time -"

"I know," Charlotte soothed. "Life isn't fair sometimes."

Charlotte asked for some water, so Aurora held the cup to her lips, and she sipped slowly.

"I'm okay with all of this actually," she'd said easing back, sinking into the bed. "I've had a full life. Lots of fun and adventure. Remember the song by Jim Croce? You know, Time In A Bottle? That's how I feel about all the people I've loved."

She ran her knot-knuckled fingers over the thin wisps of hair left on her balding scalp and adjusted the pillow behind her head.

"I've said my hearty goodbyes. Mostly tearless. But when it comes to you, I don't know what to say, so we just won't say goodbye."

Aurora dropped her head and let out a sob. She was miserable to be losing Charlotte.

"What's going on Aurora? Where have you been?" Charlotte asked.

Aurora inhaled, and hesitated breathlessly.

"Something terrible has happened. And I have to tell you. So far, I haven't told anyone. It's so bad, that I'm afraid it will alter your opinion of me greatly."

Charlotte stroked Aurora's arm and said, "First of all, nothing could ever change the way I feel about you my dear. Second, you better tell me so we can figure it out together."

"Well," Aurora said, sitting up straighter, "remember last September when we made all those little almond cakes for my Father's birthday party -"

Aurora poured the whole story out without many stops, and told it like it was. It felt like a heavy stone was being lifted from her shoulders.

Aside from her confession to her cousin, she hadn't told anyone what had happened. Aurora's in-laws were the only witnesses and they hadn't said a word. Aurora was ashamed and embarrassed. She vowed no one would know. The weight of it, was immense. It disrupted her life so much, that she knew at some point, she'd have to relinquish the burden.

***

Truly unconditional love is amazing.

Although most parents strive to love their children with clear and selfless devotion, it's hard because expectations of perfection cloud the way.

Aurora was initially afraid to tell Charlotte, but Charlotte happened to be the perfect person to confide in.

With tender concern, she held Aurora's hand and cooed, "Oh my goodness, how dreadful for you!"

Aurora told Charlotte about the classes and how discouraged she was because the gist of the issues didn't pertain to her in any way.

Charlotte frowned and her eyes darkening to a lush, deep green as she exclaimed, "Aurora! Listen to yourself. You're wallowing when you have an opportunity to do something you've always wanted to do!"

Charlotte was short of breath and asked for a sip of water. Aurora asked her to rest.

"Stop that, and think about this," she said huffing. "After all these years of searching for a good story line, a good topic for a book, you have a human-interest story, pardon the pun, slapping you right in the face!"

"Hmmm," Aurora muttered.

She wasn't sure if she wanted to share her story. She didn't think she had the guts to tell the whole world about her shameful encounter.

"If I were you," Charlotte said getting excited, pulling herself up on an elbow, "I'd bring a journal to the sessions and take notes each week. Then you could compile the data and -"

Her energy lapsed and she dropped back onto the bed, exhausted.

Aurora pulled the covers up to her friend's chin and tucked her in.

"Do you really think people would be interested to read about my misfortune?" Aurora questioned. "I mean, it's not enough of a storyline for a whole book, is it?"

"I don't know," Charlotte said mildly, "and neither do you, unless you try. But I think that if I got a chuckle out of Gumby, all the characters in jail, and the Kenny Bensen episode, then the public will too!"

***

Aurora left the hospital with a new sense of hope.

Charlotte's suggestion had considerable merit and seemed to be an interesting prospect that deserved pursuing.

***

Aurora arrived the following week half an hour earlier to meet with the Counselor. She asked for his permission to log each session in a journal.

Mr. Thera took a few moments to consider Aurora's request and then he spoke in an even tone.

"If you'd like to write about what we talk about here," he said with a serious but benevolent expression, "and you're going to refer to any specific stories, I must insist that you change their names and possibly their genders.

"Remember, these are true stories, about actual patients."

***

The next few weeks were a painful enlightenment. The vast expanse of domestic violence seemed endless. Classes were intense, and the subject matter gruesome in content. The stories were full of maliciously violent disharmony.

Aurora felt like she was being held in the grip of a vicious assault. Being forced to listen was like the hands of reality tightening around her neck trying to kill her by slow asphyxiation.

Acting in the guise of a journalist again made it slightly more bearable. Aurora had some experience from her time freelancing for a newspaper when she'd lived in Colorado.

She removed herself from the group as a participant, and concentrated on taking down the facts to report the curriculum accurately.

Now Aurora had a purpose, a viable mission to justify her being there. It also helped to placate her continual unease.

***

911 gets a call from a six-year-old girl who's pleading, begging the operator to come and get her step daddy out of the house because he's going to hurt her mommy and her baby brother. The child, although frightened, is explaining herself quite clearly. She gives her name, age, and telephone number, and says again that if someone doesn't come soon, her daddy will hurt her too, because she's locked her parents and the baby in the bedroom.

Accountability

The audio track, being played in the counseling room, seemed to vibrate while they listened to heavy pounding on a door, and a man yelling harshly, "You little shit - open this fucking door!"

It was apparent that the girl was gripping the phone close to her mouth.

"Please hurry -" she whispered tearfully into the device. "He says I'm gonna *GET IT* when he gets outta there."

Another child is crying hysterically.

"Shh, it's okay," the group heard the little girl tell the other child.

It was pathetic.

They all sat still listening with fear and loathing.

Then came a loud bang, lots of screaming and cursing; the telephone line buzzed, crackled and the line went dead.

Everyone in the room had been holding their breath.

Then the crestfallen faces exhaled slowly.

***

Mr. Thera turned the recorder off. He walked quietly to the front of the room, slowly turned to face the group, and running a hand through his hair, sighed audibly.

"After a horrendous outbreak of violence such as in a case like this, the parties are separated by the authorities.

"In most cases they reunite and return to their homes.

"In the beginning there is a renewed period of calm acquiescence and these people go through what's known as, **'The Honeymoon Stage'**."

Mr. Thera grabbed his bottle of water and started to pace the perimeter of the room.

"This starts the **Cycle** in which these situations revolve. The honeymoon period is when the great apology comes. The person whose done the damage, is in complete repentance. This is a time when they're loving to everyone and everything is guarded. They're kind and generous. This stage lasts as long as the stress level stays low."

The Counselor paused to take a long drink and continued his dialog before the class could break his momentum.

"As time goes on the parties involved go into the second stage where they become complaisant and their guards start to come down. Harsh words are not being spoken yet, everyone is still wary, but the day-to-day stress is rising, building up."

He stopped for a moment of reflection. Everyone was still tongue-tied, so he proceeded.

"The third stage of the **Cycle** is when the tension erupts and *reignites* unresolved issues. It could be that someone who has stopped drinking in this initial honeymoon period has started to drink again. Or someone's deeply concealed grievance just can't be suppressed any longer; whatever the conflict is, it inevitably resurfaces and the confrontation resumes."

Mr. Thera looked at the furrowed brows of his little audience. He seemed to want the class to listen and absorb the outline of the **Cycle**, but he did not stop talking to leave it open for discussion.

"A follow up to the last outbreak of violence is invariably on the horizon. When an altercation recurs, the same thing happens: they are separated by the authorities again, possibly put in jail for a duration of time, and then perpetually they reunite; starting the **Cycle** all over again."

He walked back to the front of the room, leaned on the edge of the portable table, and waited for a response.

Within minutes the room was a buzz.

Everyone had something to say.

"How did it turn out with the little girl?" one woman asked.

"You just described a day in my life," another woman stated.

"Does 911 react to every call?"

"Those poor children. Did they send that horrible monster away?"

"I can't believe how much of my life is like that -"

Accountability

"Ladies," said the Counselor holding up a hand in a gesture of restraining the rising dander, "let's examine some ways to counteract a situation like this if, and when, it may arise."

He handed out a sheet of paper with another wagon wheel diagram and set of statements.

The inner-circle said: **EQUALITY**.
The outer-circle said: **NONVIOLENCE**.

Each 'spoke' had a statement.
The class went through all of them.

"Negotiation and Fairness," Mr. Thera read, **"is about seeking mutually satisfying resolutions to conflict, accepting change and being willing to compromise."**

"Does anyone want to comment?"

"You know Lancel, all this talk about being fair is something I do every day. I *am* fair. I *am* loving and giving. I *am* willing to compromise, but it just doesn't seem to matter."

The well-dressed woman calmly brushed some lint off her skirt and was about to say something more, but she was interrupted by another women's testimony.

"You know, I feel the same," said a woman in the back row sitting up straighter. "I *always* try to be fair, but that means I have to change my point of view. If it's a tricky situation, I always say, 'That's okay, we'll do it *your* way', but I wish I didn't have to always do that."

"I would love to be able to just discuss possibilities with my husband," interrupted an older gal with a wiped outlook on her face. "If I could just get him to stop, look, and listen -"

"Yes ladies," said Mr. Thera, in a mollifying, companionable voice, "it must seem quite difficult at times, but we can learn to see these conflicts coming, and defuse them. Everyone CAN win.

"Let's take these sections, one at a time."

The group grumbled out of habit, but hunkered down to see where this might take them.

Mr. Thera began to read the text:

"Nonthreatening Behavior: is about being heard; the need to be valued, finding effective ways to compromise without losing your sense of self."

The women were quiet.

The clock in the hall clicked loudly, then a discussion ensued.

"*I* know who *I* am," the woman next to Aurora said, as she stood up, and faced the class like she was on stage, a sort of entertainer. "He just has to learn that who *I am*, is not his *slave*!"

Many of the women seemed to be using humor to cover up their pain.

The comedian got a few laughs and the majority invariably acknowledged their agreement at every negative comment.

Mr. Thera moved forward. "Let's look at this next part."

"Respect: Listening to her non-judgmentally, being emotionally affirming and understanding, valuing opinions."

He waited quietly for someone to comment.

"If I could get my husband to do something that I suggested, the moment I suggested it, I'd patent that formula and make millions!" said a woman with a friendly-faced grin.

"I have to plant an idea in my husband's head, very subtle, not a suggestion, just a thought, and about three days later, he'll come to me and tell me *he* has this great idea -" said another woman with whom many laughed and agreed.

The general consensus seemed to be that their opinions were of no consequence and they weren't given any recognition for all that they were capable of doing.

Accountability

Aurora thought sadly, *My gosh, and I thought my life wasn't easy. I'll never complain again.*

A sharp reality hit Aurora that William as a partner, was quite different from the descriptions these women were reporting of their significant others.

In her day to day life, she and William discussed everything. They considered anything pertaining to the children, or the household or finances, together.

And they listened to each other.

Aurora knew that she was blessed; that she and William wanted the same things out of life.

Their marriage, the partnership agreement they'd signed up for almost twelve years ago was a serious pact and an unbreakable bond between them.

The foundation of their commitment was having a strong faith and living in God's grace was their guiding force.

Having trust and respect for that hallowed power was their strength.

Why isn't there any talk of Faith in these sessions? Aurora thought. *I hear these women joke, complain, and whimper, but I don't hear anyone make a reference to God. I thought these programs were based on a GOD ALMIGHTY premise.*

Aurora was curious.

There seemed to be a sure and steady conviction that these women wanted justice and a sort of salvation, but many of them were only exacting sympathy, comfort, and condolences from the wellspring of a shared commiseration of their similar circumstances.

***

Mr. Thera continued, trying to keep the women in check. "Okay, okay, ladies, let's consider the next section."

"Trust and Support: Supporting her goals in life, respecting her right to her own feelings, friends, activities and opinions."

The Counselor regarded the stony faces staring at him.

"You know," said an older woman in a solid, meaningful voice, "I married a man who from the beginning, now twenty years ago, has thwarted every opinion and crushed every plan I've ever strived to accomplish for myself. I wouldn't even tell him about a sure bet now."

"Yeah well, if my old man was *ever* interested in what I *thought*, I'd be livin' a better life."

The woman had tried to be funny, but many others nodded solemnly in agreement.

A pretty little blonde-haired girl-woman with sky blue eyes the same color as her simple cotton dress whined with a pouty southern drawl, "I juss weeish my husband wounn't git so riled up whihn I want ta go out wif my girlfriends. He thinks weya goin' out to pick up guys and he gits real crazy mad - real jealous - ya know - I say it's not true - but he juss won't believe me."

"Ladies," said Mr. Thera, with persuasion, "you have the right to your opinions. You have the right to set your own goals in life. Do not be afraid to state them. You can achieve them without being stomped on. You all have the strength to do whatever you set out to do."

Nobody spoke, but Aurora could see a glimmer of interest in the group's ruminating eyes. She thought that maybe a spark had been ignited within them and these women saw a flicker of hope to regain the dreams and desires that had long ago been trampled. These were working women who rarely, if ever, thought about themselves. How ironic to be in a program emphasizing 'be your own person' when they'd had to be the person who did everything for everyone else.

***

Camaraderie unifies and transcends much adversity.

These women were kindred spirits with similar situations, despairs, and struggles.

They weren't weak.

They were strong and confident, away from their partners. They knew who they were and what they wanted, but what was stopping them, obstructing them from attaining those goals, was the suppressive forces in their homelife.

And they couldn't, or wouldn't, get out of that situation.

Once again Aurora was an outsider, her life a cakewalk compared to theirs.

She wrote furiously in her journal because she wanted to hide. She couldn't bear to hear any more painful expressions of the bleak realities of these people's lives.

***

Mr. Thera said that before they went forward he wanted to prepare them.

He tried to warn the class that it would indeed be a difficult section for some, and everyone should be gentle on themselves.

He said they should take it slowly.

He seemed reluctant to proceed.

Nodding his head he said, "Alright then," and he began to read the sheet in his hand.

"Honesty and Accountability: Accepting responsibility for yourself and your actions. Acknowledging the use of violence. Admitting being wrong, communicating openly and truthfully."

A wordless, disgruntled rumble like the sound of thunder way off in the distance gathered its force, and the rising protest of voices resounded and shook the walls of the little room.

Mr. Thera tried to appeal to the appalled-looking faces that were sneering at him.

"Hold on a moment ladies. I can understand your outrage. Although this section is mainly geared for the men's group, please let us look at it for your sake as well."

He paused, raising a hand.

"I've read your files, and I'm aware that most of you were *not* the true perpetrators of violence.

I'm also quite sure that for many of you the violence was begotten; probably for years you've been violently oppressed by your spouse or partner.

That in itself is inexcusable.

Let me try to explain this part of the program to you.

It is vitally important that you understand that everyone, in every situation, is responsible for their actions."

He slowly moved about the room, his expression sincere with compassion as he passed through the aisles and either gently touched an arm or a shoulder or smiled kindly into someone's eyes.

The women appeared to breathe slower, and the tension in the room seemed to be abating.

"I want you to remember the altercation that resulted in you being put into this program. I want you to consider that your acting with violence was wrong, regardless of the reasons you had to justify it."

The atmosphere in the room was subdued as each person pondered the circumstances that had brought them there.

Aurora abruptly stopped writing in her notebook.

During previous sessions she hadn't connected the material with anything that pertained to her personally, but this section hit her hard as she thought, *Oh my gosh, I've never taken responsibility for my actions. I'm at fault for the 911 call and the police coming. I put myself in this predicament because I hit William. I have no one else to blame but myself.*

***

Voices began to mingle; muffled conversations floated up like air bubbles as Aurora's own transgressions jostled inside her head.

The rest of the session was a blur.

Aurora had to admit that she wasn't the innocent victim she'd made herself out to be.

I'd been aggressive - in a fury - but for what? She fretted silently, *For the love of God - I hit my husband for disciplining our child. What was I thinking? Please Lord help me - I think I'm falling -*

***

Aurora went home and cried her eyes out.

She sniffled, snorted, and felt terribly sorry for herself. She kept reliving the scene: William's actions, her actions; like a broken record.

"If only I hadn't hit you -" she cried as she and William lay in their bed that night.

"We're not going to get anywhere with what-ifs," William said, firmly pulling her close, caressing her slowly.

"We settled all this on the telephone from the jail. I'm sorry it happened. You're sorry it happened. There's nothing more to say. Now we have to let it go and move on."

***

Daily life was busy, and the weeks went by.

The classes were slowly reducing. How many more to go?

Aurora's journal was filling up with lots of notes, her catering business was in high season, and she had little time for anything else other than her own core family.

***

Time passed, and so did Charlotte.

At the end, the family didn't want outsiders visiting.

Aurora didn't go to the funeral.

Charlotte's daughter contacted her about a week later, after she'd found a package with Aurora's name on it. Inside was a photo and Charlotte's daily planner.

The photo was of Charlotte posing in a bathing suit on top of a Volkswagen beetle that was parked on a strip of sand in Mexico. The glossy paper had browned; it had been taken when Charlotte was probably in her late thirties or forty, like Aurora. Charlotte knew Aurora had loved the story behind it.

Charlotte's escapades were the best; all the exotic travels of a woman with an uninhibited lust for life.

Her long love affair with David was often retold to Aurora (at her insistence like a child begging for a beloved fairy tale) and she felt relief for Charlotte that those sweethearts would be reunited in heaven.

The little religious book was a precious gift because they'd read many pages together, seeking answers to life's quandaries. It became a staple in Aurora's purse, on her bedside table, in a jacket pocket, just to have Charlotte's pulse close to Aurora's heart.

***

Daily devotions can be so comforting.

Aurora liked to read random pages often.

She'd been afraid there would be a terrible emptiness when Charlotte left this earth, but because Charlotte gave so much of herself, Aurora knew that her shining spirit would always be there.

Now, more than ever Aurora felt a pull to write the book, because Charlotte believed she should do it.

Accountability

The Adventuress

Charlotte at the beach in Mexico.

Chapter Nineteen: Mathematics of Battering

"One, two, buckle my shoe, three four, shut the door -"

Aurora read a favored book to her boys as they all lay with legs overlapping on the hammock in back of the house under the tall pine trees.

It was a balmy day; the sweet smell of fresh-cut grass wafted through the air as the man next door mowed his lawn.

A pile of books lay on the grass queuing for attention while the cozy group nibbled on nut bars and grapes and basked in the joy of such delightful idleness.

"Aurora -" William called from inside the doorway of the patio, "the phone's for you."

"Whoever it is, please tell them I'm busy -" she said as she smiled at her audience and turned the page of the book.

"It's Mrs. Macavey, saying she's calling you back on a date -"

"Oh, alright. Tell her I'm coming."

Aurora had to get up.

Her loyal following of clients had been dropping her name at all their social events and it had advanced her catering business considerably.

"Cooking for people is more than just a job," Aurora always said. "Creating meals for each individual's taste, is very personal."

Her career had been founded by the support of William's military comrades.

Accountability

When Aurora and William were in Germany for his second tour, William was stationed at a remote site that lacked a mess hall, fast food take out, or any other options to obtain prepared meals.

The community break room only offered a microwave, a foosball table, a candy machine, and a television set; the soldiers had to get by on their own initiative concerning their daily meals.

On William's shift, he brought whatever Aurora had prepared for him. When he heated up his meals the other soldiers would say, "Man, that smells good. Hey, I'll pay ya for that food - come on dude - how 'bout it?"

Aurora's good-natured husband would chuckle and reply that no, they couldn't buy his dinner.

This banter went on until finally William said, "Hey guys, why don't you ask Aurora if she'll cook for you? Maybe then you'll stop drooling on my dinner and we'll all get to eat."

A variety of the single soldiers hired her, and Aurora learned (from their mother's recipes) how to cook an array of ethnic meals.

Within the first year she'd gotten about eight clients.

Ten years later Aurora had a business that was booming, her marriage was solid, the boys were happy and healthy, and the classes were almost over.

So why was she feeling so anxious all the time?

***

Must get there on time!

If you're at the door, but one minute late, you won't be admitted. You'll be counted as *absent*. To amend this, you must get a written excuse (but who writes this excuse if you are not sick, just late?).

Every week you drive to the counseling center like a lunatic; heart racing, head throbbing; praying you won't have an accident, because if you're late they'll penalize you. After three times they'll revoke your current time served.

Then you'll be in contempt. They may arrest you again. Send you back to court. Then you'll have to start the program all over again from the beginning.

Rubbing her temples Aurora thought, *Geez, I can't wait for this whole thing to be over.*

Each week women came to class and announced, "Five more weeks to go -" or, "I've got three more classes and I'm outta here!"

No one talked about what the sessions covered in content. No one seemed to care whether they had tools to rehabilitate their lives. They just wanted the compulsory debt, over with.

Aurora had been going to the counseling center for sixteen weeks, and she still had the jitters if she was delayed in traffic. Whenever a siren blasted she panicked thinking they were coming for her. Aurora was sure that if she were pulled over her information would pop up in the police database and she'd be arrested again for having been arrested for domestic violence. In all likelihood it could not happen, but there was no convincing Aurora of that.

It was a tremendous strain having to account for herself every week. When she had a catering job, the date and time were planned, but it wasn't catastrophic if Aurora was running behind by five minutes; no terrible consequence. In the case of class attendance, it was the fear of the penalty that kept her eye on the clock like a maniac's phobia.

Paying forty-five dollars and the humiliation of the same inquiry wore her down too.

The probation officer seemed to relish her obligation to ask, "Have you been violent with anyone this month?"

She was stern and calculated and seemed to take personal pleasure in stating that question as loudly as possible whenever Aurora had to bring her children with her.

Once, just once, Aurora wanted to yell, "*Yes! Okay - I'm guilty - I admit it - I did it - I did the dirty deed - you can find the body parts in the deep freezer in my basement!*" and give a gruesome account of some wildly fabricated assault.

Aurora sighed.

Accountability

Her humor was becoming twisted and morbid, and dangerously close to hysteria.

***

At the next session Mr. Thera wrote on the white board in green, blue, and red markers:
"TAKING CONTROL plus **UNFAIR EXPECTATIONS** plus, **NOT TAKING WOMEN SERIOUSLY** equals **BATTERING."**

"Ladies," he started, "this is the '**Mathematics of Battering**.' Let's take it one step at -"

"Mr. Thera, can I ask you something," interrupted a small, timid-looking woman who'd never said a word in class before. "Do you ever have issues at home? I mean, you are so calm, and you seem so controlled. Have you ever had a problem with your wife or children? Do you *have* a wife and children?"

All the air slowly seeped out of her lungs as she exhaled, and she sank deep into her chair.

Mr. Thera grinned and placed a hand over his heart.

"Yes Ma'am, I do have a family and yes, we have conflicts now and again. I don't understand what it is that you want me to say?"

The little lady sat forward boldly.

"I want to know if you've ever lost control - if you've ever gotten so angry that you could hit someone - if *you* ever needed intervention - or needed help at some time - because you seem very intuitive about all this behavior."

The woman held her penetrating gaze on Mr. Thera.

"In my case, I was defending myself when I hit my husband. I was arrested, even though he's the actual abuser. I'd like to know if these sessions are the same for the men ? Do they have to confront what we're confronting? Would my husband, who really should be here instead of me, even identify what you're trying to teach us in this program?"

Aurora had also wondered, *Does the men's group see the same videotapes and witness the horrors of abuse to women and children? Do they hear the same radio dispatch where children are pleading on the phone to get someone to help them because Daddy is hurting Mommy? Do they have to admit to everyone in their group, and more importantly admit to themselves - that they're an abuser?*

"Thank you for these inquiries," said Mr. Thera as he walked to the front of the room. "This is a good time to explain the program thoroughly."

He nodded and said, "Yes, the men do go through the same outline as the women. We change the 'he' to 'she' when ever needed, but the main focus is to enlighten each party to the identifiable aspects of domestic violence, for its most effective prevention."

"Do you really think people can change?" asked a gal who had just started coming to the morning sessions.

"When pigs fly!" blurted out a woman in the front row before Mr. Thera could reply.

"Yes, I do believe that people can change," he said, ignoring the outburst, "if they get proper help."

He paused for emphasis, then said, "But, if a person is on drugs or alcohol, they are not themselves. They may seem normal in their behavior, because they are good at being a functional drunk or drug addict, but they are not a sober self. This sober self is the only person who can be helped to change. Until drug or alcohol issues are cleared up, issues of their violent behavior cannot be addressed."

"I'm sitting here, reading over this sheet you just handed out Mr. Thera, and it describes my husband to a T," said an older gal of about fifty or so.

"Where it says, **'Giving orders:'** my husband doesn't know how to do anything but give orders. 'I'm the head of the house,' he rants and raves, kind of like that loud-mouth Jackie Gleason on the Honeymooners."

That got a chuckle from the senior women who knew the actor and had seen the show.

"And here where it says, **'Being the boss:'** she continued, raising the sheet high in front of her face, "my husband even bellows, 'I'm the boss and don't you forget it'. If we disregard his orders, we have a terrible fight. It's not worth it, so we all just do as we're told."

"I know what you mean," said someone in the back row. "I just say, yeah, yeah, yeah and go about my own business."

The woman looked composed, but her hands were twitching in her lap.

Others murmured about similar situations, commiserating with each other for validation.

"And here where it states, **'Making decisions for the two of you without consulting the other person,'** continued the woman with the sheet in hand, (Mr. Thera sat down in a chair and let her take the floor.) "my husband would never consider asking me what I thought. He makes all the plans and that's it. I've never been consulted on anything, whatsoever."

"But wouldn't it be nice to have your own opinion heard?" Mr. Thera asked standing up.

"No one would be listening," said another woman quietly, her voice barely audible.

"But wouldn't you like to try?" he persisted as he walked the length of the room.

"Have you ever tried talking to a roaring tiger? Do you think a plea would be heard before the tiger attacks his prey?" asked the same woman who'd confronted Mr. Thera prior.

"About this statement," said a small, woman with a quiet demeanor, **'Being possessive, keeping track of where the other person is, whom they talk to and what they do:'** I have to admit that my husband is this way, but I've never questioned it before. I've always thought that he wants to know where I am because he cares, not because he's checking up on me."

"Are you serious, girl?" barked an angry-looking woman in the front row, turning to face the quiet woman head-on.

"Do you really think that if you told him you were going to a friend's house and then changed your mind, and went to the mall instead, and he found out, he wouldn't haul your ass out, drag you home, and kick the shit out of you?"

"Well, it's never gone to that extreme - as yet -" whispered the shy woman, a bit stunned.

"Well mine does that to me - and worse," declared the angry woman without self-pity.

Everyone stopped talking.

The class was silenced by her candor.

That raw bit of information physically shook the whole assembly.

Confessions were the worst.

No one seemed to know how to react when a woman revealed something private.

Hearing these truths be told was hard enough, but it was even more disheartening knowing that in all probability their situation wasn't going to change.

Mr. Thera, spoke gently, "Ladies, it's unfair expectations that get us into trouble with our partners -"

As he continued to talk about being realistic in the expectations we have of others, Aurora's mind wandered as she thought to herself, *Of course we have expectations –*
we expect our partners to love us and help us,
we expect our children to be respectful and learn,
we expect our friends and family to share our lives –
And they have expectations of us as well.
Why would any of those expectations be unfair?

***

Aurora thought about the angry woman who had revealed the state of her homelife and approached her after class.

"Pardon me, I don't mean to intrude Ma'am, but I thought that maybe, well, maybe I can help. I mean, I'm concerned, concerned for you. Could we - would you - like to sit down somewhere and talk?"

Accountability

The woman shrugged dropping her shoulders heavily.

"No thanks," she said with a quick huff and a smirk, "I don't need to talk to anyone. Especially someone I don't even know. So get off my case and stop meddling in affairs that don't concern you."

Then she turned on her heel and strutted away.

Aurora took a slow, deep breath, and let it go.

***

When the classroom was empty, Aurora approached the Counselor. "I was hoping to ask you a few theoretical questions, Mr. Thera," she said, trying to sound businesslike.

He waved her into his office as she was saying, "About the program. As I'm sure you've seen, I've been writing down what's being said in class each week. I'm forming an outline for a book about abuse, and I'd like to show it to you."

Aurora hung in the doorway, unable to enter and take a seat.

He didn't press her to come in, but sat down at his desk and cordially replied, "Why yes, Mrs. Sabel, I would be very interested in seeing what you've written. Let's make an appointment and we'll sit down and take a look, alright?"

Aurora thanked him and walked out of the building elated. Even though she wasn't able to help the first person she sincerely tried to assist, she could still be removed from the course as a participant, and continue to attend simply as an observer.

Aurora was trying hard not to be *in* the program; insisting she was only there to collect data and set up the framework for her book.

Chapter Twenty: Criticism and Manipulation

Writing an article for a column, is much easier than trying to compose a whole book. The inverted pyramid works well for impact, but it's hard to build volume if the subject matter isn't exhilarating, suspenseful, or scare-you-out-or-your-seat horrifying.

Although the sessions were gruesome, the stories compelling material, and documenting the program as a participant a good viewpoint, writing any variation of the program would be redundant. Possibly offensive. Maybe even plagiarism.

Aurora wanted to be earnest; she wanted the body of work to have a solemn appeal so that she would be *heard*. She was like a fanatical missionary who's forged deep into forbidden territory and come through the labyrinth of fearsome realities bursting with the energy of an Evangelist who seeks to enlighten; maybe even save other people's souls.

Aurora had no notion about saving her own soul; she didn't need help, she thought. She was fine.

***

Aurora sat at her desk fiddling with the small stack of notes she'd compiled to discuss with the instructor, trying to glean correlations between her past and present worth writing about.

Accountability

At eighteen, Aurora took a break after finishing high school, and ran off to Colorado; a beautiful place for a hiatus. Boulder, the unofficial headquarters of the Grateful Dead, was a laid-back place and Aurora saw right away, coming from the east coast, that the west coast was a different world.

The northeast was the stomping ground for a rat race of business dressed, sneaker shod, professional wannabe's rushing to make their careers. Whereas Colorado, was a slow and steady walk in the park.

"Hey dude, take it easy, let's just chill," was what the happy hippy-like people in faded jeans and tie-dyed shirts said as they put off the day's responsibilities until further notice.

New York City had been Aurora's neighbor, (an hour's drive from her home in Connecticut) having every kind of food, fashion, or freak imaginable.

Table Mesa, a suburb of Boulder, had the glorious snowcapped Flagstaff Mountain (viewed from her bay window). It was (and is) the home of Celestial Teas, the Mork and Mindy show, and it was like stepping back ten years. There was a feeling of being on holiday or returning to a time of innocence that was so inviting about the cozy little 3.2 beer selling college town. Life was simple man, *cool*.

Aurora had gotten a chance to work at the local paper there called, the Daily Camera. The newsroom smelled like stale coffee and charcoal cigarettes and bustled with opinionated, sometimes pompous writers who thought nothing of holding court and pontificating on any current hot topic.

It was exciting to hear Editors yell at journalists, "Is your copy done - it's got to be out and proofed by five - what? Well hop to it then - it's marked for tomorrow's edition!"

Aurora did a bit of layout and paste-up; merely a green horn, but she was enthusiastic and showed that she would do any menial job, if it taught her something about the business.

After pestering the editor for half a year for an assignment, she was given a tough subject to write about.

Seeing her name at the bottom of that article and getting recognition from some of the staff who had mentored her, had boosted her resolve to pursue becoming a writer.

***

It had been a boastful proclamation by Aurora's parents, that she would become a writer.

The choice she'd made the Christmas of 1972 when asked what she wished for, had been the cause.

Every trendy twelve-year-old girl wanted Farrah Faucet Hair, light blue eye shadow, or embroidered bell-bottoms.

Aurora wanted a typewriter.

Every modern twelve-year-old girl wanted David Cassidy's autograph, a Magic'8' Ball, or a Carpenters album.

Aurora wanted a thesaurus and dictionary to go with her typewriter.

Her parents beamed. They bragged to everyone within earshot, that their daughter would be a writer. Aurora was given elaborate writing tools, and she tried to be properly reverent about the forced vocation, although frankly, she couldn't fathom being a writer like her favorite author, Laura Ingalls Wilder. She was a bright-eyed kid who only wanted what the popular girls had: chunky metal braces and a pair of wire-rimmed glasses like John Lennon.

Her early years in rural Connecticut, had been a relatively happy time; a kind of Utopia.

Aurora's father had designed and built a modern house, nestled on an uncultivated two-acre parcel of land, in New Canaan. The neighboring lots were unoccupied at the dead-end circle, making rolling meadows with tall uncut grass fields an enchanting playground. The wonders of nature, were magical. The woods in the back of the house was a wild frontier. Aurora and her siblings acted out, 'Star Trek' and chipped shiny chunks of mica off a rock the size of a Winnebago, calling out, "We've got the lithium crystals Captain - beam us up Scottie!"

Accountability

They held tightly onto the thick braid of a rope swing that hung forty feet up from a huge Oak tree. They teased and called out, 'I-dare-you!' when they treaded over the fat trunk of a rotted tree that lay across a little winding stream. They scooped gooey green globs of jellied frog's eggs into a bucket of fresh water.

It was a marvelous, care-free time in Aurora's family's life.

For a while anyway.

Aurora's home-life, revolved around many forms of art.

As graduates of Carnegie Melon, her father was an accomplished artist and industrial designer, her mother was an artist and ballet teacher, and they both worked from home. The house was a busy place filled with her parent's projects. Huge sheets of plexiglass lined the walls in her father's workshop, ready to be cut by the vast table saw that let out a high-pitched scream when he created massive models for his work.

Theatre people came to discuss stage sets that he would design and build for plays like, 'Man of La Mancha' and children of various ages tromped downstairs to the ballet studio where her mother taught classes. The sound of flutes, French horns and violins could be heard upstairs when she choreographed 'Peter and The Wolf' for a recital.

Their parent's paintings showed in galleries, and hung on the spacious walls of their contemporary house.

When their children complained, 'I'm bored -' either of Aurora's parents would be given to say, "Okay then, let's do a project - what would you like to work with today?"

Aurora and her siblings were encouraged to use many art mediums. Various cameras were available and a dark room in her father's studio was ready for developing or they could paint on paper or canvas with water, oil, or acrylic paints, sew fabrics, glue scraps of plexiglass, mold clay, whittle wood or carve on linoleum blocks.

Aurora remembered carving a 3D sun with a smiling face. She'd used acrylics to make various colored prints.

She recalls how proud she was that her father hung them in his studio for some years.

Aurora's parents were excellent teachers. Individually they taught with creative energy and gave much in encouragement, but sadly, they were a disaster as companionable partners and never found an amiable way of cohabitating and parenting together.

Aurora's father grew up in a strict household, ruled by his strong, unyielding Italian father. Aurora never knew her paternal grandparents, but she'd heard enough to know that she would have feared her grandfather.

Aurora adored her maternal grandparents of Hungarian heritage; a different culture and religion all together, where loving attention was given in heavy doses. Aurora was happy when her grandparents visited, but when her family went to their little apartment in Woodmere, Long Island it was even better.

Stepping across the threshold of that cheery little place where her mother grew up, gave Aurora a warm feeling of belonging. Hanging out in the tiny kitchen, or sitting elbow to elbow straddling the legs on the gateleg table in the dining room, or laying on the bed her mother had slept in as a child, or looking through the photos in the family albums or sneaking into her grandparent's bedroom to poke through their stuff while the grownups sat in the elegantly furnished living room drinking coffee, made happy butterflies dance in Aurora's tummy.

The atmosphere was refreshing in that place, the air not so dense as in her own house. In comparison, her family life had an underlining, *chill*.

Although Aurora's parents were attentive, they never exhibited love or affection towards each other. She'd never seen them hold hands, kiss, joke or laugh together. They never seemed to work *together*. They didn't converse or communicate.

Aurora's mother was active and present, but her father was, most of the time, busy and unavailable.

Accountability

He seemed to be easily agitated; mostly concerned about deadlines and finishing monumental projects. He was a proud man. Benevolent when his rules were abided. Tyrannical when they were not.

Their family lived in the same house; a wonderful house, but it had never felt like a home.

***

Their divorce had been a long, bitter battle that left everyone groundless; like falling down an elevator shaft and never hitting bottom.

As was the way they conducted themselves, her parents didn't gather the children together to explain anything about them splitting up.

Aurora's father just loaded his car one morning, making ready to leave as the sun was rising. He was going to walk out without a word, but then he turned and saw his barefoot little girl standing on the front deck in her white cotton night gown; her arms crossed with a questioning look on her face.

"Where are you going?" Aurora recalls asking her father; the man she idolized and adored.

Aurora's father had looked around the yard and then way off into the distance. After nodding slowly he pointed at the painting of Icarus that hung in the entrance of his house; the house that he so painstakingly designed and built by himself, and said, "I want you to have Icarus, Sweetheart. Watch over it. Keep it safe for me okay?"

***

'Time heals all wounds.' Quoted by someone who'd obviously never been through divorce.

Aurora's version: 'No time heals a variable pain completely.'

***

It took a long time for Aurora to come to terms with the sorrow of her family breaking up. She'd put out of her mind, the disharmony that had been in their everyday lives.

As the weeks went by and the content of the sessions jarred her memory, she realized that Power and Control issues had been abundant in her home, and her father had held all the power.

She closed her eyes and could vividly see his disgruntled face, that frown of disdain when he criticized, corrected, or gave a command and would say, "There is God. And there is me. And if you don't do it my way, you're doing it wrong."

Aurora frowned herself, remembering how they were all cowed by him and had to obey. She found herself recalling many times when her father had reprimanded her mother for the way she did things but hadn't given her credit when she had done something well. It pained her to remember the dread and anxiety they all had of him.

As a teacher, Aurora's father was conscientious, indulgent, and encouraging. He was contemplative and thoughtful, always offering valuable advice on how to create even the most childish of endeavors. But as a parent, he was condescending and often a potentially foreboding figure.

Ah, and she'd forgotten about the stick.

Aurora was baffled that through the earlier discourse about the rule of thumb, it hadn't dawned on her about the stick.

A force to be reckoned with in discipling his children, her father would say, "I'm going to count to three and if you're not doing what I've asked you to do by then, I'm going to get 'The Stick' and you'll know that I mean business."

He never once hit them with the long narrow stick that was sanded and stained and polished to a high glossy sheen. It was stored prominently in front of the silverware; when the wide drawer opened and slowly slid on the rollers it was set on, the sound of the low metal squeal sounded the call.

That alone was enough to send Aurora and her brother and sister dashing down the hallway to hide in their rooms.

Most of the time, he only had to threaten to get the stick, to put them all into a fright.

Being under a dictatorship within which they'd lived, had not, at that time, been subject to question.

There was no other role model to compare it with.

Aurora assumed that every father was strict. Fathers had to be strict and commanding to teach their children well.

***

Aurora was a bit overwhelmed by all those memories. What she had been learning in the sessions opened up doors that she'd closed a long time ago. Now though, she could see connections with those same issues from her own history.

***

"Few of us can give or take criticism well in any context," said Mr. Thera, standing in front of the class at the twenty-first meeting. "Criticism from loved ones, though, can be constructive. Since they know you best, loved ones are able to offer helpful hints for change and growth. Of course, how helpful the criticism is, depends on how that person delivers it."

"I know what you're trying to say, Lancel," said a woman in the middle row, "but when my husband tells me what I'm doing wrong, he doesn't say it in a constructive way, he yells at me! You're barking up the wrong tree if you think *that* will change."

"Criticism doesn't have to be a source of friction, Mary, when both partners are striving to learn, refine or improve upon their relationship and themselves. It's a good tool to achieve such goals, it just needs the proper presentation to be effective."

He waited with papers in hand.

"That's a fairy tale, Lancel," said a woman in the back. "Do you really believe that crap?"

"I think you're being unfair," said a small young woman fidgeting in her seat beside Aurora. "He's just trying to explain that we can change things, or help our partners to change, if we talk things out and make suggestions. Am I right, Lancel?"

"Ladies," he said, as he handed out the next packet, "let's take a look at this."

The top sheet said:

To deliver or receive constructive criticism. Determine the motive for the criticism.

"Are you angry about other things and using this argument as a smoke screen?

"Are you disappointed in yourself and projecting it onto your partner?

"Do you try to manipulate other people to feel better or advance your own means?"

Before Mr. Thera could expound on his opening statement, a woman turned towards the class and blurted out, "My husband should read this! Even though he wouldn't get it, he sure has these issues. He always starts an argument when he wants to get out of the house. He makes a big stink, criticizing me and the kids about *nothing*, so he can storm out and stew at a bar.

I know he's disappointed he can't find work, but it sucks that we've got to go through this *hell* every time his frustration gets the better of him."

"My old man does the same thing," another woman said. "He'll say something just to start an argument, and when I rise to the bait he'll say, 'See, you can't get along with anybody,' and then he makes a big scene insulting me and hightails it out of the house!"

Aurora sat listening intently and suddenly she remembered a stint like that with William.

Accountability

After her second miscarriage, Aurora sank into a deep depression.

Although William tried to get her to snap out of it and join the living world, Aurora's spirit had died on the operating table when they cut out the ectopic pregnancy in her fallopian tube and severed all her hopes.

Her grief was too much for Aurora, and the despair that William had, losing not only his chance at fatherhood, but his now estranged wife as well, left them both feeling there was no other option but to separate.

Aurora moved to the second floor of a friend's country cottage upstate and William took the couch at his sister's place nearby.

They spoke but once a week, during William's Sunday shift at work, and Aurora began hormone therapy to correct the Endometriosis that was causing the miscarriages.

Six months into their separation and at the final phase of her treatments, Aurora called William (on a Tuesday).

"Hi Lovey -"

"Aurora?" William had questioned, "What's up? Are you okay? Why are you calling me during the week - are you sick? I can catch a train within an hour -"

"No honey, everything's good," she'd said sweetly.

"Better than good actually. I just had my last shot, and even though the doctor told me I should have three normal cycles before we try - I'll be ready - my *body* will be ready to make a baby in six weeks!"

William had hesitated, but only for a moment and said, "Okay then - let's do it!"

They hadn't seen each other in six months.

They hadn't touched each other in almost a year.

Their rendezvous was at Aurora's mother's house; she had been asked to house-sit while her folks were out of town.

That weekend they had sex in every room, on every surface, for three solid days.

Joyfully a baby was conceived; and William moved into the cottage with Aurora.

William's sister's friend was having a party.

Aurora didn't want to go because it would be rowdy, and she needed to be quiet and rest. She was into her second trimester; the longest she'd been with child, so her prayers and her primary objective was to be positive, stay healthy, and let nature run its course.

Aurora had asked William to stay home with her, but he'd wanted to get out of the house saying he felt cooped up. They'd quarreled, and he'd said snidely, "It's just a small group of people having a little party Aurora, it's not likely that you'd contract a life-threatening disease from anyone."

The argument had escalated to a point where William, in a huff, had stomped out of the house.

And he didn't come home that night.

***

Aurora grabbed a tissue from her purse and dabbed her eyes as she remembered waking up at three in the morning to the sound of wheels crunching on the dirt driveway. She'd gone to the living room window that was above the front porch and saw a woman's face behind the steering wheel of the car that's lights were illuminating the path to the house. She'd heard Willian trying to get his key into the lock, jiggling the door.

A tear fell down her face as she remembered the silence, then William turning and walking slowly, getting back into the car. Aurora remembers the headlights diminishing as the car drove away.

***

Not knowing how to deal with it or where to turn, Aurora had called her in-laws in California. They were vocally sympathetic, but reserved about being critical of their son.

Aurora sighed recalling how violently she'd retched in the toilet; how hard she'd cried; how exasperated she'd been.

Accountability

At eight o'clock that morning she'd called her sister-in-law to see if she knew where William could be.

"He's not here Aurora," she'd said with a long drawn-out yawn. "My brother does what he wants; you know that. It's none of my business."

Aurora remembers disengaging the phone feeling deeply wounded by her cold, dispassionate indifference.

***

William had trundled up the rickety stairs at about two o'clock that afternoon. He'd walked past Aurora sitting at the freckled Formica dinette table, took a shower, and went to bed.

That evening, he'd found her resting on the couch rubbing her stomach.

"Aurora, I just -" he'd started to say.

But Aurora held up her hand.

"I don't want to know where you've been," she'd said shaking her head with great sadness. "I don't want to know what you've done. I just want you to take me to the doctor tomorrow, so you'll see what you've lost."

William had slept on the couch that night.

They'd woken without a greeting and went through their morning rituals of showering and dressing morosely.

They'd had a silent breakfast and gotten into the car without a single word said.

They'd taken seats in the overcrowded waiting room; finding separate chairs at opposite ends of the room.

Aurora winced recalling how betrayed, lost and alone she'd felt.

Looking back at that horrible escapade, Aurora saw clearly how William had manipulated the situation and built up a 'fight' so that he could leave.

The worst of it was that his initial actions, had paved the way to more disreputable actions, which had led to a complete fall out.

Their marriage had almost crumbled from that incident.

***

As fate would have it, the prenatal visit had an indelible effect on William.

It put him in a state of awe.

The image on the screen, that thumping truth, that pounding heartbeat, pierced through his and it was as if the sea had parted, that William saw and embraced the miracle.

Aurora shifted her weight on the seat.

She remembered how she'd insisted that William go to confession before she would consider remaining with him.

He'd gone to see a well-seasoned priest, and they'd talked for a long time.

William had been full of repentance, consigned to be a better man for the sake of his unborn child.

His infidelity was never mentioned again.

It seemed so long ago, that devastating episode, but Aurora would never forget what she'd said to William the day their child was born.

In the hospital room while William stood mesmerized by the precious baby in his arms, Aurora had nestled under the covers and studied him.

Quietly she'd called out, "William -"

"Yes?" he'd said absently, his eyes glued to his beautiful son.

"If you ever cheat -" she'd inhaled deeply, "or dishonor - or take for granted what God, in his mercy has given us, I'll take that priceless treasure and vanish - you'll never see us again."

She'd wiped away the tears and let the air out of her lungs slowly. "Do you hear me?"

Without looking up, William had nodded solemnly and said, "Yes Aurora, I hear you."

***

Accountability

Aurora thought, while the session droned on, about how she interacted with William.

She knew that he could be controlling, even if it was camouflaged in a kind way.

He did what he wanted, whenever he wanted, and as long as Aurora didn't cross his line, or get in his way, everything functioned for them.

William had given her an amiable speech at the beginning of their relationship.

"Do what makes you happy Baby, and let me do the same," he'd said grinning. He'd acted like it was a joke, but it hadn't been a joke.

"If you don't get in my face and try to run my life, everything will be fine, but if you try to control me, you won't like it."

Aurora was a strong-minded person, who didn't hesitate to say what was on her mind.

For that reason, there was conflict as much as unity, between her and William.

Their individually powerful personalities were often unwilling to yield to the other's demands.

***

Mr. Thera drew their attention back to the sheet, reading:

"Determine any difficulties you may have in hearing criticism from your partner.

"What are your past childhood patterns? Perfection is a common one.

"Are you so concerned about pleasing others that you become hard on yourself?

"For example, your partner says, 'Why did you do that?' but you hear, 'You're a bad person, a total failure and I may not want you.'

"You can blow a little criticism way out of proportion without intention."

"Mr. Thera," asked a young woman leaning forward to get in his face, "how can I ask my boyfriend to treat me differently, or talk to me differently, when he does it all the time. He thinks it's cool. His friends treat their girlfriends the same way. I've even seen his dad treat his mom like shit too."

"Suzi, you can get your point across, if you choose the right way to go about it. On the next page you'll see:
"DOS and DON'TS on CRITICISM.
"Let's look at that."

They all shuffled the papers to get to the same page as Mr. Thera read:

"Pick an appropriate time when your partner is receptive, relaxed, and -"

"Oh, man!" howled a lady in the back. "That's right - find an appropriate time - but when? He's never home!"

Another woman chimed in.

"When he's receptive? Oh, yeah, that'd be when he's sleeping - ha - and relaxed? He's only relaxed when he's stoned drunk - You've gotta to be kidding me. This ain't never gonna happen in my house!"

Mr. Thera, raised his voice overriding the caustic dialog and continued to read aloud:

"Be specific about the exact behavior.
"Talk about one thing.
"Focus on the behavior, not the personality."

"Do you mean to say," said a cynical sounding woman, "that if we try to be specific, our husbands will respond, change their personality and our lives will be great? You serious?"

Many women snorted, sniggered, and nodded their heads, but they listened further.

Aurora sat silently thinking, *Yes - it's possible.*

Accountability

She wanted to say, *I do it with William a lot. He'll sting me with a comment, then I'll retreat - angry. But I'll go to him later and let him know what that comment did to me. He'll listen, and although he doesn't say he's sorry - he'll know why it hurt me.*

But she didn't say that. She just scribbled in her journal.

Aurora sensed that the group was getting riled up, but Mr. Thera remained composed. He ignored their animosity and continued reading the words clearly, waving a hand in the air.

"When you criticize someone, try to mention the positive things you know about them also."

He paused long enough to let the words sink in.

"Understand why you feel the way you do. Invite an explanation. Stay in control. Don't be overly emotional."

"Overly emotional!" yelled a woman from the right side. "If I whisper, he yells. If I plead with him to calm down, he goes into a rage. If I try to be kind and understanding, he thinks I want something. I can't win."

"Yes, you can," Mr. Thera soothed. "You have to stay in control. No matter what. You have to walk away from a situation if it is becoming volatile. You can readdress the issue at a later time. Try it, it will work."

He walked towards the front of the room, looked at the women, and read on.

"Separate facts from feelings - don't stretch facts to support your view. Know when to stop. Don't beat a dead horse or nag."

Right after he said the last word, a slender woman in about her fifties said quietly, "I'm always being called a nag. If I make one small comment or bring up a sensitive subject, I get labeled 'nag' every time."

Aurora shrugged her shoulders and sighed.

Suddenly she remembered a book she'd read and thought, *You have to pick the right time to talk to your man. You have to know when he goes into his cave. You have to give him time to accept new ideas. Didn't anyone read 'Men are from Mars; Women are from Venus'?*

She considered saying that to the group, but she didn't have the courage.

Some women got up to refresh their coffee cups, some just sat in their seats and waited, lacking a response.

Mr. Thera said, "Let's try to get through this, shall we?" and continued to read:

"Offer forgiveness and offer options for how you would like to be treated."

"You know Lancel, these words sure are pretty on this paper. It would be a wonderful world if this could happen. But the reality is, this isn't possible. Men will always control women, and women will always have to bear the brunt of it. That's just the way it is."

"I think you're wrong," Aurora blurted out before she could stop herself. "It may not be possible for the whole world to change, but your world can, just because you make it change." Aurora was trembling, but she also felt that she had to speak up.

"What do you mean?" the woman next to her asked.

"I mean that every day we have a choice," Aurora began passionately. "I read somewhere that life is ten percent what happens to us and ninety percent how we react to it. Our attitude can make or break any situation. Our attitude can change our world. If something is not right, it's how we react to it that can keep us there or motivate us to move on."

Just when Aurora thought she could resume being a wallflower, another woman turned to her and accused, "What are you doing there anyway - writing in that notebook?"

Aurora thought they all knew what she was doing.

Her face flushed; she was embarrassed.

Everyone turned towards her.

The shield of a literal reason for being there suddenly fell away, and she was exposed.

Completely naked.

"I'm writing things down so that I have a better understanding of the program," Aurora said flatly, hoping that none would inquire further.

"But I thought you said that you were writing a book for women?" said a woman that Aurora had interviewed a few times.

"You're writing a book about us - for people to read?" asked another woman that Aurora hadn't seen before. "Are you going to write about what we discuss here? What we say confidentially in this place? You're writing about our lives?"

"Well -" Aurora started to say when Mr. Thera interrupted.

"Now ladies," he said in a calming voice, "Mrs. Sabel is here to go through the program herself, to participate with us, and learn what she can for her own benefit."

Aurora wasn't fooling anyone.

She had issues, just like them.

She thought, *I can't just sit on the sidelines - I have to participate like the rest of them.*

"I'm sorry," she said feebly.

"But no one asked me if I wanted to be in a book!" said the insulted woman. "I don't want my life broadcasted! Who said you could come here and assume we would all agree to that?"

"I didn't assume anything," Aurora tried to say. "I just wanted to get different perspectives, so I've interviewed a few women over the last couple of weeks. That's all I've done so far -"

"But you didn't ask us!" she interrupted. "You can't do this to people. We're entitled to our privacy! You can write whatever you want, say anything about us and we wouldn't be able to do a thing about it."

"But I won't do that," Aurora stated quietly. "I'm just jotting things down for background information."

"Ladies," Mr. Thera interjected, "let's get back to the worksheet. No one's privacy is being breached. Mrs. Sabel is here to do the program, just like everyone else. Her taking notes and talking with others just may help other women in similar situations in some significant way."

The woman grumbled but let it drop. The rest of the group seemed to be undecided, eyeing Aurora with sideways glances.

Mr. Thera pressed on. "Now, getting back to the next part. Let's review these suggestions:"

"In a situation where there is a conflict of interest, don't generalize by saying: 'You never' or 'You always .'

"Don't personalize by calling someone names or saying: 'You're a bad person'.

"Don't make things worse by saying: 'You'll always do this' or 'You'll never change.'

"Don't blame.

"Instead, take responsibility for yourself by saying to your partner: 'I get upset when you' -"

The session went forward although the suggestions for staying in control and trying to communicate with one's partner seemed to be the most frustrating, and most unattainable exercises in the program so far.

"You know, this is all a bunch of shit," stated a woman without scorn.

"I wish I could do like it says on here on the sheet:

"Don't call names or swear, don't allude to a family member by saying something like, 'you're just like your mother' but I'd be the only one making the effort," she said, with a sigh. "I've tried to watch what I say to my husband, but he still hammers me. He's just that way. You can talk until you're blue in the face, Lancel, but it won't change my life."

Accountability

Round and round it went. The whirlpool of disheartened souls turned and churned. They were so caught up in their own turmoil, they'd forgotten all about Aurora and her intrusion into their lives. Every woman had a negative response. Every woman was tired of trying to better a situation that was evidently without hope, because every woman seemed to feel trapped.

What Mr. Thera was trying to get across to the group, would have been valuable tools for people who were in full cooperation with their significant other, and had a mutual intention of bettering their lives, together. But these women lived with partners who proved to have no intention of doing things differently. These women were convinced that their lives would never change.

It seemed like they felt condemned with weary resignation to remain in an impossible situation.

***

To Aurora, the fundamental dynamics of her relationship with William differed from the women in the group because they *did* communicate. Not always with sparkling clarity or decisive definitions or positive results, but they *tried*.

Aurora could see parallels between the issues they discussed in class and her home life. She realized she didn't merely empathize; she could actually relate.

Still, she had to admit that nothing she wrote, even with her naive, 'The sun will come out tomorrow' overtures, would make a significant difference.

No sharp, persuasive argument or positive intervention would ever be enough to affect these discouraged women.

Chapter Twenty-One: Open Negotiation

"Mr. Thera?"

The door to the counseling center pushed open easily after Aurora knocked, but received no reply, and gently leaned on the handle. "Hello - is anyone here?"

The front room and adjoining reception area smelled like freshly brewed coffee, but the receptionist wasn't at her desk, and the ringing telephone wasn't being answered.

Aurora had planned to meet Mr. Thera in his office the following day.

The previous session had been so depressing, that she had all but abandoned the idea of writing the book, but after reworking the outline she had for him to critique, her optimism had been rekindled.

She'd arrived a few minutes earlier than scheduled, and seeing that no one was around, went into his little office and sat down on a chic upholstered chair.

She absently traced a shape on the swirling pattern and evaluated the area.

The design of the room looked like it had been well thought out. The plush deep green carpet looked new. The low coffee table and chairs looked inviting. Soothing colors of pastel landscapes hung on the walls, presumably to take one's mind off their troubles.

At least for the duration of a confidential meeting with Mr. Thera at any rate.

And why not, Aurora thought. *He's a sincere, thoughtful man.*

Aurora had seen from the first session, how confident and self-assured he was of where he wanted to take the group through his lectures.

He was a man of strong convictions who conveyed them quite effectively utilizing his quiet demeanor.

***

"Thank you, Mrs. Daily, I couldn't have gotten all that stuff to the trash without your help," said Mr. Thera to the rotund, middle-aged female aid before walking into his office.

"Ah, hello, you're here already."

He was welcoming as he sat down next to Aroura.

"How are you today, Mrs. Sabel?" he asked kindly.

"I'm fine, thank you, Mr. Thera," Aurora answered automatically, her tone a bit stiff.

They smiled at each other, both vacilating; the silence in the room afloat like a hot air balloon hovering, suspended; each waiting for the other to initiate the conversation.

"So, what would you like to talk about today?" he finally asked.

"Talk about?" she questioned. "Oh, I'm not here to *talk* to you - I don't have anything to *discuss* - I just wanted to show you my outline - for the book idea - remember?"

Aurora inhaled deeply, and waited.

When he didn't respond, his eyebrows raised as if he wasn't sure what she was talking about, she continued.

"I feel very strongly, that by telling my story, and infusing your program's guidelines, I can empower women. Help them. Maybe change some people's lives."

He nodded and asked, "And what have *you* gotten out of the program so far, Mrs. Sabel?"

Aurora looked at him taken aback; the question was too complex to make a quick reply.

Flash backs of the classes, the women's outbursts, the intrusive memories of her past - all raced through her head. *What have I gotten out of the program so far?* she thought. *What do I think of the program, really? Well, I've done twenty-one weeks - I have five more to go. I have five more payments of twenty dollars and one more payment of forty-five dollars and I'm done.*

Those were the first things she thought, but she didn't say any of that.

She wanted to say, I *can't wait to be done with all of this and get on with my life* - but instead she said, "Oh, I think the program is great, it's -"

"Yes, yes," he said as he waved a hand openly, "but what has developed or changed for *you* so far?"

Aurora's head filled with plausible answers.

She wanted to sound authentic; to reveal nothing, but still be honest.

"Mr. Thera, I have to say, that is, I believe that although the sessions have been quite informative, all I've gotten from this whole ordeal is that I realize, without a doubt, and know in my heart, that I don't belong in this program at all."

There, Aurora said it.

The weight had been lifted; the curtain unveiled; there was nothing left to hide.

She watched his face go from an inquisitive expression, to a broad smile.

Clearly, he was mocking her.

Obviously, she had said something of which he found quite amusing.

"Well, that's fair if that's what you believe, I guess, but surely it's not the whole picture," he said calmly.

Feeling incited by his silent reproach to defend her statement, she said, "Okay, first of all, this program is for abusers."

She sat up straighter in the chair squaring her shoulders, and said resolutely, "For your information, and public record, I'm not in that category."

Accountability

The room seemed to be shrinking.

His seat seemed closer to hers than a few minutes before, so she sat back a little and said, "Second, most of the group are struggling with drug addiction and alcohol abuse. I do not drink, nor do I do drugs, so I'm not in that category either."

Aurora inhaled, getting ready to conclude her speech.

"Finally, it's for women who need an alternative, a strategy to survive in their dysfunctional lives and their toxic marriages with their abusive husbands, and I don't fit into any of those categories either. So, as I tried to tell you before, I don't believe this program pertains in any way, to me or my circumstances, at all."

"I can understand how you might feel that way," was his nonjudgmental rebuttal.

Aurora looked intently at Mr. Thera.

He calmly held her gaze, breathing in and out slowly.

Further conversation seemed redundant.

Aurora could hear the clock on his desk tick in the stillness of the room.

After a while Mr. Thera nodded and got up to open the door.

Aurora felt that she had no choice but to get up and follow him.

In the doorway, his eyes crinkled as he smiled and said, "Let's meet again in two weeks' time. And see."

Before Aurora could respond, he gently ushered her out the door.

***

For six days, Aurora thought about her talk with Mr. Thera.

***

"Good morning ladies," said Mr. Thera in a cordial greeting to the class the following week.

"Today we're going to do a worksheet that requires you to form two groups. Let's do this in the back of the room. The questions are addressed to men, I use them in their group, but I'd like to do the exercise with you, so if you'd just change it to 'he' where it states 'she', we can get started."

The women split up and, in a few minutes, apprehensive faces were waiting for instruction.

Mr. Thera walked to the center of the room and addressed the groups.

"Please go through and review each question with your group before choosing the box you want to check. You are not being evaluated on any of this, so be honest and it just may reveal a few things.

Please read the whole sheet first for a general overview, then you can discuss your answers."

The sheet said:

WHAT IS OPEN TO NEGOTIATION:

The instructions were to mark a box of either:
Open To Both Sides
Not Open Partner Decides
Not Open You Decide

Mr. Thera spoke to the groups offering the top page's introduction.

"An issue is open to negotiation if it is not entirely one person's right to decide.
"It's open to discussion, but not negotiation, if it is only one person's right to decide."

He waited for a response.

"Oh, this is going to be a hoot," one woman said, her eyes alight with mischief.

The class read every entry on the sheet, changing the, he's to she's, where applicable.

Accountability

Which friends can he/she spend time with?
Which friends can you spend time with?
Who cooks / cleans on weekdays?
Who cooks / cleans on weekends?
Who finds a sitter?
Who pays the sitter?
Will he/she drink or use drugs again?
Will you drink or use drugs again?
Will he/she get a job or change jobs?
Will you get a job or change jobs?
How will the children be disciplined?
When will the children be disciplined?
Can he/she go on a trip without you?
Can you go on a trip without him/her?

Laughter filled the overcrowded room, as the women went down the list. They had a good time, just good fun, poking at their lives.

"Oh, this one's good," said the woman to Aurora's right. "Who cooks and cleans on weekdays - yeah, right - who *else* cooks and cleans on weekdays, weekends, holidays, my own birthday -"

"No this one's better," cackled another woman grinning with good humor. "Who finds a sitter? Who goes out? If we ever go anywhere it's to the park or the pool hall and the kids come with -"

They skipped over the one that read: Will he/she drink or do drugs again. There was no comment from either group.

"Oh, I love this one," giggled another gal waving the paper above her head. "Will he get a job? I ask him that every day!"

"Wait ! How will the children be disciplined and when - is *mine* girls," bellowed an older woman whose broad smile pronounced the spidery laugh lines at her temples. "Which children are they referring to, is what I want to know, because I have two in their teens and one oversized child to discipline, every day!"

They united in boisterous laughter at the line that asked, "Can you go on a trip without him?"

The joint response of both groups cackling loudly was, "Oh yes! Absolutely! In a heartbeat!"

It's a powerful thing, women united, Aurora thought, and wrote in her notebook as she watched the groups play around.

These women weren't as desolate as she'd thought they were. Their situations were not terminal. They could find a way out of their private prisons, if only for a while, through the combined effort of joined acceptance. They were intelligent, caring, humor and hope-filled individuals who deserved to be treated with a lot more respect.

Aurora had to admit that she admired them in the way that they could look and laugh at themselves. She knew that they weren't so blind as to believe in miracles, but maybe, just maybe, it was possible for them all (including Aurora) to come to terms with the notion that they had the right to turn difficult situations into possibilities, within *their* control.

Thinking about the questions on the sheet, Aurora thought, *Every day I have to negotiate.*

Aurora sat still, privately confronted by the fact that she argues her point of view with William all the time. She wants her way, and he wants his. She wants things done a certain way and he has other ideas.

Aurora thought, *We may go about reaching a compromise differently because we don't hit each other, but there's still the same struggle for power. I know I like being in control. I always think my way's the best way, so I don't negotiate well.*

Negotiation is an essential part of any partnership, but not many people are good at it.

Humor aside, the group was beginning to get the picture, that how one negotiates, makes a difference in coexisting with one's partner.

Although she hadn't been able to admit it, Aurora realized that she needed to take stock of things. She needed to reevaluate - herself.

Part Three: Acceptance

Laura Strobel

Chapter Twenty-two: Accountability

Accountability: *noun (Merriam-Webster Dictionary)*
The definition of accountability is taking or being assigned responsibility for something that you have done or something you are going to do.

Accountability: *noun (Cambridge Dictionary)*
The fact of being responsible for what you do or say and being able to give a satisfactory reason for it.

Accountability: *noun (Collins English Dictionary)*
The state of being accountable, liable, or answerable: an obligation or willingness to accept responsibility or to account for one's actions.

***

Being married should have been like floating on a cloud, every single woman's dream of security and stability.

Living in Europe should have been the adventure of a lifetime.

Having sex with a handsome, ardent lover morning, noon, and night (often more) should have been like a steamy, romance novel.

One would have thought.

The seventy-five-minute, high mass at the Catholic church in Wilton, Connecticut was, although a little lengthy, beautiful. Peach colored roses, wisps of greenery and baby's breath adorned each end of the pews.

The organ sounded majestic.

The one hundred and twenty well-wishers standing as the bride and her father moved gracefully down the center aisle, probably all had tears in their eyes as Mendelssohn's 'Wedding March' played on.

My father squeezed my hand; the hand that he'd held when I was a child. The hand that he hadn't held in over fifteen years, and said leaning in ever so slightly, his minty breath seeping through my veil, "Sweetheart, if you're not sure about this - you don't have to -"

I saw William at the alter in his dove grey morning suit grinning. The four bridesmaids nodding with toothy smiles in their dark green taffeta tea length dresses and pearls. The four bridegrooms not looking at me, standing stoically erect, joking, and chuckling through the sides of their mouths. My beloved grandmother waving to me in her standard wedding attire, (She wears the same dress to every wedding; the guests in the photos decipher who's event it was.) standing next to my impeccably dressed mother dabbing her eyes with a tissue.

As we approached the front of the church I saw William's grandmother turn, bow, and tip her hat to me.

My steady hand tightened around my father's clasp. Without reservation I replied, "Yes daddy, I'm sure."

***

For overseas assignments, the military provides HOLA (housing allowance) and COLA (cost of living allowance) and issues a quantity of American made housewares like, beds and lamps, couches and chairs, refrigerators, stoves and washing machines, according to the soldiers marital status, and if family members have accompanied them.

Accountability

William, as a single soldier, was issued a small dining table, one chair, a five-foot-long olive-green couch, a small cubical chair to match, a coffee table, a stove, a washing machine and dryer, a refrigerator, one bedside table, one lamp and a narrow single bed.

We slept in that bed, after I'd joined him on his second tour in Germany; body and limbs entwined every night, for about eight months.

A single soldier has to obtain written approval from the company commander to marry. William had put in for this request without my knowledge, so when he came home the night he got his orders, sat on our bed, and whispered, "Wake up little girl, you're getting married -"

I thought he was joking.

I was pretty angry when I sat up, pushed him away, and said, "That's mean William - waking me in the middle of the night to tease me - why would you think that'd be funny?"

William had chuckled. He'd hugged me and said, "No really Aurora, I mean it - it's no joke - I got my permission statement today - we can get married."

I'd scrutinized William with knitted brows, searching for any sign of deceit, any sign of dishonesty and found only a candid expectant grin. Becoming giddy, I'd said, "Well if that's the case mister, then you'd better do this the right way - go on - get down on one knee and ask me properly - then you'll have to call my father."

William had laughed, gave me a peck on the cheek, slid off the bed and rearranged himself in a kneeling position.

His expression became serious, his hazel eyes shining as he took my hand and asked, "Aurora, my love, will you marry me and be the mother of my children?"

I happily answered, "Yes-yes-yes!" hugging his thick neck, kissing him all over his face.

Then William made the call.

I imagined that my father was standing at the easel in his studio with paint brush in hand, scrutinizing his current endeavor.

I pictured his face coming out of the trance when the phone rang.

I was sure that he'd been a little annoyed wondering who'd be calling at nine o'clock in the evening (it was three am for us) when he took the call.

I silently tugged on William's arm urging him to let me listen and as he held the phone between us, I heard my father clearly say, in a fairly irritated tone, "Hello?"

William greeted him warmly, made a few pleasantries and conveyed the point of his call.

My father was commanding.

"Alright William, you've proved to be an admirable guy. You have my blessing. Now I'm holding you accountable."

***

The Deutsche Mark currency exchange in American Dollars in 1988 was about two to one. US soldiers overseas were picking up Mercedes, BMW, Audi, Porsche, and Volkswagen vehicles by the tons. Buying anything on the economy was like playing with funny money. Converting the cost felt almost like stealing, getting items for about half the price in dollars.

The USO offered vacation packages for very little money, to travel by bus to see Europe. These special deals were for military personnel, their spouses, and immediate families. They included your hotel, breakfast, lunch and dinner, sightseeing tours, and leisure hours to shop, relax and do as you pleased. Some of the tours were for a three-day weekend, some of them were for a week. All of them offered interpreters to guide your group throughout the trip.

I had been very interested in traveling through Germany and into neighboring countries this way. It seemed like a safe, no-hassle way to sit back and let someone else get us to where we wanted to go. We needn't be burdened with mapping out routes, obtaining border passes or stopping for gas, but William would have none of it.

Accountability

He'd said, "Man, Aurora, I work with Americans all day, why would I want to go on vacation and spend my free time with them?"

We did take quick trips to go skiing with some of the guys from his site. That was fun. We also checked out castles and meandered through medieval towns nearby; and that was fun too. But we never took a *real* vacation because William didn't want to be penned in. He wanted the freedom to do as he chose, spontaneously.

"Let's just go-with-the-flow -" is what he said all the time.

***

But I was married now. I wanted to plan - *everything*.

***

At the age of twenty-eight, I was ready to make a happy home. Since my parents split up, I'd craved for, and clung to, the dream of getting married and having children of my own. I was committed to doing a better job than they had. I thought that I could make everything perfect, but I didn't have a handy book of insights as to how the dynamics of a marriage functioned.

The fairy tale was that I had my prince, but the reality was, I wasn't sure how to handle him.

We got along well on a daily basis, William, and I, both being genuinely positive people. Every day was a good day.

Lust was a major factor in our bond. Lust and good humor. We laughed a lot and played house with a passion. We had no financial burdens. We were young and free.

Sometimes though, tension underlined our bliss.

I was a woman whose maternal instincts had kicked into high gear. I was ready to nest.

William at twenty-five, was still quite headstrong.

He didn't abide borders or boundaries outside of his military obligations.

When he'd asked me to marry him, and be the mother of his children, William hadn't meant the children we'd have someday, he'd meant the children we would make right away.

But that didn't happen.

What started out as a sex filled, easygoing relationship with all the joy of simple love, became, over the next three years, constrained by the effort to attain our goal.

I was diligent monitoring my cycle, jotting down my temperature readings to notate the optimal time to conceive, but it didn't assist much to facilitate our cause.

Oh, we had sex as often as we'd always had and mostly during those hot-blooded passionate embraces, we didn't think about trying to make a baby.

But still, the reality of failure every month when I had to tell William that I wasn't pregnant, sucked.

***

Most people seem to be more balanced after they marry, and the commitment issue is over.

Some people though, like William, continue to waver. Because our marriage hadn't advanced in the direction we'd both hoped it would go, William began to question whether we should stay together.

One day he declared, out of the blue, that he didn't want to be married anymore.

"It's not you," he'd said sighing with genuine remorse. "It's that I just can't do this anymore. I love you, but I can't breathe. I don't want to hurt you, but I can't play this game anymore."

It was quite a shock.

"Can't play what game?" I'd asked, incredulously. "Is this just a game to you? I thought we were *happy*. How can you say that you don't want to do this anymore when we've been trying to have a family?"

I couldn't accept failure or the fact that he wanted out.

"I know," he'd said quietly. "I can't explain it. I just can't do it anymore. I'm sorry."

And then he'd left. Walked out the door.

He left me standing there weeping like a despondent child who'd been recklessly abandoned and left out in the cold to fend for herself.

When it happened that first time, I'd pleaded and cried, "Please, William, don't do this! We have to stick it out - I'm sure that everything will be better when I get pregnant."

He'd sighed heavily then and said, no he couldn't stick it out and no it wouldn't get better.

Days passed with him sleeping in the guest room, and I thought we were splitting up.

I tiptoed around the house like a timid little mouse, hoping that he would come around, take it back, and we'd be okay. I was sickened and humiliated by the thought of our marriage being over.

I continued to cook and keep house, not knowing what else to do, and after a while William became friendly towards me again. He acted like nothing had been said about us breaking up. He joked and teased me. Lovely sex and laughter resumed, but a few months later he did it again; he repeated that he was sorry, but he didn't want to be married anymore.

When that storm blew over, I exhaled in relief, but kept my guard up. When it happened for the third time, I changed my response to him.

We were in the woods with a group of friends on a bumpy dirt path, riding mountain bikes. It was a brisk fall day; the cloudless blue sky, the sound of the wind and the smell of pine trees, made me feel *alive*.

When we'd stopped riding to wait for the others, my husband turned to me, and as I smiled at him, he sighed and said, "I'm sorry, I don't want to do this anymore."

"Do what?" I'd asked growing unease. "What do you mean? You want to leave? You don't want to ride bikes anymore?"

William had waved his hand between the two of us and then he'd lowered his head with grave finality.

"No - I mean this - *us*."

Here we were, on this lovely day, out with these nice people, and it'd come back to *this*.

Inside I grew furious, but outwardly I remained calm.

I inhaled deeply and replied unemotionally, "You know what William, I think you're right. I don't want to do this anymore either. Let's just get through the day and we'll make arrangements for me to get out of here as soon as possible."

I hesitated briefly, then peddled off to meet the others; left him in the dust with his bullshit.

For the rest of the day I ignored him.

I kept close to the lively group and tried to enjoy their company, keeping the intense friction that was bouncing off William and I, at bay.

William tried to approach me to talk a few times, but I waved him off and went to the others to joke around, seeking refuge.

By the end of the day he was nipping at my heels, pleading with me to talk to him. The more distance I put between us, the closer he tried to come. The more I pushed away, the more he advanced.

I was thrilled with the power I held, and I admit, retribution was sweet seeing him suffer to learn that he couldn't play around with me; he had to be held *accountable*.

It took me over a week to rescind my plans of leaving (I didn't want to appear too easy).

He never attempted another stunt like that again.

It wasn't until the subject matter in the program broadened my view, that I was able to see that there had been many situations between William and I where we'd struggled with control issues.

For months I'd been hearing about other people's state of affairs, never comparing any of it to my own life. But now I could see patterns that correlated with my past and coincided with the material being discussed in the program.

Accountability

We were asked to bring the police report to the twenty-third session. We were told to be ready to explain our case and respond to questions from the class.

I sat, not on the outside of the circle anymore, and readied myself to be subjected to the scrutiny of my peers.

"To be accountable means to acknowledge and take responsibility for one's actions," said Mr. Thera to the anxious eyes staring back at him. "Let's begin, shall we?"

The room smelled like sweat; the only noise was the rustling of papers.

Heads nodded and faces looked grim as the reports were being read, but no one had a question or a comment. The cases varied in the form of abuse, or the condition of the victim, but all of the reports had the same common denominator in that the woman had reportedly attacked someone, without provocation.

I had been so worried that I would be called upon to tell my story, but when I realized my turn would not come up, I admit that I was a bit disappointed.

Self-righteousness began to overpower me with all of the passion and determination of a preacher who believes in the cause; believes that he will vindicate himself if he can prove the falsehood of others.

I was sure that if I told my sordid tale, these women, who had become my comrades-in-arms, would absolve me of any wrong-doing by saying how outrageously contemptible the law's intervention had been, and how sorry they were for me.

It's probably better that there hadn't been time for me to speak, because the high horse I was standing on wasn't very solid.

***

At the end of the class session we were given a 'take home' assignment to be reckoned with the police report.

The directions were to write a brief paragraph after each statement explaining and qualifying yourself.

In three separate boxes were these sentences:

"I have physically and emotionally battered my partner.
"I am responsible for the violence. My behavior was not provoked by my partner.
"My partner does not owe me forgiveness for admitting my use of violence."

"Is this one of those papers that we need to change the 'he' to 'she' Mr. Thera?" asked a woman holding the paper by her fingertips like it was dirty.

As the other women looked apprehensively to Mr. Thera for his answer, I felt sure that they all had the same thought: *My husband should be answering these questions - not me.*

***

I took the paper home, and then reread my report.

My particular episode was accurately documented, but it had been a singular incident, while these statements had the tone of *plural* in their nature.

***

"I'm sorry you have to go through all this," William said after scanning the page.

We were out in the patio, watching the boys splashing each other in the shallow end of the pool.

"I couldn't sit through all this self-examination; I'd have told them to -"

"You'd have told them to what?" I snapped, "To fuck off? That sounds like something you'd say. But William, I've had no choice. I've been physically forced through these sessions for the last twenty-three weeks."

I scooped up the sheet and huffed into the kitchen.

I began cutting onions which stung my eyes.

Swiping the tears with the edge of my apron, I tossed the onions into a big pot with oil, and stirred them aggressively.

The boys scooted past me heading to their rooms to change with towels dragging, leaving a trail of water from their wet suits.

William came in and sat down at the counter.

I added button mushrooms, cut up chicken, and stewed tomatoes to the pot. After seasoning the dish, covering it, and setting the timer for one hour, I started to make curried rice.

I turned to William and said, "The first part was horrible listening to how physical abuse shatters lives, but these last few weeks we've been talking about the fact that each individual has to be accountable for their own actions."

Going to the fridge, I pulled out salad makings and started to chop some celery.

"Even *I* can relate to that kind of logic now that the physical assaults are behind us. Since we've started to discuss behavioral modifications on how to *communicate,* it's become very interesting."

Wiping my hands on a towel and picking up the paper, I said, "Look at these statements. Okay, the first one isn't how *we* are, because we don't hit each other, but I did strike you without provocation, and it was an act of violence. I have to be accountable for that."

William came around to my side, drawing me into his arms.

"Oh, come on Aurora, I was never in danger. I'm the man of steel."

His grip tightened like a vice and we chuckled. He leaned in and kissed my lips, then he worked his way along my neck. While clutching me with one hand, he tugged at my blouse with the other, and buried his face in my bosom. He turned me around and tried to bend my body forward, pressing himself against me.

I chided him saying breathlessly, "Please lovey, I'm *cooking,*" and pushed him away while straightening my apron.

William sighed, gave my backside a little pat, and plunked himself down on a stool.

"I think what makes us different is that we don't hold grudges," I said smiling broadly.

I picked up the finished salad and took it to the table.

"Oh, don't get me wrong," I said playfully wrinkling my nose. "I can recall every injustice done to me, by you. I even remember when we first got together and you said, "If you want this to work out Aurora, you'd better take the word 'FAIR' out of your vocabulary - because it may not always be fair - do you remember saying that?"

William laughed.

"Did I say that? To you?"

Then he nodded because he did remember saying it.

"But I let that kind of stuff go -"

I reached over the counter to stroke William's hand. "Because you're there for me. You've shown me that we can survive anything."

I held his gaze and hoped that he could see in my eyes, the love I had for him as I said, "But William, these women don't get that kind of validation."

"Who knows what happens to people," William said, quietly. "You know Aurora, guys want to be appreciated as much as women do. Maybe the woman was different in the beginning. Maybe she was happier, more carefree, but then she changed after they got married."

He got up to get a glass of water.

"Maybe the guy got more attention before the kids came along, but then he was ignored because his wife was too busy. Who knows?"

He set his glass on the table and looked at me. His expression became reflective.

"A man beating a woman is inexcusable, no if, ands, or buts about it. Nothing in the world could constitute justification for that."

William fetched the dog's food out of the cabinet and filled their bowls.

Accountability

"I think most guys, me included, just want to be treated with respect. It's hard to hear someone tell you all the time that you're wrong, but it's even harder to admit it to yourself. It takes two to make a marriage - man, listen to me," he laughed, "I sound like an ad for couples anonymous. But really, you know what I mean."

"Geez, honey, that's exactly what the program's about, but these women are dealing with major demons called: Drugs and Alcohol. They can't talk to someone who's out of it. How can they make any kind of progress when their partner doesn't remember the conversation?"

I sighed and said, "William, these women have been abused for *years,* and the first time they tried to do something about it, it landed them in jail."

I got out the dishes and silverware and started to set the table. Turning to William, waving a fork in my hand, I said, "It's sad to say, but a program won't fix them. A six-month crash-course on anger management, just isn't enough."

"I think you're wrong," William argued taking the silverware out of my hand, and setting them around the table. "Okay it may not fix everything, but it's a start. I know that you've never seen conflicts like you've described to me, but I have, and I'll tell you, as low as a man gets, deep down he wants to get up. With help, he can get up."

William scratched his head.

"Nobody wants to hear what a failure he is, Aurora. Every man hates constant nagging. A man who feels beaten down either becomes mean or numb. Neither is good, but it's what happens."

"It hasn't happened to *you,*" I said with doe-eyed admiration. "You haven't become mean or numb and I nag at you - a lot!"

I set the last plate on the table and moved toward him. I slipped my arms around his trim waist, tilting my head back to be kissed.

William wrapped his arms around me, enclosing me within the cavity of his broad chest.

Stooping to look into my eyes he said with a chuckle, "Because I play a lot of sports!" And then he kissed me passionately.

***

"William -" I asked after we'd cleaned up the kitchen, settled the boys in bed and retired ourselves, "why do I have to pester you before you help me with something?"

I adjusted the pillows and sat up.

"I mean, it would be so much easier if you would just -"

"The thing is -" William said rolling on his side, propping an elbow under his chin with a glint in his eye, "you've got ants in your pants Baby. You want the job done right away, and I do things on my own time, not yours.

You may pester me to get things done, but I don't work for you. I keep telling you that. If you ask me to do something, I'll be happy to do it. I just don't have the same sense of urgency, that you do."

"But William, it's not *urgency* to want something to be done within say, a day or a week. It frustrates me that you let time pass, and it doesn't get done - then I end up doing it."

"It's not that way all the time, Aurora, but sometimes I'm doing something else, and you want me to stop what I'm doing to help you with one of your projects, and I don't want to stop what I'm doing, just to assist you with one of your crazy ideas -"

On and on we went. Bantering, joking, teasing, and *communicating*. I felt so lucky.

Chapter Twenty-Three: Control Log

We did the last writing assignment in class, during the twenty-fourth session.

"Be honest ladies, this exercise is to show you that the river of human nature runs both male and female currents," said Mr. Thera with a smile on his face. "And remember, it's for our eyes only so you can take it and go with it as you will."

Everyone was given a pen and the sheet of paper on a clipboard. The title of the paper was called: **Control Log.** We were instructed to breakdown a given situation in which we had controlled our partner.

A rush of feverish chatter sent the majority of women into a verbal frenzy of remembered experiences when they'd gotten the upper hand (for probably one of the few times in their lives, I imagined). The animated exuberance and electric energy these recollections created in the women illuminated their flushed faces and made them seem more carefree, but I remained subdued because my memory bank was empty. How had I manipulated my very clever husband? How had I tried to control a situation? When had I ever gotten the upper hand?

The only time I could think of had not been serious, only an amusing test of wills.

Setting the paper on my lap I read the first sentence and began to write.

1. Briefly describe the situation and the actions you used to control your partner:

My husband wanted to take our foosball table to a housewarming party. Not a super bowl party, or a barbecue, but an elegant catered affair. I thought it was inappropriate to do this, so I took the legs off the table and hid it in the garage.

2. INTENTS and BELIEFS: What did you want to happen in this situation?

I wanted my husband to realize that it wasn't his party, and it wasn't his program, and it wasn't his decision whether playing foosball was part of the activities.

3. What beliefs do you have that support your actions and intents?

I wanted to be respectful of our friends celebrating their new home, so I took it upon myself to judge what was appropriate, and tried to inhibit my husband's plan.

4. FEELINGS: What feelings were you having?

My feelings were that it was a housewarming party! I felt that my husband was only thinking of what he wanted to do and not what the gathering was about.

5. MINIMIZATION, DENIAL AND BLAME: In what ways did you minimize or deny your actions or blame your partner?

I blamed my husband for being selfish and disrespectful to the hosts of the party.

6. EFFECTS: What was the impact of your action:

My husband just laughed and thanked me for making it easier for him to load the table into the car.

7. PAST VIOLENCE: How did your past use of violence affect this situation:

I haven't used violence in the past. There was no violence involved in this situation.

8. NON-CONTROLLING BEHAVIORS: What could you have done differently?

I could have driven to the party separately and ignored what my husband wanted to do. Or, I could have asked him to ask the hosts if he could bring the foosball table to their party.

***

In the grand scheme of things, my little vignette was ridiculous; absurd really. Although it was humorous, it did bring to light the fact that I could be as controlling as the next person.

Issues that I'd denied having any relation to, did confront me and I thought, *I often want William to do something, but he wants to do something else. The important thing that I have to remember is that it doesn't have to be a war if we disagree. With a concerted effort, we can both hold fast to our beliefs, even if they don't coincide.*

I was flabbergasted to have gotten so much from what I thought was a silly little exercise.

***

What I had to admit, even if it was only to myself, was that I manipulated situations as much as William did.

I usually found a way to do the things that I wanted to do.

I smiled inwardly recounting the times I 'Did It My Way'. I almost laughed out loud remembering when we moved into our house.

We were planning to landscape the front lawn.

William had insisted that I wait for him, but I'd gone ahead and transplanted the forty-five overgrown silver-tip shrubs that were climbing the exterior walls of our new home. I'd cut the four-foot-high beasts in half and moved them, having dug forty-five holes down the length of our lawn. I was sore and bedridden the next day.

William had reprimanded me for my impetuousness when he'd carried me to the toilet, but he did admit that it looked great.

My eyes wandered around the room and I grinned silently baring my teeth at no one in particular as I recalled numerous times when I'd disobeyed William's authority.

I love doing big renovations, what William calls, 'Aurora's creative outlets'.

William isn't as spontaneous as I am. He has to think things through, take his time; measure and plan and contemplate an idea.

I jump right into a job after an initial overview of the plan.

***

Before I went ahead and tiled the boy's bathroom and our front stoop, William had been emphatic that there weren't enough leftover tiles from the job that we'd done together tiling the 20 x 24 - foot living room - but there was.

And he was pleased when it was done.

I couldn't remember if I'd asked William about painting the whole interior of the house. I'd wanted to retain that wonderful feeling of being on holiday after we'd come home from a trip to the Bahamas.

The Bahamas is an enchanting oasis of tropical colors, mostly peach and turquoise. It felt like we were living in a dull beige box after we returned from that island.

Accountability

So, one morning after William had left for work, I mixed leftover buckets of blue, green and a bit of yellow and painted the walls of our dining room and living room, *turquoise*.

When William walked through the door that evening, he'd gasped. His unflinching smile and comment in answer to my questioning look was, "Uh, yeah, okay, so you did it - wow - that's some color - but if you like it - it's nice - kind of like living in an aquarium - but nice."

***

I stopped asking my husband for permission to do my projects when I recognized the pattern.

Every time I proposed something, anything that involved changing or moving or redoing something, I encountered opposition from him.

Every time.

Every time.

Any of *my* ideas for a makeover, or a bid to remodel, was met with William's automatic response, "No, that's not a good idea."

Sometimes he'd sigh heavily and say, "Okay Aurora, but please, wait until I'm home and I can help you."

Mostly, he'd hesitate, like he might acquiesce, but then he'd simply say, "Man, Aurora, it's not a good time to do that right now."

After years of struggling and fighting for my way, I learned to simply say, "Okay Lovey."

Then I'd wait until he was either gone for the day or away on business, and go ahead and do the project that I'd planned, disregarding his stubborn, negative attitude.

I always ending up doing what made me happy, and William always admired the work that I'd done.

Funny, huh?

William wasn't blind to the fact that I needed to *create*.

It stemmed from my childhood.

So why did he oppose me every time?

My cheeks flushed thinking how William acted when he was controlling. When we'd begin a project together, and I needed help, William would explain the process and put me on the right track.

Then I'd say, "Okay, I've got it, I can do it now."

Then he would act a bit offended and say, "Sure, go ahead, knock yourself out."

He'd watch for a bit and then walk away.

And he wouldn't come back.

Not even to check on how things were going.

I would end up finishing the job on my own.

Even though he was a bit cruel in that way, I was so wrapped up in what I was doing that his absence was negligible.

I could recall many times when he'd abandoned me at a job, but I smiled inwardly remembering the one time that it wasn't his fault.

We'd ordered six yards of white gravel, bought some rolls of heavy black plastic, and rented a sod cutter to clean up the grass area around the pool.

When Hurricane Opal hit the panhandle of Florida that weekend, William and his team were sent on a five-day mission to restore communication lines.

That left me to do the job.

I nodded to myself remembering how William had told me resolutely, to wait. He'd said that it was too much of a job for one man to do, let alone a little person like me to handle.

But I couldn't stand by while fire ants infiltrated our swimming pool area. I had to get rid of the huge mounds of sand that housed the hungry devils and clear the space for my children to play freely, so I hitched the sod cutter to my shoulders and sheared twenty-five rows of grass. I rolled them up, tied them, and stacked them along the driveway. After laying the black plastic around the whole pool area and securing it with heavy metal stakes, I shoveled and flung the massive heap of gravel, raking it evenly everywhere.

It took four days to complete.

Each day working my way closer to that end result had been exhilarating. It had been a personal triumph.

William had been utterly without words when he saw what I'd done.

He'd hugged me and kissed me, and we'd laughed when he told me what the man from across the street had said: "Man, me and the other guys on the road watched your wife working every day in your yard, and I have to say - you're the envy of the neighborhood!"

***

A lot of good stuff came out at that second to last session.

Some of the women had humorous stories to share and they were as amusing as the ones I'd recounted only to myself. These women weren't too proud or too ashamed of themselves to tell their tales.

It was a wonder to see that the group appeared to have gotten as much out of the exercise as I had. I saw a hope-filled-light shining on the faces of these women.

Maybe they weren't doomed to live in a prison of hopeless confinement, because vital keys had been put into their hands to liberate them from that life of anguish.

Mr. Thera's lectures seemed to be getting through, to all of us.

***

Mr. Thera tried to explain that most of the things we argue about are insignificant. "If you can recognize that anger comes from old primary feelings that have been re-stimulated, you can walk away from a fight and take a time out."

He tried to wrap up the assembly with pointers about getting your thoughts and feelings heard without violence, but he was talking to the wrong group.

At home that night, I showed William the worksheet; showed him how I'd dragged his name through the dirt.

He laughed.

Not much bothers him, he just goes with the flow.

***

I couldn't recall what had happened with the foosball table. I didn't remember seeing it at our friend's house; not in their open workshop-garage or on the spacious lanai near their pool.

When I asked William about it, he said, "Oh, yeah, I never took it out of the car."

Chapter Twenty-Four: Self-Talk

An opportunity for a job in Germany, presented itself to William in the early part of June. It was a chance to work on some state-of-the-art telecommunications equipment that few people in America had knowledge of.

He was excited and had all but made up his mind to take the job.

I wasn't so keen on the whole deal.

I still had a lengthy list of questions William had to answer before his ship could sail.

"Yes, of course I'll have a set contract," he answered impatiently. "It could be for six to twelve months. Up to twenty-four months."

William blinked slowly at me with an air of self-assurance.

"*Okay* - so who else is going? Is anyone bringing their families?"

"Well, Schmidt isn't bringing his family, and Johnny isn't bringing Marianne, but another guy, Debowski, is bringing his wife and their three-year-old daughter."

"Well, I'm not thrilled about you going there without us. Even six months is a long time."

"You know, I've been thinking that too. I want you and the boys to come. So we'll have to rent the house and put things in storage. I'm just not sure it's worth all that trouble for only a few months -"

"You know William," I interrupted, "this is a bit too unsure for us. Are you really considering quitting your job in Tampa, at your current salary, to go off to Germany with only a tentative plan?

"I'd be doubling my salary, Love," William said trying to entice me. "And, even if it's only for a short time, it's an opportunity that's not offered often. I'd be a fool to pass it up."

"Well, you may have to pass it up, big guy -"

Once again, we were at odds.

Once again, we were at an impasse; his will against mine.

With all things considered though, it was a significant opportunity for William; and if we could go with him, it would be a great adventure.

I prayed in earnest that we could go, that we'd have a new beginning; start a new chapter in our lives. I was desperate to run away. I would have been willing to leave with only a suitcase if I could get rid of the constant anxiety that was following me like a dark shadow.

It was hard to think about our future plans without having to face the fact that no matter where we were, whether we stayed in Florida, or went off to Germany, I still had personal issues that haunted me.

I wasn't sure if I would ever be the same again, or if I could make a new start anywhere, at all.

***

The twenty-fifth session was about to start.

My thoughts were on talking with Mr. Thera after class, so I didn't hear the woman's question.

"I'm sorry, were you talking to me?" I asked politely, coming out of my fog.

"I said, are you really writing a book? How about interviewing me? I have a real whopper of a story I'd like to tell -"

The woman's bobbing head, and bright eyes annoyed me.

"Actually," I said, surprising myself, "my plans may be changing. I'm not sure if I'll be writing a book after all. You see, I may be leaving the country -"

"Oh, leaving the country, wow. I've always wanted to travel. Where are you going?"

Before I could respond, Mr. Thera addressed the class. "Ladies, I'm sure that you are all well aware, having counted each week diligently, (many women giggled) that this term concludes in two weeks."

A rumble of hoots bounced off the walls of the little room. Grinning faces beamed; their heads nodding in agreement.

Mr. Thera nodded and smiled kindly at their animated expressions. He waited for the group to quiet down and held up his hand.

"I want to give you two important sheets about self-talk and your personal rights. They may be good resources for you in the future."

The first sheet's title was:

SELF-TALK

Both research and experience show that when people with anger problems change their self-talk, their anger de-escalates, and they regain control.

When you notice yours escalating or start to feel angry, take a Time - Out and read these statements to yourself:

* **I don't need to prove myself in this situation. I can remain calm.**
* **As long as I keep my cool, I'm in control of myself.**
* **No need to doubt myself; what other people say doesn't matter.**
* **I'm the only person who can make me mad or keep me calm.**
* **My anger is a signal. Time to talk to myself and to relax.**

* I don't need to feel threatened here. I can relax and stay cool.
* Nothing says I have to be competent and strong all the time.
* It's O.K to feel unsure or confused.
* It's impossible to control other people and situations.
* The only thing I can control is myself and how I express my feelings.
* It's O.K. to be uncertain or insecure sometimes.
* I don't need to be in control of everything and everybody.
* If people criticize me, I can survive that. Nothing says that I have to be perfect.
* If this person wants to go off the wall, that's his/her thing.
* I don't need to respond to his/her anger or feel threatened.
* Most things we argue about are stupid and insignificant.
* It's O.K to walk away from this fight.
* It's nice to have other people's love and approval, but even without it, I can still accept and like myself.
* People put erasers on the ends of pencils for a reason; it's O.K to make mistakes.
* People are going to act the way they want, not the way I want them to.

The little hand-out was full of pertinent insights.
Self-Talk - hmm, I thought.
The first two lines about remaining calm and staying in self-control were concrete, viable suggestions, but not that easy to do.
Could I make use of these rational guidelines while issues were so hot at home?

Decisions had to be made, and the window of opportunity for me to give my opinion would be fleeting. I had to have a quiet resolve to get my views across. I was worried that I was too headstrong, and couldn't stand up to the challenge. I had to find a way to communicate with William, and not start a fight.

Throughout the session, while the others discussed the worksheet, I contemplated my options.

William was going to take the job in Germany, that was for sure. He would take us with him, if we could work it out, but he was going none-the-less.

I knew there was no chance of discouraging him, once the offer had been put on the table, and his pals were going as well.

Now, it was simply about logistics.

Should the family go; dogs and all? Or should we let him go, and man the fort while he was away?

It would be a lot to do, packing up the house, putting what we didn't take with us into a storage facility.

If William were going right away, all that burden would fall on me.

I would have to find a realtor to rent the house. I'd have to get a crew for the pool and lawn care. It would be a lot of work. And it wouldn't be cheap, bringing all the things I started to think I needed.

When we brought our goods back from Germany the first time, it had been on Uncle Sam's bill. This would be much different. We had to be thrifty and practical.

Was it worth the expense and trouble?

I was adamant that if we did go, the boys should attend an international school, where they would be taught in English. I wanted them to be able to matriculate back into the American school system, once we returned.

William had argued that he wanted them to go to a German school, so they could learn the language quickly and make neighborhood friends. He wanted our boys to integrate into the new culture as seamlessly as possible.

He wouldn't budge on his view that they had to be immersed swiftly. He also wanted them on a German soccer team. He was confident that they'd be successful fitting in right away.

I wasn't so sure about any of it.

***

"Mr. Thera-" I called in a high-strung voice, as I knocked on his open door after class. "Excuse me, but do you have a few minutes? Could you clarify a few things for me?"

He was sitting at his desk reading a file. He nodded at me, and I entered.

Resting a hand on the upholstery, I leaned on one of the designer chairs. My eyes darted around the room as I looked at him expectantly.

As if reading my nervous expression, he asked, "Is there something I can help you with Mrs. Sabel? You look as if you're a bit spooked."

I refused to sit down in the seat but started right in.

"I was wondering about the police report. Do I have a record now? I mean, let's say I go to renew my passport for example, do I have to admit that I've been arrested? Am I a felon? Am I in some global system? Will all this be erased once I finish the program? Am I bound to this country or can I leave any time?"

There was so much tension oozing out of me, that it probably looked like I might burst. I was sure he could see my heart pounding through my blouse. I could feel that my face was flushed, and it was hard to breathe normally.

"Mrs. Sabel, are you all right? What's happened? Why are you so stressed out? Come and sit down and let's talk about all of this."

Mr. Thera motioned for me to take a seat.

I plopped down hard on the nearest chair and started to cry.

He slowly rose and came toward the adjacent seat.

Accountability

He handed me a tissue box as he sat down beside me. He folded his hands in his lap and waited silently while I composed myself.

After I blew my nose, took a deep breath, and dried my eyes, I said, "This last sheet you gave us is great. I can really use it. This part of the program has been enlightening. Did you write all that stuff yourself?"

His eyes smiled at me as he laughed. He seemed to have such an easy way about him. Not a thing, vexed him.

Not one time had I seen his mood change. He was as calm as a steady stream, as sure and dependable as a solid foundation.

"What's going on Aurora?" He asked quietly, gently touching my arm.

It was the first time he called me by my first name.

Every woman, save me, had called this man by his first name throughout the entire course, but I couldn't bring myself to address him that way.

He had always been informal with the group, but I had remained formal with him. His cordiality had the effect of an invitation to a private party, but I'd never wanted to be admitted to that party.

Looking at the mild-mannered man, how the corners of his eyes crinkled as he coaxed me with a placid smile, I suddenly had the urge to let it all out.

In a squeaky voice I said, "Mr. Thera, I need your advice. My husband has an opportunity to work overseas. I think our family can accompany him, that is, if I'm not confined to the U.S. Am I? Am I a felon? A criminal? Will my record be on file for the rest of my life? I'm mortified to even *think* about taking a job because every job application asks if you've ever been arrested. I'm too afraid to volunteer at the elementary school because they run a background check and police report. My records are in some kind of database, right? I can't tell you what a strain this whole ordeal has been on me; the stress it has put on my life. I don't think I'll ever recover."

Mr. Thera raised a hand to stop me. His facial expression seemed to be a cross between amusement and pity. He cleared his throat and began to explain things to me.

"First of all, Aurora, when you signed up for the Diversion Program, all charges were dropped. There is a record of your arrest, but you were never convicted of a crime. You are not a criminal nor are you a felon. It's true that you are in the system, but you should not hesitate to go forward with your plans. You're free to live anywhere in the world and do anything you wish to do. Does that ease your mind?"

Those were the words I wanted to hear, but I wasn't completely satisfied. I needed more assurance that there were no more tricks up anybody's sleeve, or any last-minute surprise addendums.

I closed my eyes and a wild image flashed in my mind. I heard a shrill voice beckon me from the murky depths of a dank subterranean office at the last official stop I had to make.

"You're not free yet Mrs. Sabel," the menacing creature said. "We neglected to mention that you still have to do 10,000 hours of community service by cleaning up the highway -"

And I imagined a long, slimy, purple pulsing tentacle, twisting through the doorway, its suctions thrusting a pitchfork and a glowing orange vest at me.

Get a grip Aurora, I said to myself as I pulled oxygen deep into the cavity of anxiety constricting my chest.

I focused on Mr. Thera and said, "So, next week is my last session and that's it? I report to the probation officer for my last payment and that's all I have to do? Don't I get a graduation certificate or something? Won't I receive a written statement from the authorities stating that I fulfilled the requirements? Will I ever, really, be able to put all this behind me?"

Appeasing me was clearly his intention when Mr. Thera smiled and said, "Yes, you will be getting a letter in the mail, following the end of your term. It will state that your twenty-six-week contract with this program has been completed. But, frankly, that's about it."

I could see that he wished he had more to offer.

"Ohhhkay," I answered slowly, struggling to digest the information. "So, let me get this straight; to understand this fully. I am under no further obligation; I have no structured guidelines; nor do I have any restrictions on where I go, or where I live."

"Right."

"And I don't have to come back in a year or so for an update on my personal status."

"Correct."

"All right then, so, that's great."

But it wasn't great.

It wasn't over.

It would never be over.

There was a police report with my name on it forever.

I'd have to lie on every application where the question asked, 'Were you ever arrested?'

At least I could mark 'NO' on the box that asks, 'Were you ever convicted of a crime?'

But I couldn't face the humiliation of having to explain things to a possible employer. What would I say?

"Well, yes Ma'am, to tell the truth, I was arrested, one time, but not convicted of a crime. The details? Oh, it was merely a misunderstanding. You don't really want to know, do you?"

I couldn't imagine ever applying for a job again.

I tried not to think about that as we moved the conversation to current events.

"Tell me Aurora, about this chance to go - where? Europe?" he asked kindly, with genuine interest.

"Well, it's all a bit overwhelming, Mr. Thera," I said as I leaned back in the seat, suddenly exhausted.

"Then you should just take a moment to collect yourself," he said. "I have time. We can talk, and figure it out."

He was so openly friendly that I felt compelled to pull myself together and comply.

We talked for a while, as two acquaintances do sometimes, and I relaxed under his calming presence. We touched on the subject of the book idea and I confessed that it wouldn't be something I'd start if we were leaving the country. He assured me that whenever I wanted to begin that endeavor, he would gladly help in any way.

For a moment I thought we were done.

As we sat quietly, he began to speak.

"To reach people through a program like this is nothing less than profound, but sometimes I don't think it's sufficient, or that I'm actually reaching them-"

"Oh, but it *is,* and you *are* -" I tried to say, but he waved a hand at me.

"No, let me finish. Sometimes, I can actually *see* that I'm not getting through. It's like a vacant parking lot; no one's there. Too much damage has been done; the wreckage is total."

"Well," I said in earnest, "I have to admit that in the beginning, the program's content did shock me. I was impressed at how you kept your cool, lecturing to a group of hostile women. I was one of them, in fact. At first everyone was so angry; ironic don't you think? As the weeks passed though, there was a change. The tone improved as we began to really hear what you were preaching: that with the right attitude, one can alter an intolerable situation."

Mr. Thera smiled modestly at me.

He seemed to be considering my words.

"Thank you for the vote of confidence," he said quietly, "but these women need much more than this program. Next week when we discuss alternatives to lifestyles, I'm hoping that it will be an eye-opener for some of the women who are in desperate situations."

He got up, poured two glasses of water from a slender plastic bottle, and offered me one.

"These women need to find a way out. Either by AA, NA,

counseling, or a divorce lawyer. They need help right away. I'm truly afraid for some of them. I worry about all of them."

Trying not to upset the flow of dialog, I grabbed the bottle to refill our glasses and waited. I had a strong feeling that probably for the first time in his career, Mr. Thera was talking to a 'patient' about his patients. He was single-handedly dedicated and driven by his principles, but like any Therapist or Counselor, I'm sure that he conferred with others. I felt privileged that he was talking to me about his work; releasing what seemed to be a burden on his mind.

"The abuser doesn't remember the details of the assault," he continued nodding his thanks. "He doesn't want to know what he did. He only tries to justify his actions. When the abuser finds that his partner is changing, and past behavior isn't working, the conflict can move to a terrible level, possibly fatal. In most situations there's no hope of reconciling; no chance of a healthy recovery. I have to make it clear to these women that they have the power to take back the control. That's the hardest lesson for them to learn."

Lines I had never noticed before were prominent on his forehead. I wanted to reach out and put my arms around him, but I knew that it wouldn't be appropriate, so I just held his gaze, and nodded at him encouragingly.

Mr. Thera went to his desk and sat in his swivel chair.

"They all agree they shouldn't be treated like garbage, but they stay because they believe that they have no other alternative. My toughest job is making these unfortunate women understand that they have to leave for the violence to end. It's hard to watch them go after each session. I pray for their safety. I hope they can survive their circumstances and show up for class the following week."

I looked at his troubled face. There was nothing I could say, not a word that could soothe his disquiet. He had a tough job. A mostly thankless job too, because every woman resented (at least in the beginning) being put into the program knowing they were not the ones who really needed the counseling.

His was an admirable, pastoral kind of vocation.

I wondered briefly why he had chosen this profession, and thought that maybe something that had happened in *his* past, had led him here.

It was quiet and peaceful in his office. The clock's ticking set a metrical beat that lent us to our individual thoughts.

At one point Mr. Thera got up and went to the door.

I rose and went to face him at the threshold. We were at eye level as we smiled at each other. He wasn't much taller than me, but oh, he was a giant of a man.

As I extended my hand, he took it and gently held it in his cool palm. I could feel that the sense I had of understanding, compassion, and friendship, was mutual.

"I'm sure you'll make the right choices, Aurora."

He gave my hand a squeeze and let it go.

"I appreciate that, Mr. Thera. I have a lot to think about."

I started down the hallway.

"Sometimes I hear your words at the oddest times," I said, turning around. "And in the strangest places too! You *have* made an impact, I wish you could see that, but I guess you'll never really know, because no one comes back to say thank you, do they?"

He chuckled and said, "No, we hope that no one comes back."

***

After we said goodbye, I walked out into a gorgeous, sunny day.

People were bustling about, going forward on their quests. The confidence with which they moved, like being mechanically propelled, moved me. They appeared to have no doubt, going forward knowing exactly where they were headed, confident in obtaining their objective.

I wanted to feel that kind of inner resolve, that sure-footed, innate sensation of *knowing.*

Chapter Twenty-Five: Me, Myself, and I

Going to Munich, had been a foregone conclusion.

Oh, William listened to my concerns, or at least he looked right at me while I was talking. Still, he'd gone ahead and taken the job, and we were going with him.

Plans for the big move were underway.

We needed to hire a realtor to rent and manage the house, employ a moving company to send our valuables overseas, pack up the items that would go into storage, and find a permanent home for our house guest.

Our house guest was a small dog that I'd found tied to a 'NO PARKING' sign outside the Thrift Store.

***

My first secondhand store experience at the age of ten, led to a lifelong addiction.

The tiny white Thrift Store stood alone on a little hill, at the end of Main street. The old fire station's faded red and white brick building was its only neighbor. It stood crooked, defying gravity for ages, on the slope down the road.

My eyes popped with wonder as we pushed open the creaky glass-paned door and entered the clapboard house.

My mother, her face aglow, gave me a few dollars and said, "Take your time Aurora - it's like a treasure hunt." She also said in earnest, "Be careful. If you break it, you buy it."

I stepped onto wide pickled floorboards that gave in a little by my weight, and my jaw dropped in awe.

In a corner stood an old-fashioned cupboard. Its little doors and drawers were open displaying platters and mismatched dishes, tarnished silverware, jugs and bowls, saucers and teacups and fine linens with beautiful hand-stitched embroidery.

One wall had racks stuffed with clothing. Dresses, jackets, sweaters, and blouses dangled on the top row. Pants and skirts overlapping, hung underneath.

On the other side of the 12x12 room, an entire wall was filled with books. Thick green and brown faded canvas bound books, colorful-looking children's books, books of every size and shape.

In the center of the room was an open-shelved cube. Among delicate vases, China dolls and picture frames, I found a beautiful carved wooden music box.

I picked it up and was admiring it when an ancient-looking woman with snow-white hair, a face as wrinkled as a walnut, and the bluest eyes I'd ever seen smiled nicely at me.

"Oh, that's a great find," she said. "You don't see workmanship like that anymore - let's take a look underneath to see what it costs."

She took the box from me and turned it over. The price $2.50 was scrawled on a tiny white sticker.

The woman nodded as I grinned and said, "I'll take it."

From that moment on, it was like a moth to the light that I felt drawn to thrift stores.

***

So, this dog was tethered outside the thrift store one morning that prior September of 1999. I noticed her as I entered the store for my weekly shopping spree, and when I left an hour later, the honey-colored dog was still there. I felt bad for her and had an impulse to find the owner; to find that person who'd left an animal out in the heat, but I didn't.

Accountability

I bent down, petted the dog, and said, "Don't worry little one, your owner will come back soon."

Then I left, and went about my day.

On my way home from grocery shopping that afternoon, I drove past the thrift store and the dog was still tied up outside.

I don't know what compelled me, but I turned the car around, swung back into the parking lot, stopped a moment to pet the dog, and marched with intent into the store.

Standing at the register was a pair of large, aging twin sisters. Although they wore identical size 3x powder blue pants and floral blouses, their social skills were not the same.

The friendlier one told me the story when I inquired about the dog.

"The poor dear, she's been out there all day. People have been coming and going and no one's claimed her. We gave her some water, but we're closing soon, and I don't know what to do."

The woman put a hand to her forehead. With doleful eyes she said to her uninterested-looking twin, "Gee whiz, that poor, poor doggie. What ever shall we do sister?"

***

That was nine months ago.

I couldn't put it off any longer, I had to find Ginger a home because we couldn't take two dogs to Munich.

William had been lukewarm when I'd brought the dog home saying that it would be temporary, but he'd understood that I couldn't have walked away and left her there.

The boys were thrilled to have a pal for Ranger, but our sweet-natured black Labrador's reaction, had been mostly to pout and growl at the little dog.

Within days of posting a cute photo and info about Ginger around our neighborhood, a young family bustled into our house, scooped the dog up, (literally) and whisked Ginger (they loved the name I gave her) off to her new home.

"A twenty-foot container could cost anywhere from 2,000 to 3,000 dollars," said the young man smiling. His hands sank deep into the pockets of his faded green trousers as he bounced enthusiastically on his heels.

"Wow, that's amazing," he said, assessing the wall of boxes that I'd assembled in our dining room. "I've never seen anyone do that before - I mean, pack and stack stuff up so uniformly. You even marked the dimensions on the floor and up the wall - dang, that's cool."

Daryl, I assumed that his name was Daryl, although the company shirt he was wearing with the name Daryl sewed on the patch above the left pocket was at least two sizes too big for him, secured the paper on his clipboard, and began to write. While filling out the order sheet with my name and address, he eyed me soberly.

"After we list the other goods you're going to ship, we can set a date to pick up the boxes."

His eyes scanned the wall of boxes.

"After we weigh them at the warehouse, adding an estimate of the furniture and other items, we'll choose your container. After we check cargo availability, we'll send you the bill and set a moving date."

Our boxes were picked up the next day and a week later a letter arrived with the figures.

"Yes, good morning Patty," I said in response to the operator's scripted telephone greeting, "you can help me. I'd like to speak to Daryl, or a manager please."

I was put on hold; made to listen to orchestrated showtunes. It seemed like the whole score of 'Hello Dolly' had played before I heard Daryl's voice come onto the line.

"Hi Mrs. Sabel, how are you today?"

"I'm fine Daryl, but I think there's been some kind of mistake with the final bill."

Daryl hesitated so I plunged in.

"When we first talked, you said that the cost would be anywhere from 2,000 to 3,000 dollars, am I correct?"

Before Daryl could get a word in edgewise, I continued.

Accountability

"Then we made a list of the furniture, paintings, and other items, and you said that it didn't look like all that much. Do you remember saying that Daryl?"

Again, he didn't respond quickly enough so I shot out, "But now I'm looking at a bill for 4,600 dollars Daryl. Why on earth has the final cost exceeded the initial estimate by so much?"

At first, I thought that we had lost our connection, but then the heavy sighing at the other end of the phone made it evident that Daryl was trying to find an appropriate answer. I heard papers being rustled. I heard Daryl inhale and exhale.

"I have the docs right here Mrs. Sabel. There's a notation. I see that the boxes weighed in much heavier than expected. What did you pack in them, rocks? Let me check the numbers and get back to you, okay?"

I waited all day for Daryl to call me back, but he didn't.

I wanted to call the company and talk to one of his superiors, but I didn't.

The boxes weren't packed with rocks, they were packed full of *books*. More than six boxes were dedicated to Scholastic books for my boy's continuing education.

With the understanding that my children would be attending a German school, I wanted to ensure that they had all the tools to keep up with the curriculum in the states, so I purchased learning logs in Math and English and home reader books, from beginner to the fifth grade.

Sometime in the afternoon of the next day Daryl called. It was apparent from the tone of his voice that he was pleased and excited.

"I have good news Mrs. Sabel," he said. "The rate has been changed to book freight and volume. The new balance due is 3,600 dollars."

With genuine sympathy for Daryl's efforts on my behalf, I said as kindly as I could, "That's all well and good Daryl, but it's still not what we talked about and it's still not a workable number for me. Please return my boxes and I'll look into another shipping company."

This time his hesitation was so brief that I had the feeling he was getting ready to jump hoops.

"Hold on," he said drawing a deep breath, "I'll get back to you."

The final cost came in at 3,200 dollars.

I stayed with Daryl and his company because of how hard he'd championed for me in trying to honor the original estimate.

Plus, he already had my stuff.

***

A red corvette pulled into my driveway and a slender, well-dressed woman got out of the car. She straightened her black pencil skirt, fluffed the collar of her white sleeveless blouse, and smoothed her frizzy coiffed hair. Reaching into the car she grabbed a tall plastic cup capped with a pink straw and an unzipped tan-colored brief case stuffed with loose papers that were flapping recklessly.

I wondered, as I spied from behind the curtain in my dining room, who or why someone had told her that that shade of salon blonde, was attractive.

Usually I am not that critical of others.

Let people do as they will, is my motto.

But this woman, who was pivoting in my driveway, sucking on the neon-colored drink, surveying my property, made me mad.

I had been pacing the floors of my house for forty-five minutes, waiting for the realtor. I'd gone in and tidied my bedroom, and straightened the pillows on my bed that didn't need straightening. I arranged the shower curtain in the bath, to show the garden tub.

Sitting in their room, the boys watched me wander in; following me with their eyes; still gripping their Legos, as I picked up Kermit the frog and moved him, and then put him back on the shelf that he always sat on.

I prepared a table and made tea that got cold.

Accountability

I laid out homemade cookies, but returned them to the tin with a huff after eating two of them while I was waiting.

The doorbell rang right as I was opening the door.

I caught her arm just as she was slipping backward off the landing.

"Hold on, I've got you," I said pulling her up onto the front stoop.

"Oh, what a lovely home you have," she said almost tripping over the threshold of my house. "It looks small from the outside, but the high ceiling and the stone fireplace are a nice surprise!"

With genuine charm she introduced herself, (no excuse was given for her tardiness) and Mae Belle and I began to move through the rooms.

Nothing defuses animosity better than flattery.

I was appeased by her compliments about my home and we became fast friends.

After reviewing the terms of the agreement, I signed the documents for her company to represent us.

After calling a few agencies, I'd gone with Remax, because the man on the phone with the heavy southern accent sounded competent. His voice had bellowed with force to assure me, "As sure as rain we'll take care of ya Ma'am. We'll get yur house rented faster than you can shake a rattlesnake!"

As I looked around my home, memories fluttered my heart and tears crept out of the corners of my eyes.

"I hope that you'll find a loving family who will enjoy this house as much as we have," I said, struck by emotion.

"That's exactly the kind of people I'll find to live here, Mrs. Sabel. No worries about that."

We parted on amiable terms.

I closed the door and sighed. I was sad to leave our home, but it would be good to go away. Far away

While going through my desk the following week, I found the second sheet that Mr. Thera had given us at the previous session.

We hadn't been able to go over the text in class, so he asked us to find a quiet place and take some time to read through it ourselves.

I went out to our pool area and tucked my legs up Indian style, on one of the deck chairs. It made me smile to hear a bunch of kids squawking and hooting it up in our neighbor's pool on the other side of the fence. A cool breeze carried the smell of lilacs that was as soothing as a gentle massage. Sparkling sun-kissed rays glistened on the water's surface, and made tons of tiny dancing diamonds. I closed my eyes; happy to be in the security of my home.

I unfolded the paper in my hand. It said:

PERSONAL BILL OF RIGHTS

* I have the right to ask for what I want.
* I have the right to say no to requests or demands I can't meet.
* I have the right to express all of my feelings, positive or negative.
* I have the right to change my mind.
* I have the right to make mistakes. I do not have to be perfect.
* I have the right to follow my own values and standards.
* I have the right to say no when I feel unsure or it is unsafe.
* I have the right to determine my own priorities.
* I have the right not to be responsible for other people's problems.
* I have the right to expect honesty from others.
* I have the right to be angry with someone I love.
* I have the right to be uniquely myself.
* I have the right to feel scared and say, 'I'm afraid'.
* I have the right to say, 'I don't know'.
* I have the right not to give excuses or reasons for my behavior.

Accountability

* I have the right to make decisions based on my feelings.
* I have the right to my own needs for personal space and time.
* I have the right to be playful and frivolous.
* I have the right to be healthier than those around me.
* I have the right to be in a non-abusive environment.
* I have the right to make friends and be comfortable around people.
* I have the right to change and grow.
* I have the right to have my needs and wants respected by others.
* I have the right to be treated with respect.
* I have the right to be happy.

After reading the last line, I felt a bit saddened because it seemed obvious that these basic rights were rudimentary.

I thought, *Every woman should know that she has the right to be happy.* Our *lives hang in the balance when there's uncertainty or an absence of self-love.*

I must believe in myself; that I'm entitled to pursue my own happiness. It's the force that drives me. It's how I get up, pull myself together and face the world every day.

I couldn't say if I'd changed much in twenty-six-weeks. Nothing monumental showed as a revised version of me. I was definitely more conscious of stopping to think before I opened my mouth. I tried to douse, and defuse, any sparks from flying, and *discuss,* rather than *argue,* my point of view. I worked on being calmer when I expressed myself, and I found that William seemed to be more receptive to me because of this change in my delivery.

Oh, I was still that fearless, headstrong woman who would undoubtedly rant and rave at times; that being part of my charming personality, but I noticed that if I controlled my temper, I could articulate my desires, hopes and dreams more effectively.

Before my last session I opened a disturbing letter that had been sent to William. I opened it, as I open all mail, regardless to whom it is addressed.

Noting from where it was sent, I sat down at the kitchen table amongst the unfolded laundry and shuddered as I read:

Dear William Sabel,

The defendant named above is receiving pretrial diversion supervision in agreement with the Hillsborough County State Attorney's Office. This agreement states that the defendant shall take no action or engage in any conduct which may endanger the safety of the victim or family members of the victim and shall be completely law-abiding during the term of this agreement. It is very important that you contact me if this defendant is in violation of the conditions described above. If she/ he commits any violent act against you or others, please immediately contact law enforcement. If you have any questions, please feel free to contact me at the number below.

Signed: Probation Officer.

I didn't show the post to my husband. I threw it with a vengeance into the drawer with all the other documents I'd compiled to prove how absurd the whole incident was.

I tried not to dwell on what it inferred, but it frustrated me knowing that I was still being monitored like a criminal.

I was under surveillance in case I slipped off the edge, and reverted to felonious acts again.

***

The class was quite cordial, that last day before summer break.

The sun's dazzling rays shined through the upper window in the room and crowned the heads of the women in the group with little halos.

Accountability

Everyone's spirits were riding high.

An atmosphere of joyous emancipation rang through the animated congratulatory smiles because of the reprieve.

Part of the class would continue in the fall to finish up their required terms. Some like me, would be done and gone, without much fanfare.

When we all finally settled down and formed a small circle, part of the group spoke enthusiastically about their future. A few of the younger women could barely contain their excitement boasting new resources of enlightenment.

"I've been going to AA meetings every night for the last two weeks, and boy, my husband gets an earful when I get home. The stuff they talk about is so positive, and I can see the same patterns in my life listening to some of the other people's stories."

"I'm doing that too, which nights do you go?"

A buzz of conversation reverberated in the room.

"I've decided to pack up the kids and go to live with my mother," a small timid young gal blurted out. "I won't be threatened any more, and I won't have my babies frightened either."

The conversation abruptly stopped, and all eyes went to this pitiful broken doll. She had been watched with concern for many weeks. It was visible that quite often, she had it rough. She would come into class with her face caked with make-up, and solemnly wave a hand to defer any explanation when someone asked her how she was doing, even though it was grossly apparent, that things were not going well. Everyone knew she needed to break away from the violence.

With a staunch resolve she assured us, "This is it. I've made arrangements. My mom is coming for me and the kids tomorrow."

Some of the women got up and hugged her fiercely in a cluster of motherly energy chanting, "GOOD FOR YOU! YOU CAN DO IT!"

I looked over at the woman and prayed, *Dear God, please help her be strong, and follow through with her plans.*

After everyone quieted down and returned to their seats, Mr. Thera gave us one, final paper. It was only a small block of words, but it had a weighty feel to it.

I read the paper in my hands, a knot forming in my throat.

I am responsible for my choices and actions.
I am responsible for the way I prioritize my time.
I am responsible for the level of consciousness I bring to my work.
I am responsible for the care with which I treat my body.
I am responsible for being in the relationships I choose to enter or to remain in.
I am responsible for the way I treat other people: my spouse, my children, my parents, my friends and associates.
I am responsible for the meaning I give or fail to give to my existence.
I am responsible for my happiness.
I am responsible for my life - materially, emotionally, intellectually, spiritually.

"Ladies, pretty soon you'll be on your own," Mr. Thera said with a warm smile. "I'm sure you won't miss me, or this place, or these lectures, but I do hope you'll walk away from here, having gained something.

"The intended purpose of this program, has been to teach you, and make you aware, that you are directly responsible for your own actions."

He looked out at the wide-eyed faces.

"What you do, where you go, and how you make your life work for you, depends almost solely, on you."

With a countenance of kindness in his eyes, he continued.

"If you come from a rough past, and it's repeating itself in your present, you may have to make some drastic changes to ensure that it doesn't continue in your future."

He paused to take a deep breath and exhale slowly.

"These changes may certainly be painful to start with, but the long-term effect it will have on you and your children could save your lives."

He walked to the front of the room and faced the group.

"I don't want to seem morbid, but you must realize that getting out of a violent home, or away from a violent presence, is the first step towards taking responsibility for your life, and the lives of your children. Sometimes there is no other way."

His expression was solemn, his arms at his sides.

"You know, deep down in your heart if something can be fixed, made more tolerable, or not. It is not a bad thing, to walk away. It is not a terrible thing, to admit that it won't work, and you cannot go on the way things are.

"Have the strength to say so. Have the courage for your self-preservation and the welfare of your children, to say so."

He sighed, but then he nodded and moved on.

"Shelters and abuse centers are out there to assist you. If you need help, call me. If you want to get out of a bad situation, I can aid you. Don't stay in a life-threatening place thinking you have no alternatives. I can give you a list of facilities that may be useful. If anyone would like to have this, please come to see me after class. Remember, be good to yourselves, you deserve it."

He slowly walked around the room making eye contact with each one of us. His gaze held warmth and concern.

"I wish you all a happy, healthy life. Thank you."

With a rumbling roar, the class rose, knocking over chairs in a stampede to embrace him.

He was visibly moved.

Laughing, he stood still and let them come to him.

As the group of women tugged and hugged him, they sang in unison, "Thank you Mr. Thera, you've been great!

It was the end of a long haul.

I stood back and watched the others acknowledge what Mr. Thera thought he hadn't succeeded in giving: hope and a chance to heal.

The acclamation was more than a small consolation; he could see, and feel, that he had gotten through to this group. And many changes would be possible for them.

I was really glad that they praised him so highly; he had deserved that tribute.

***

What would happen to these people out in the real world was anyone's guess, but I could gather, with my own eyes, that the women who'd started there twenty-six weeks ago, were not the same pitiful souls, that were walking out the door six months later.

They were stronger more empowered individuals, with the weapons of self-pride, and self-preservation, to fight against their oppressors.

It was hard not to be impressed by the whole program.

It had accomplished its purpose in making us, *conscious*.

Sometimes, it had been brutal.

Sometimes, it had been really sad.

Learning to understand the patterns of abuse, and how to change situations to break the cycle and reinstate new values to live by was invaluable.

The trick was to hold fast to those encouraging insights, and use them with fortitude when the daily struggles, inevitably, would occur.

Chapter Twenty-Six: Faith

I rushed into the probation office, ready to make my last payment, and dash out of there without another word.

No such luck.

"She'd still like to see you, Mrs. Sabel," said the clerk who had been cheerful and kind to my boys and me every time we'd come in.

I thanked her for that kindness, and signed in.

The entire six months coming to this dismal place, the mandatory sign-in validating that I had not left the county (or country) or been violent with anyone had been humiliating, embarrassing, and annoying. It had been a constant slap in the face, to use the pun; an ugly incessant reminder of what a farce the whole affair had been from the very start.

The result of this personal assault, again the pun intended, was not wholly without effect as to the course my life has taken. It definitely sends a soul on the road to redemption, regardless of how one may struggle against the lessons along the way.

Why though?

Why was I forced to experience this?

The definition of 'redeem' states: To regain possession by paying a specified sum, or pay something off in full.

Well, I'd paid the debt and fulfilled the requirements.

Now all I wanted was to leave the whole episode behind me, and regain possession of my life.

I found my probation officer busy as usual, absorbed in her work.

With the intention of levity, I called in a sing-song tone, "Hell-oh, anybody home?"

She glanced up and motioned for me to take a seat.

I watched her fiddle with some files, rearrange some papers, neither of which needed her undivided attention, and at that point my objective to be pleasant vanished.

Her subtle, arrogant gestures, renewed my conviction that she was a totally sour, spiteful person.

"So, Mrs. Sabel, have you been violent with anyone this month?"

She put down her pen and studied me.

I'm sure if there were a Lie Detector on the premises, she would have gone to get it, just to mess me up one last time.

I was on the verge of saying something really shocking like, *'Okay, you've got me, I confess, I killed them all -'* because Sharlee Stone, the ice-queen of all time, had from that very first encounter, tried to unhinge me. But I knew that I had to hold my temper.

"I'm happy to say that I've been vindicated," I said mockingly. "I did *so* enjoy our meetings each month, but as I've fulfilled my agreement, we won't be seeing each other, ever again."

I stood up and headed swiftly toward the door.

"I want you to know, Mrs. Sabel," she said, watching me as I reached the threshold, "that although you think you've had it rough all these months, it's been a relative picnic for you, because you don't have any underlining issues."

She sighed and said, "I am glad for you that it's over, really. I can see that for your kind of person this isn't reality, but for ninety-nine percent of the people that come through those doors, it is a vicious reality, and my asking if they've been violent with anyone each month, is less an assault on their character, as a way to keep them within the rules and guidelines of society. You can never understand this, I can plainly see that."

Accountability

She put her head down, indicating that we were done.

"You probably won't believe me," she said, looking up again, "but I do hope that you have a good life, you and your children. I mean it. Just stay away from situations that got you here in the first place. Enjoy your freedom."

I waited until she went back to her work and made haste, literally running out the door.

***

Six months.
Twenty-six weeks of unending stress.
Rushing to the class, not missing an appointment.
Paying regularly.
The loathsome probation officer.
OVER WITH.
I was done.
DONE.
Finally, I could have my life back.

***

I got the confirmation letter in the mail the following week. Actually, it was addressed to William again, but I opened it, acknowledging the same address as before.

It read:

Dear Mr. Sabel,

This letter is to inform you that Aurora Sabel has met and satisfied all treatment requirements. If you have any questions or concerns regarding her behavior in the future, please feel free to contact me.

Signed—Victim Liaison

Victim Liaison! Geez!

It was the last and final insult that my future behavior would be anyone's concern.

William would get a kick out of the letter, I was sure, but I packed it away with the rest of the documents I'd compiled and put it out of my mind because the case was closed now, and I was free!

What a heady feeling of relief that was. Now I could truly put it all behind me and go forward.

But what about all those other women? I wondered. What would happen to them during the interim between summer break and the fall session? Would there be casualties in their personal wars? Would they survive and be successful, the ones that wanted to change their lives?

I believe that we were all touched by Mr. Thera's lectures, but was that enough? Did the program do anything for anybody, really?

Yes, I believe it had.

The actual transition from shock, resentment, and denial, to empathy, acceptance and understanding, had been gradual, but the end result was what Mr. Thera had sought to achieve.

We gained a broader perspective with empowering tools. The lessons in those classes can help anyone in a relationship, not only a hostile one. Who wouldn't benefit from a little guidance where relationships are concerned?

***

Oh, you can be sure, that if I'd had a choice, I would *never* have done the program, but there's no denying that I walked away with a keener awareness of *cause* and *effect*.

The fact that I have to be accountable for my own actions, is a solid principle to adhere to.

I continually reiterate to myself that what I do, what I say, and how I say it, directly affects those around me.

My aim is to be mindful of that every day of my life.

Accountability

"Life does not require us to be the biggest or the best. It only asks that we try."

(The quote on Mr. Thera's business card)

Postscript

I wonder if you got it - the whole *feeling* of what I've tried to convey in this tale of mine.

Did I enlighten you in portraying the chaos and indiscriminate forces of domestic violence?

Did I show you a vivid birds-eye view of this other world, and clarify misconceptions?

Or did I only entertain your curiosity with those morbid stories?

Have I opened closed doors, affording you to see parallel situations in your life?

Or has it been just a lot of *talk* on a vast and unsurmountable subject?

Will any of this have an effect on you?

***

It's been almost too many years to count since I went through this horrible experience. The vivid (and shocking) reality that domestic violence dwells rampantly within our society, is still surreal to me. My everyday life, although hectic, is not without harmony.

***

I can still recall the women I encountered. Some of the officials were very kind, but it's the women from the group that stay sharp in my mind. Their desperation, their pain, and their determination to pull themselves up, made an everlasting impression on me.

I wonder if Mr. Thera is still there, worrying about every person who crosses his path. His program, and what he does for people in distress certainly makes a difference; I can attest to it, having experienced his powerful positive strength firsthand.

Accountability

Aren't you a little curious about what happened to me and my family?

We did move to Munich in 2000, and we lived there for almost two years.

The boys went to a German school, and became fluent in less than six months by joining a soccer team, and playing with the children in the neighborhood. We went through all of the scholastic books (five years' worth) within the twenty-two months that we lived there. The boys were way ahead when we returned to the states in 2002.

We were back in our house in Florida for six years, and then William was offered another opportunity to work for the Department of Defense, in Germany.

In 2007, we moved to Stuttgart.

The boys attended high school at an international school, both graduating with an impressive International Baccalaureate. They're off pursuing their individual dreams now, in different parts of the globe; bright-eyed, worldly young men.

I went to work at the school in 2009; ten years was long enough to hide. I was asked many questions before being hired, but not if I had ever been arrested, or convicted of a crime. The American military base supplied a local police report. I was relieved that it proved my status as a sponsored spouse because I'm not 100% convinced that a stateside record of me isn't still out there in a database somewhere.

I provide support from pre-kindergarten to the fifth grade, when the teacher's assistants are out, so everyone know me. Up and down the halls I'll hear someone ask, "What's yummy this week?" because I teach cooking classes as well.

And what about my husband and me, you're wondering?

Well, we're older, having been married for thirty-plus years now. We laugh a lot, and still play house with the passion and zeal of newlyweds.

I admit that we've had fights during our life together, but nothing like the domestic scenario (that word again) that sent me to jail.

I try to use the methods from the program when we argue, but mostly, I'm too riled up at that moment to utilize them.

Still, I think we're more tolerant of each other as the years go by. I've certainly honed my sense of fairness in any dual. And neither of us are so quick to accuse, or judge each other, anymore.

I'm sure that I will always have discussions, debates and disagreements with my grown boys and my husband. Every day brings new challenges concerning power and control issues coexisting with those headstrong men with which I share the same living space.

It isn't easy.

It isn't always fun.

And I wouldn't change it for anything.

***

Sometimes I think back on that brief interlude in my life. That troublesome time when I was all but driven out of my mind from the shame and disgrace of being taken to jail. The degradation of being cast with people the likes of which I thought I had nothing in common.

I know that in no small way, that program and Mr. Thera's lectures, changed my views.

Having searched deeper inside myself, I think that I have a clearer understanding of what makes me act and react the way I do in all of my relationships.

***

I can recall those I'd come across on my journey.

I remember the overzealous young policeman who became genuinely deflated when he realized that his superior had misrepresented the judicial system by that unwarranted arrest. The kind-spirited Jamaican matron of goodwill, who took me in her arms and left the scent of roses in her trail was a Godsend, and my gentle giant must have been an angel.

Accountability

What would I have done without Kenny urging me to keep the faith? Or the judge who read the report, saw the law's breach, and sent me home. To top it all off, the self-empowered, kindhearted Counselor who, on a stupendous mission, taught with a passion to help the helpless see a brighter future.

It makes me shake my head with scorn to remember that horrible probation officer, Sharlee Stone. Part of me wants to send her an invitation to our thirty-fifth wedding anniversary celebration, but she probably wouldn't remember me. She had a job to do, I realize that. But surely she could have had a little more compassion, or empathy or restraint. Or at the very least, she could have been a little less abrasive.

***

What do I do differently to justify Mr. Thera's program?

Ah, well, old habits are hard to break, but I do consider how I want to represent myself.

I hold myself accountable for my actions, and reiterate to myself, that I am the one responsible for my life - materially, emotionally, intellectually, and spiritually.

Laura Strobel

"There, but for the grace of God, go I."
(Quote by John Bradford - circa 1510 - 1555)

Group Discussion Questions

What aspects of the author's story could you most relate to?

What do you think about the way the police handled the situation in Aurora's particular case?

Did certain parts of the book make you uncomfortable? Did this lead to a new understanding or awareness of some aspect of your life you might not have thought about before?

Did you find the list of Self-Talk exercises a useful tool to help reinforce your strength in yourself?

How has reading the Personal Bill of Rights affected thoughts of yourself and your life? Do you consider your needs, desires, hopes and dreams more than you did before reading it?

Have any of the events in this book ever happened to you or someone you know?

What did you find surprising and most interesting about the facts introduced in this book?

Why was this title chosen for the book? Does it convey the main argument of the story?

How does the cover art reflect the theme of this book? The author sees it as a society of unique, colorful people, intermingling in harmony. What do you see?

If this book were to be made into a movie, who would you cast for the main characters?

Laura Strobel

Accountability

{Pullout Page}
SELF-TALK

Both research and experience show that when people with anger problems change their self-talk, their anger de-escalates, and they regain control. When you notice yours escalating or start to feel angry, take a Time - Out and read these statements to yourself.

* I don't need to prove myself in this situation. I can remain calm.
* As long as I keep my cool, I'm in control of myself.
* No need to doubt myself; what other people say doesn't matter.
* I'm the only person who can make me mad or keep me calm.
* My anger is a signal. Time to talk to myself and to relax.
* I don't need to feel threatened here. I can relax and stay cool.
* Nothing says I have to be competent and strong all the time.
* It's impossible to control other people and situations.
* I can only control myself and how I express my feelings.
* It's O.K. to be uncertain or insecure sometimes.
* I don't need to be in control of everything and everybody.
* If people criticize me, I can survive that.
* Nothing says that I have to perfect.
* If this person wants to go off the wall, that's his/her thing.
* I don't need to respond to his/her anger or feel threatened.
* Most things we argue about are stupid and insignificant.
* It's nice to have other people's love and approval, but even without it, I can still accept and like myself.
* People put erasers on the ends of pencils for a reason; it's O.K to make mistakes.
* People are going to act the way they want to act, not the way I want them to act.

Laura Strobel

Accountability

{Pullout Page}
PERSONAL BILL OF RIGHTS

* I have the right to ask for what I want.
* I have the right to say no to requests or demands I can't meet.
* I have the right to express all of my feelings, positive or negative.
* I have the right to change my mind.
* I have the right to make mistakes. I do not have to be perfect.
* I have the right to follow my own values and standards.
* I have the right to say no when I feel unsure or it is unsafe.
* I have the right to determine my own priorities.
* I have the right not to be responsible for other's problems.
* I have the right to expect honesty from others.
* I have the right to be angry with someone I love.
* I have the right to be uniquely myself.
* I have the right to feel scared and say, 'I'm afraid'.
* I have the right to say, 'I don't know'.
* I have the right not to give excuses or reasons for my behavior.
* I have the right to make decisions based on my feelings.
* I have the right to my own needs for personal space and time.
* I have the right to be playful and frivolous.
* I have the right to be healthier than those around me.
* I have the right to be in a non-abusive environment.
* I have the right to make friends and be comfortable around people.
* I have the right to change and grow.
* I have the right to have my needs and wants respected by others.
* I have the right to be treated with respect.
* **I have the right to be happy.**

Laura Strobel

Accountability

Printed in Germany
by Amazon Distribution
GmbH, Leipzig